D1236299

Time To Write

William Sidney Porter

Time To Write

How William Sidney Porter Became

O. Henry

Trueman E. O'Quinn Jenny Lind Porter

EAKIN PRESS
Austin, Texas

THOMPSON-SAWYER
PUBLIC LIBRARY
QUANAH, TEXAS

Library of Congress Cataloging-in-Publication Data

Porter, Jenny Lind.
    Time to Write.

    Includes 12 short stories written by O. Henry while in prison in Columbus, Ohio.
    1. Henry, O., 1862–1910 — Criticism and interpretation. 2. Prisoners as authors. 3. Prisoners' writings, American — Ohio. I. O'Quinn, Trueman E., 1905–. II. Henry, O., 1862–1910. III. Title.
PS2649.P5Z77 1986   813′.52   86-1979
ISBN 0-89015-547-X

"Prison" photograph of O. Henry reproduced by permission of *The Saturday Review of Literature* (Dec. 1933) and copied by Bill Malone who also photographed the manuscript of "A Fog in Santone."

Photographs of O. Henry in the Austin years and of buildings associated with his life are reproduced by permission of the Austin History Center (Travis County Collection) and the Texas State Library. The mature portrait of O. Henry is printed through the courtesy of the Greensboro Historical Museum, while the photographs of O. Henry furniture were taken by Jim Flinn of Seattle, Washington.

COVER PORTRAIT BY DAVID DAMM

FIRST EDITION

Copyright © 1986
By Trueman E. O'Quinn and
Jenny Lind Porter

Published in the United States of America
By Eakin Press, P.O. Box 23066, Austin, Texas 78735

ALL RIGHTS RESERVED. No part of this book may be reproduced in any form without written permission from the publisher, except for brief passages included in a review appearing in a newspaper or magazine.

ISBN 0-89015-547-X

To

Hazel Hedick O'Quinn

and

Lawrence Evans Scott

The young William Sidney Porter in Austin (c. 1887), age 25, "Uncut to pattern." Five feet seven, with chestnut brown hair, blue eyes, and a mustache, the writer made many friends in Texas. He spent a third of his life in Texas and made it the setting of more than fifty stories.

Austin History Center, Austin (Texas) Public Library

Contents

William Sidney Porter, age 35, April 1898, the prison photograph. "He set out to challenge failure and to unlock the imprisoned splendors of his creative imagination."

Courtesy of *The Saturday Review of Literature*

Acknowledgments

Grateful acknowledgment is made to the Manuscripts Department of The University of Virginia's Alderman Library for permission to quote the "Whistling Sam" fragment (#7457) from its William Sydney Porter Collection; to Dr. Decherd Turner and the Harry Ransom Humanities Research Center of The University of Texas at Austin for the quotations from O. Henry letters which are in their archives; and to the Texas State Historical Association for allowing us to use portions of an article by Judge O'Quinn, "O. Henry in Austin," which appeared in *The Southwestern Historical Quarterly* (October 1939).

The twelve stories of O. Henry printed herein have all, after seventy-five years, come into the public domain, and each version is that of its pre-1910 original magazine appearance, with the exception of "A Fog in Santone," which Judge O'Quinn owns in its manuscript form. It was initially copyrighted by Witter Bynner in 1910.

Special thanks go to Ann Bowden of the Austin Public Library and the Austin History Center, to which Judge O'Quinn gave his fifty-year collection of O. Henry first editions and furniture; to Bill Moore, director of the Greensboro Historical Museum, Greensboro, North Carolina; to Sara Bolz and the O. Henry Museum staff in Austin; to the Ohio State Historical Society in Columbus, Ohio, for the prison records; to Mrs. Oliver H. (Adriana) Orr of Washington, D.C. and Mrs. J. B. (Gray) Golden of Austin, Texas, for their expert research assistance; to *The Saturday Review of Literature* for permission to print the O. Henry "prison" photograph first published therein by Christopher Morley (1933); to Dr. Dorman Winfrey and the Texas State Library; to J. Hubert Lee; and to Dr. Miguel González-Gerth of The University of Texas.

Judge O'Quinn has devoted a large part of his life to the study of O. Henry. In the 1920s and 1930s, he had the foresight to interview every person in Austin who had some significant connection with O. Henry, and the Judge's essay, Part I of this volume, is based upon his first-hand knowledge of Austin and Texas history, his career as a lawyer and appellate judge, and his personal notes on the talks he had with Herman Pressler, Charley Pickle, Harry Hofer, C. M. Bartholomew, Edmunds Travis, Lawrence K. Smoot, Laurence Ledbetter, the members of the Kreisle, Maddox, Morley, and Ward and James families, as well as with Howard Sartin, whose father, Guy, married O. Henry's only daughter. The Judge also traveled to Weaverville, North Carolina, to interview Sara Coleman Porter; to Baltimore, Maryland, for talks with Paul Clarkson, O. Henry's great bibliographer; and to Cotulla, New York, Greensboro, and New Orleans, in study of his favorite author.

Dr. Porter's essay, Part II, is her original interpretation and analysis of the twelve stories which O. Henry wrote in prison. Its title, "The Imprisoned Splendor," comes from Browning's *Paracelsus:*

> There is an inmost centre in us all,
> Where truth abides in fullness. . . . and to know
> Rather consists in opening out a way
> Whence the imprisoned splendor may escape,
> Than in effecting entry for a light
> Supposed to be without.

For quotations from the works of O. Henry other than the twelve prison stories, we are indebted to Doubleday, Page, and Company, publishers of the memorial edition, *The Complete Writings of O. Henry,* Garden City, New York, 14 volumes, 1917. We also wish to acknowledge the following works which have contributed greatly to O. Henry scholarship and our own understanding of his life:

The Letters of Harry Peyton Steger (1899–1912), Published by the Ex-Students Association of The University of Texas, Austin, 1915.

Coleman, Sara Lindsay, *Wind of Destiny,* Doubleday, Page and Company, Garden City, New York, 1916.

Jennings, Al, *Through the Shadows with O. Henry,* The H. K. Fly Company, Publishers, New York, 1921.

The Mentor (A special O. Henry issue) II: 1, February, 1923, containing Margaret's tribute to her father.

Seymour, Charles, *The Intimate Papers of Colonel House,* Houghton Mifflin Company, Boston and New York, 2 vols., 1926.

Smith, Arthur D. Howden, *Mr. House of Texas,* Funk and Wagnalls Company, New York and London, 1940.

Travis, Edmunds, "O. Henry's Austin Years," "O. Henry Enters the Shadows," and "The Triumph of O. Henry," in *Bunker's Monthly, The Magazine of Texas,* for April, May, and June, 1928.

Maltby, Francis Goggin, *The Dimity Sweetheart, O. Henry's Own Love Story,* Press of the Dietz Printing Co., Richmond, Virginia, 1930.

Stratton, Florence, and Vincent Burke, *The White Plume,* or *O. Henry's Own Short Story,* E. Szafir and Son Co., Beaumont, 1931.

Davis, Robert H., and Arthur B. Maurice, *The Caliph of Bagdad,* D. Appleton and Company, New York, 1931.

Williams, William Wash, *The Quiet Lodger of Irving Place,* E. P. Dutton and Co., Inc, New York, 1936.

Long, E. Hudson, *O. Henry, The Man and His Work,* The University of Pennsylvania Press, Philadelphia, 1949.

O'Quinn, Trueman E., *O. Henry's Own Trial,* The Steck Company, Austin, 1940.

Raymond, Dora Neill, *Captain Lee Hall of Texas,* The University of Oklahoma Press, Norman, 1940.

Copeland, Fayette, *Kendall of the Picayune,* The University of Oklahoma Press, Norman, 1943.

Langford, Gerald, *Alias O. Henry,* Macmillan, New York, 1957.

Kramer, Dale, *The Heart of O. Henry,* Rinehart and Company, New York, 1954.

Arnett, Ethel Stephens, *O. Henry from Polecat Creek,* Piedmont Press, Greensboro, North Carolina, 1962.

Current-Garcia, Eugene, *O. Henry (William Sydney Porter),* Twayne Publishers, Boston, 1965.

McLean, Malcolm D. "O. Henry in Honduras," *American Literary Realism,* The University of Texas at Arlington, Summer 1968, 39–46.

Arnett, Ethel S., article about O. Henry, *Greensboro Daily News,* September 14, 1969. Description of O. Henry's wedding to Sara Coleman.

O'Connor, Richard, *O. Henry, The Legendary Life of William S. Porter,* Doubleday and Company, Garden City, New York, 1970.

Gallegly, Joseph, *From Alamo Plaza to Jack Harris's Saloon, O. Henry and the Southwest He Knew,* Mouton, The Hague, Paris, 1970.

Sibley, Marilyn McAdams, *George W. Brackenridge, Maverick Philanthropist,* The University of Texas Press, Austin and London, 1973. A fine chapter on O. Henry expands an earlier article published in *The Southwestern Historical Quarterly,* "Austin's First National Bank and the Errant Teller," April 1971.

Indispensable and unique are C. Alphonso Smith's *O. Henry Biography,* Doubleday, Page & Co., New York, 1916, which contains the first story of O. Henry's imprisonment, and Paul S. Clarkson's *A Bibliography of William Sydney Porter (O. Henry),* The Caxton Printers, Ltd., Caldwell, Idaho, 1938.

There are hundreds of reference books, small volumes, pamphlets, and association items in Judge O'Quinn's collection at the Austin History Center; however, substantial O. Henry scholarship exists in the books listed above, and we are grateful for permission to quote them from time to time in our work. Unfortunately, almost all of these books are out of print, and some, like Clarkson's *Bibliography,* are very scarce indeed.

Our deep appreciation goes to our families for their enduring support and help — to the Judge's wife, Hazel, and their two sons, Kerry and Trueman, Jr., and to Dr. Porter's husband, Lawrence Evans Scott, who commissioned both David Damm's remarkable oil portrait of O. Henry striding away from Belle-meade in the character of "Whistling Dick" and also the excellent photographs of the O. Henry Collection taken by Jim Flinn of Seattle, Washington.

Portrait of the mature O. Henry. "I write about people who have crossed my lifeline."
Reproduced by permission of the Greensboro Historical Museum,
Greensboro, North Carolina.

[I]

O. Henry's Unending Trial

Trueman E. O'Quinn

The title of this book comes from the mind and words of Dr. Walter Prescott Webb, distinguished professor of history, author, and editor, who very early became a reader and admirer of the works of O. Henry (William Sidney Porter). It was at the supper table of the Town and Gown Club one evening that Dr. Webb pointed out how Will Porter, while working as drug clerk, bookkeeper, draftsman, bank teller, and newspaper writer, produced only two or three short stories of merit, but that during the three years and three months Porter worked in prison at Columbus, Ohio, as pharmacist at first and later as bookkeeper, he produced a dozen or more short stories by which, in the words of Dr. C. Alphonso Smith, Will Porter "passed from journalism to literature." Dr. Webb turned toward me and said, with significant emphasis, "Those twelve stories should be gathered into an anthology entitled *Time to Write,* for it was the first time Porter had actually had time to write."

When Will Porter arrived at prison in Columbus, Ohio, on April 25, 1898, he did not know that he carried with him an asset that would afford the time he needed to write while in prison. Asked to state his occupation, Porter clearly thought of his last full-time employment as columnist and feature writer on the Houston *Post* and answered, "Newspaper writer." Then, as if prompted by a mystic inspiration, Porter added, "I am also a registered pharmacist."

Nearly seventeen years earlier, after working two years in his Uncle Clark Porter's drug store in Greensboro, North Carolina, under the tutelage of his Uncle Clark, Will Porter became officially recognized under the statutes of North Carolina as a registered pharmacist on August 30, 1881.

The prison officials did not need a "newspaper writer," but they could use a pharmacist in the prison hospital, located some one hundred yards outside the prison walls, and promptly assigned Porter to that duty the day he arrived at prison. Porter was never assigned to a cell in prison, but slept, ate his meals, and worked in the hospital. After doctors on duty retired for the night, Porter became the "night nurse" for prisoners in the hospital and in their quarters in prison. In time Porter became a trusted friend of the doctors, and it was through Dr. John M. Thomas, chief physician at the prison, that Porter obtained transfer from the pharmacy to the office of C. N. Wilcox, the steward, located four or five blocks from the prison, where he became a bookkeeper and private secretary to the steward. There Porter slept, and also ate his meals with the staff. After working hours, ending at four o'clock in the afternoon, Porter was a "trusty," permitted to go out in town, visit his doctor friends in their homes, or go to the local beer halls for refreshment.

In correspondence from Columbus, Porter described his ample desk and other working facilities in the steward's office. Obviously, Porter wrote a substantial number of the twelve stories in this work while in the steward's office. Dr. Charles Alphonso Smith, in preparing to write the first biography of O. Henry, published in 1916, found among Porter's personal effects a notebook Porter kept at prison, in which he listed ten stories in the order they were written, but did not include two stories which are known to have been published prior to making entries in the notebook. These stories were "Whistling Dick's Christmas Stocking," previously published in *McClure's Magazine* for December 1899, and "Georgia's Ruling," published in *Outlook* for June 30, 1900. The ten stories found in the notebook and the two stories published prior to the notations in the notebook constitute the twelve stories included in this work as representative of Porter's passing "from journalism to literature."

Many persons no doubt think of O. Henry as a Texan because he spent one-third of his life in Texas and at least fifty of his stories have Texas settings, but he was born on September 11, 1862 in Greensboro, North Carolina. Very accurate accounts of his family and boyhood in Greensboro may be found in C. Alphonso Smith's *O. Henry Biography* (1916) and Ethel Stephens Arnett's *O. Henry from Polecat Creek* (1962). Mrs. Arnett's genealogical chart shows that

O. Henry was a direct lineal descendant of the royal Stuarts of England, with distinguished American relatives among the Shirleys, Sidneys, and Worths.

His mother was Mary Jane Virginia Swaim (1833–1865), the daughter of Abia Shirley of Princess Anne County, Virginia, and William Swaim, who became editor of the Greensboro *Patriot*. O. Henry was in many ways very like his mother, a gentle, witty girl who painted and sketched, wrote poetry, and graduated from Greensboro Female College. Ironically, her graduating essay was entitled, "The Influence of Misfortune on the Gifted."

The father of O. Henry was a beloved Greensboro physician named Dr. Algernon Sidney Porter, the son of Sidney Porter and Ruth Worth Porter. When O. Henry was three years old, his mother died of tuberculosis, and Grandmother Ruth took in Will, Shirley Worth (called "Shell"), and David Weir ("Bunnie"), the latter a child who died as an infant. Before he went to Texas, Will Porter made his home with his spirited grandmother, his doctor father, his Aunt Lina (who taught school and encouraged his love of books), his brother Shirley, and his Uncle Clark Porter, who lived at home until his marriage in 1873. The Porter residence was at 440 West Market Street and later at 426 West Market Street.

Will experienced a normal boyhood in a sleepy Southern town, skating, swimming, fencing, boxing, fishing, reading, playing the violin, and sketching. He was so talented as an artist that friends urged him to pursue this gift and make it his career, and indeed, Thomas Nast, the well-known illustrator, offered to train him as his protégé. All of his life, in North Carolina and Texas and New York, O. Henry continued to use and enjoy these special talents he must have inherited from his mother: music, art, and poetry. For example, a very famous book, Wilbargers's *Indian Depredations in Texas* (1889), is totally illustrated by Will Porter. An affidavit by N. A. Rector in The University of Texas archives dated November 10, 1932, proves the accuracy of this statement: "We employed Mr. Will Porter to draw the engravings. . . ." The General Land office files in Austin contain numerous maps and documents enlivened by Will Porter's charming sketches of jackrabbits, windmills, cowboys, and even the statue atop the Texas State Capitol.

By the time O. Henry left Greensboro for Texas at age nineteen, his major gifts were apparent: the gift of art, the gift of music, and the gift of storytelling. He had already met and admired the "Magnolia" girl who would become his second wife, Sara Lindsay Coleman.

Will Porter went to Texas in March 1882 at the invitation of his

Greensboro friends, Dr. and Mrs. James K. Hall, who had three sons in Texas. Dr. Hall thought that the sunny Texas climate might be the perfect cure for Will's persistent, racking cough. Two of the Hall sons had a deep and lasting impact upon Will Porter's life — Lee ("Red") Hall, the Texas Ranger (1849–1911), and Richard Moore ("Dick") Hall, land commissioner of Texas (1851–1927). Will spent two years on the Dull–Hall ranch in LaSalle County near Cotulla. There he devoured the Hall's well-stocked library and absorbed the lore and passion of an entire region. From these years he took the inspiration for many an unforgettable Texas story and many a delightful character: Jackson Bird — the Pinkeyed Snoozer, Baldy Woods, Poky Rogers, Dry Valley Johnson, Chicken Ruggles, the Cisco Kid, and Lonny Briscoe. In three months' time Will Porter learned to speak perfect Spanish. He was already writing stories, though he seems to have destroyed them all, and there is no question that in two years this keen master observer of human nature stocked his mind with the thousands of accurate details which make his Texas ranch stories so convincing and so truthful.

On a record made in the early days of this century, O. Henry's soft Southern voice may be heard saying, "People ask me how I write my stories. I write about people who have crossed my lifeline." Not only to the student of O. Henry but even to the most casual observer of his stories, if comparison is made with the characters and incidents of Porter's own life, it quickly becomes obvious that O. Henry etched with accurate design the pathos, humor, hopes, ambitions, loves, successes, and defeats of his own dramatic life. Even at the height of his remarkable writing career in New York, O. Henry continued to tell the story of Will Porter.

Will Porter spent sixteen years in Texas, of which nearly twelve years were lived in Austin.

He went to Austin from the ranch in the spring of 1884, when he was not quite twenty-two years old. Dick Hall had sold out and moved to Florence, in Williamson County, but Porter stopped off in Austin, where he remained, except for about nine months in Houston and less then seven months a fugitive, until April 1898, when he was taken away to serve a five-year sentence for alleged embezzlement of bank funds. Will said that he never took any money and that all his troubles might be traced to the slipshod manner in which the First National Bank — for fifteen years — had conducted its business.

Let O. Henry introduce us to the man whose thorough, unrelenting methods as a bank examiner were the undoing of Will Porter, paying and receiving teller of the First National Bank of Austin:

Indecision had no part in the movements of the man with the wallet. He was short in stature, but strongly built, with very light, closely trimmed hair, smooth, determined face, and aggressive, gold-rimmed nose glasses. He was well dressed in the prevailing Eastern style. His air displayed a quiet but conscious reserve force, if not actual authority. . . . Perry Dorsey, the teller, was already arranging his cash on the counter for the examiner's inspection. He knew it right to a cent, and he had nothing to fear, but he was nervous and flustered. So was every man in the bank. There was something so icy and swift, so impersonal and uncompromising about this man. . . . He looked to be a man who would never make nor overlook an error.

The bank examiner in this story, "Friends in San Rosario" (*Ainslee's*, 1901), is called "J. F. C. Nettlewick" and described as "one of Uncle Sam's greyhounds" — clearly the F. B. Gray of Will Porter's experience. Notice that O. Henry's own name is represented by "Perry Dorsey the Teller," for it cleverly conceals and yet reveals all the letters of his last name, Porter.

In "A Call Loan" (*Everybody's*, 1903) the bank examiner reappears as a

. . . dyspeptic man, wearing double-magnifying glasses [who] inserted an official-looking card between the bars of the cashier's window of the First National Bank. Five minutes later the bank force was dancing at the beck and call of a national bank examiner.

But we shall hear more of the bank matter, for it is a tragic scene in the last act of the drama of Will Porter's life in Austin during the closing years of the nineteenth century. A prologue is not inappropriate at this point to give a thumbnail picture of Porter's years in Austin.

In 1884, when Will Porter arrived in Austin, the capital had a population of 10–12,000. The old capitol was destroyed by fire in 1881, and a new Texas State Capitol was being constructed, a building Will Porter saw dedicated on May 16, 1888. From the Capitol he could see the Governor's Mansion, built in 1856 and designed by Abner Cook. In 1884 the occupant of that mansion was Governor John Ireland, but in 1898, when Porter faced trial, the governor was Charles A. Culberson, whose brother was none other than R. U. Culberson, the federal district attorney prosecuting Will's case! At one time it looked as if Porter's friend, Dick Hall, the land commissioner, might occupy the Governor's Mansion, but he was narrowly defeated in the governor's race by James Stephen Hogg, a man

O. Henry described as "a large flesh-colored man about the size of two butchers. He is self-made, ambitious, and perspires easily."

Will Porter made his home for the first three years in Austin with the Joe Harrells, formerly of Greensboro, at 1008 Lavaca Street. That home has been demolished, but I managed to preserve the beautiful old curly-pine mantel with its beveled mirrors and gave it to the Austin History Center. Will used to sit before this fireplace, which was in Mrs. Harrell's upstairs, southeast sitting room, reading and writing some of his early stories. In May of 1884 he went to work for Morley Brothers Drug Company at 203 East Sixth Street, but he soon tired of the routine world of the pharmacy and transferred to the Harrell Cigar Store. The 200 block of East Sixth Street is also important in Porter's life because of the Roach and Hofer retail grocery and feed store, located at 211 East Sixth Street. From that address, in 1897, Will Porter sent out and sold to McClure's Syndicate his first story accorded national circulation, "The Miracle of Lava Canyon" — a story not found in O. Henry's collected works, though in prison he rewrote it as "An Afternoon Miracle." Some years back I was fortunate to acquire the typescript of "The Miracle of Lava Canyon" with corrections in Porter's own hand as well as the desk at which he composed this story. Never again did he sign the name "W. S. Porter" to a story.

In the fall of 1885, Will Porter became a bookkeeper for Maddox Brothers and Anderson, a real estate firm run by John W. and Frank M. Maddox and Charles E. Anderson. After their marriage, Will and Athol Estes stayed with the Andersons for about six months, and Charles Anderson's son was one of Porter's closest friends. I bought the large walnut desk which Will Porter used at Maddox Brothers and placed it in the collection I gave to the library.

In 1886 R. M. Hall was elected land commissioner for Texas, and on January 12, 1887, Porter became a draftsman in the General Land Office, where he remained for four happy years, resigning January 21, 1891. Will had many friends among the draftsmen, and they used to walk down the hill from the Land Office to buy bread and delicious Sally Lunns at the old Lundberg Bakery at 1006 Congress Avenue. This stone building, the setting of O. Henry's "Witches' Loaves," in which Porter is doubtless the "young man smoking a pipe," stands in its original location to this day and has been charmingly restored.

On July 1, 1887, Will married Athol Estes in the old Richmond Kelley Smoot home at 1316 West Sixth Street, a home still occupied by Dr. Smoot's granddaughter, Jane Smoot, who has deeded this historic place to the City of Austin. Dr. Smoot was the pastor of the First Southern Presbyterian Church, where Will — a light bass, Athol, and Athol's mother, Mrs. Peter Roach, sang in the choir. The twenty-four-year-old groom and the seventeen-year-old bride — Will's "Dimity Sweetheart" — hired a city carriage in front of what is now the Littlefield Building at Sixth Street and Congress Avenue, obtained a license, and drove out to their minister's lovely home. Lawrence K. Smoot, age twelve at the time and later official reporter of published opinions for the Supreme Court of Texas, was a witness to the wedding.

Frances Goggin Maltby writes in her book, *The Dimity Sweetheart,* that Will may have first seen Athol at the laying of the cornerstone of the new Capitol in 1885 when Athol represented her class at that ceremony and placed in the cornerstone both class mementoes and one of her long, golden curls. That evening Athol had to iron her ruffled dimity frock again and restyle her hair because a sudden shower had soaked her dress and curls — and she was going to a dance given by the Austin Grays, a militia company which included one Will Porter! This incident may have been the inspiration of O. Henry's "The Purple Dress."

Will and Athol settled into a small "Honeymoon Cottage" at 505 East Eleventh Street, and they were living there when their newborn son died in 1888 and when their daughter, Margaret Worth Porter, was born September 30, 1889. I purchased this cottage and later made it possible for the City of Austin to acquire it to be made into a youth center in Wooten Park adjacent to Lamar Boulevard, but it was destroyed by a fire set by vandals in 1956. I did save the white pomegranate from the yard at 505 East Eleventh Street (Athol and Will used to place cuttings from this shrub on their little boy's grave), and its "descendants" are alive in my own garden to this day.

From the home on Eleventh Street, Will and Athol moved to 308 East Fourth, across the street from the Roach family. This home was moved to Fifth Street (now the O. Henry Museum), and it was for this cottage that Athol bought muslin curtains and wicker chairs, using the money Will had saved to send her to the World's Fair in Chicago, because she said she loved home and Will more than any trip she could possibly take. Her sacrifice is the source of the celebrated O. Henry story, "The Gift of the Magi," where the young wife Della cuts off her long hair and sells it in order to buy her husband a present. Tuberculosis claimed Athol July 25, 1897, and O. Henry's only child, Margaret, also succumbed to this disease, in

1927, in Banning, California, having been married only a few days to Guy Sartin.

It was in 1891 that Will Porter became a teller in the First National Bank of Austin, a building designed by Abner Cook and located on the northwest corner of Sixth Street and Congress Avenue. The bank building was torn down and replaced by another which itself has been removed to make way for the One American Center's thirty-two story structure. Again a bank has come to that corner, but very few, passing by, remember that Will Porter's tragedy began here.

Will remained with the bank until late in December 1894, but in the meantime he had started a weekly newspaper, *The Rolling Stone,* which began publication in the spring of 1894 and ran about a year, discontinuing publication in April 1895.

In October 1895, Will Porter went to Houston, where he was on the staff of the Houston *Post* until late in June of the following year.

Early in 1896, Porter was arrested on an indictment for alleged embezzlement of bank funds during the time he was teller for the First National Bank. The case was put off on Porter's motion until the July term of federal court at Austin.

Porter sent his wife and child to her parents in Austin and sometime after his last Houston *Post* column appeared Monday, June 22, 1896, he left Houston and caught a train for New Orleans. He did not reappear in Austin until the following January, 1897. Mrs. Porter was seriously ill and died in July 1897, and her husband did not stand trial until February 1898. He was convicted, and in April of that year left Austin for Columbus, Ohio, never to return to Texas, even after he had served a prison term reduced for good conduct from five years to three years and three months.

Thus, briefly, we have the salient facts concerning the years Will Porter spent in Austin, Texas. How those years left their mark upon his life is the theme of the remaining pages of my discussion.

It was in Austin that Porter had his first taste of social life as a young, eligible bachelor. It was here that he married and here his two children were born. It was in Austin that Porter spent the formative years of his writing career. He sold his first short story while living in Austin, and he contributed to newspapers and minor periodicals around the country. It was here that he published and illustrated and wrote most of the material for *The Rolling Stone.*

It was in Austin that Porter suffered his great misfortune and public disgrace. It was from Houston that he fled as a fugitive from justice, and it was to Austin he voluntarily returned to face the ordeal of his trial. In Austin he laid to rest his first-born and buried his wife as a broken-hearted husband. It was in Austin that Will Porter ran the gamut of emotional experience from joy and love to sorrow and humiliation.

From prison Porter went to Pittsburgh, where Margaret and the Roaches, her grandparents, were living, and from there he went to New York, where he lived the rest of his life and died June 5, 1910. From 1901 to 1910, O. Henry enjoyed popularity and success as a writer, drawing heavily upon his experiences in Texas, and particularly, in Austin.

One of the most colorful descriptions of Austin in the 1880s has been furnished me by a man who formerly lived in Austin and who became an intimate friend of Will Porter:

> In Austin I met many of the nicest young men of the town. I had as my intimate friends Walter Wilcox, Dave and Joe Harrell, William Sidney Porter, Bert Randolph, Joe Cavalier, Sherm Drake, Ed Byrnes, Joe McCarty and many others. . . . Austin was a gay place in the 80's. I guess we added some to the gay little things that happened there or thereabouts. We certainly went places and saw things. The old burg was filled with cowmen, flush of money, rearing to spend it on gambling, booze and the women of the night. We trailed and piked along with this bunch of high rollers. We were cronies with Bud and Tobe Driscoll, Miel and Alf Mienel, Alex Casparis, Billy Searight, and other top-notch night rounders. We played Faro, Chuckaluck, Keno, stud poker, and roulette at Ben Marshall's or Bill Perkins'. We drank and had good credit with Dave Hunter, the Iron Front, Fritz Hartkopf, Texas Siftings, Charley Cortissoz, and dear old Doc Muntick, who could look you in the eye and prescribe a pick-you-up that would put backbone on a rope.
>
> For good food on open account we had Tom Looke, Billie Salge, Simon and Billeisen to fall back on with a sure welcome. Miss Georgia Frazier, Miss Dixie Darnell and Miss Sallie Daggett were night hostesses, pandering to depraved tastes with the *tout ensemble* of various culls on the hoof. Our clothes were tailored to a nicety by Mr. Raymond Renz just to our tastes and on long credits. Well, you know men will be men, so we deny these things.
>
> During this time we did a lot of boating and swimming in the Colorado River. . . . We made many happy excursions for hunting and fishing. . . . On one of our trips Ed Struber, while we were splitting a keg of beer, hit upon the happy expedient of naming our boat after some prominent citizens and collecting $50 for the honor. It worked fine for a time. Our noble craft bore in succession the names Major Wheatley, Major Burke, the Charles Hicks, and then finally the A. P. Wooldridge.
>
> During all of this time we were mingling with and enjoying

the society of Austin. We danced at the old Turner Hall until our collars wilted. At times we had Germans which called for evening clothes. As for inaugural balls, they were all-night revels, never to be forgotten.

This man speaks of the cattlemen and the money they spent in Austin. What does O. Henry say of these?

> . . . In those days the cattlemen were the anointed. They were the grandees of the grass, kings of the kine, lords of the lea, barons of beef and bone. They might have ridden in golden chariots had their tastes so inclined. The cattleman was caught in a stampede of dollars. It seemed to him that he had more money than was decent. But when he had bought a watch with precious stones set in the case so large that they hurt his ribs, and a California saddle with silver nails and Angora skin *suaderos,* and ordered everybody up to the bar for whiskey — what else was there for him to spend his money for?

And Austin of the 1880s and the 1890s, what was it like, according to O. Henry? In reading the following passage, one may substitute the word *Austin* each time San Rosario is mentioned, and one then arrives in Austin, Texas, on a train and starts walking up Congress Avenue to Sixth Street.

> . . . The westbound stopped at San Rosario on time at 8:20 A.M. A man with a thick black-leather wallet under his arm left the train and walked rapidly up the main street of the town. . . . After walking a distance of three squares he came to the center of the town's business area. Here another street of importance crossed the main one, forming the hub of San Rosario's life and commerce. . . . Upon one corner stood the post office. Upon another Rubensky's Clothing Emporium. The other two diagonally opposing corners were occupied by the town's two banks, the First National and the Stockmen's National. . . . ("Friends in San Rosario")

O. Henry has moved the post office to Sixth Street and Congress Avenue. He has changed the name of Scarbrough and Hicks to Rubensky, and he has moved the old State Bank three doors west on East Sixth Street to get it on the corner opposite the old First National. With these slight alterations, he has returned to the Austin he knew so well.

Now examine Austin of the late 1880s as viewed from a window of the old General Land Office where Will Porter spent four happy years:

> . . . The Land Office capped the summit of a bold hill. The eyes of the Commissioner passed over the roofs of many houses set in a

packing of deep green, the whole checkered by strips of blinding white streets. The horizon, where his gaze was focused, swelled to a fair wooded eminence flecked with faint dots of shining white. There was a cemetery, where lay many who were forgotten, and a few who had not lived in vain. And one lay there occupying very small space, whose childish heart had been large enough to desire, while near its last beats, good to others. ("Georgia's Ruling")

The grave O. Henry saw in this striking picture perhaps was that of Athol, whose unfaltering faith in Will Porter must have been a consolation to him and a refuge long after her untimely death. It also probably represented the grave of his small son, buried like Athol in Austin's Oakwood Cemetery.

Another O. Henry story, "Bexar Scrip No. 2692," contains a description of the Land Office.

Whenever you visit Austin you should by all means go to see the General Land Office. As you pass up the avenue you turn sharp around the corner. . . and on a steep hill before you, you see a medieval castle. You think of the Rhine; the "castled crag of Drachenfels"; the Lorelei; and the vine-clad slopes of Germany. And German it is in every line of its architecture and design. . . . even now, when you enter the building, you lower your voice, and time turns backward for you, for the atmosphere which you breathe is cold with the exudations of buried generations.

Designed by C. C. Stremme, the General Land Office where Will Porter worked was built in 1857 and until 1918 housed the myriad documents and maps pertaining to land transactions in Texas. Today the old Land Office contains the museums of the United Daughters of the Confederacy on the first floor and the Daughters of the Republic of Texas on the second floor. O. Henry's desk is still there.

A prized acquisition for my collection was a domino table used by Will Porter and one of his Land Office friends, Charles ("Count") Scrivener. It is a round walnut table with shelves where one could place a sandwich and a drink while he dealt the cards or played dominoes. I also located and bought a second "O. Henry" table, this one quite famous because it was given full-page writeups in the Houston and Dallas papers. O. Henry — when he was Will Porter — playfully cut a notch in this round table to show that it was *his* place to sit in Zerchausky's old Bismarck Saloon on Congress Avenue. O. Henry's chair, which matches the table, was luckily kept with it.

It is surprising to see that even with the modern buildings

which have sprung up in recent years in Austin, with the exception of the First National Bank, most of the major structures associated with Will Porter's life remain — his second home, the Land Office, the Old Bakery, the Smoot home where he was married, St. David's Episcopal Church where he sang in the choir, the Texas State Capitol (scene of "Art and the Bronco"), the Federal Courthouse where he was tried, and the old Millett Opera House (now the home of the Austin Club) at 110 East Ninth Street, where he and Athol sang in musicals like "Pinafore" and where Will even choreographed a folk dance by making sketches of the proper movements of the dancers.

And of Texas, whose capital was Austin, what did O. Henry have to say?

> In Texas you may travel a thousand miles in a straight line. . . . Clouds there sail serenely against the wind. The whippoorwill delivers its disconsolate cry with the notes exactly reversed from those of his Northern brother. . . .
>
> The Legislature convenes at Austin, near the center of the state and, while the representative from Rio Grande country is gathering his palm leaf fan and his linen duster to set out for the capital, the Panhandle solon winds his muffler above his well-buttoned overcoat and kicks the snow from his well-greased boots ready for the same journey. All this merely to hint that the big ex-republic of the Southwest forms a sizable star on the flag, and to prepare for the corollary that things sometimes happen there uncut to pattern and unfettered by metes and bounds.

Among the things uncut to pattern in the history of O. Henry are the numerous legends, unfettered by metes and bounds, which have grown up around the life of William Sidney Porter in Austin. He was not a great writer when he left Texas, but achieved fame long after he had been forgotten by many residents of the capital city. Many of these persons, in an attempt to reconstruct for inquiring newspapermen and other writers the events of Porter's life in Austin, were, in their anxious desire to please, guilty of supplying missing chapters from the great fund of the human imagination!

Furthermore, for some of these errors, O. Henry himself, or, to be more just, the people who made him talk of himself against his wishes, might be held responsible. Once in his life Porter allowed himself to be interviewed. Driven by his literary associates to reveal something of his past, he made some remarks which, put together by a clever newspaperman, formed an amazing narrative, partly true, partly misleading, and very largely pure "spoofing." Numerous writers relied on this account in discussing the life of the author whose work was so widely known and who was so little known himself. Not until his work had been translated into many languages and he had published two books — not until he had been free five years — was it known outside of a little circle of friends that the famous author was really W. S. Porter of North Carolina and Texas.

And so legends cluster about the writer even to this day. It is no easy task to winnow the chaff from the few grains of truth in the many tales still circulating in Austin about Porter. A typical story is the one told by a highly respected citizen whose graphic account of how he took Mrs. Porter and Margaret to the train when Will was leaving to serve his term in the penitentiary and of this sad leave-taking, would move one to tears if it were not for the fact that everyone else seems to know that Athol died almost nine months before Porter was taken away to prison and that Margaret did not learn that her father had been in prison until she was a grown woman.

The most amazing legends about Porter have come from his mysterious movements during the nearly seven months he was a fugitive from justice after he skipped his trial set for July 6, 1896. Biographers admittedly know little of O. Henry's movements during these months. But his trail can be reconstructed from his stories. He definitely went directly to New Orleans from Houston, and later he wrote six stories with a Crescent City background, one of them written in prison — "Whistling Dick's Christmas Stocking." It was plain that Porter remained in Central America long enough to absorb a great deal of the spirit of the land and its people. His first book, *Cabbages and Kings,* had for its principal locale the "volatile republic" whose capital "lay at the sea's edge on a strip of alluvial coast."

Al Jennings has been the cause of numerous references to Porter's associations with fugitive outlaws, train robbers, and stick-up men in Central America. But in this Jennings obviously is making a thing of whole cloth, for he tells of celebrating the Fourth of July with Porter in Salvador on July 4, 1896. That was only a few days after Porter left Houston for New Orleans, and the next July 4 Porter was back in Austin sitting at the bedside of his dying wife.

Unimportant as literary productions, Jennings's books in which he relates these fabrications have been used as source material by practically all later biographers of O. Henry. Moreover, his verbal reminiscences have crept into many books, magazine articles, and newspaper stories. As a result, the history of O. Henry, as accepted by millions of his admirers today, is in part a fairy story, doing justice neither to the life nor to the character of the real man.

Another myth still extant in Austin is that the police officers and other authorities by common consent agreed to lay off Will Porter after he came back to Austin until after Mrs. Porter's death. The slightest investigation of the real facts will convince anyone that such was not the case. In *The Caliph of Bagdad* (1931) we read that when Will Porter returned "so keenly in sympathy were the police and other authorities of Austin with his little wife, condemned to death and fighting her battle, that they not only ignored his presence in the city, but also privately sent him word that if he kept out of sight during his wife's illness they would not molest him."

An Austin professional man told me: "The officers did not bother him as long as his wife was sick. They left him alone until after her death. I remember the officers coming to the house and taking him away right after the funeral." An Austin business man provided me with this piece of fiction:

> Porter was in the Travis County jail after he came back to Austin, but was released on his own recognizance to attend his wife's funeral. Emmett White was sheriff at that time and when word came to him that Mrs. Porter was dying, Sheriff White sent for Will Porter in his jail and brought him into the sheriff's office in the living quarters in the old Travis County jail. There he told Porter that he was going to permit Porter to go on his own honor and on his solemn promise to return, in order to be with Mrs. Porter in her last hours. As soon as the funeral was over, Porter returned voluntarily to the jail, where he remained until after his trial in 1898.
>
> The reason I know this story is true [the man continued] is because Porter himself told it to me. Either the day of the funeral or the day after. . . . I was passing down an alley back of the Roach home, where Mrs. Porter had been staying. . . . I saw Will Porter sitting on the back porch with his little daughter in his arms, and I got down from the wagon and went in to offer him my sympathy. . . . He was one of the most broken men I ever saw, and it was on this occasion that he told me about Sheriff White letting him out of jail on his honor.

I have personally examined the court records in the federal district clerk's office in Austin, and I find that the judge of the court filed an order on February 12, 1897, giving Porter the right to file a new bond. Porter had returned to Austin in January and was represented by the law firm of Ward and James, who, on the same day that the court entered his order permitting the bond to be filed, filed a new bond signed by G. P. Roach, Mrs. Porter's stepfather, and Herman Pressler. On the first day of the same month Porter's attorneys had filed motions to quash the indictments against Porter, and on the following July 3 a subpoena was requested in Porter's behalf demanding the bank books in court.

Porter was out on bond during all these months. He was not in the Travis County jail, and neither was he hiding out from the officers; nor were they with common consent permitting him to remain a fugitive under their very noses. Everything was entirely regular.

This naturally brings us to the trial of W. S. Porter for alleged embezzlement of funds of the First National Bank of Austin. Many persons have asked me whether I believed Porter to be guilty of the charges on which he was tried. I have examined every paper on file in Austin and have read the entire record in the Circuit Court of Appeals at New Orleans, to which Porter's case was appealed in the fall of 1898. Technically everything was regular, but none of us has any way of knowing today what evidence the jury had before it. No transcript of the testimony was made, and the court reporter who took the testimony down — the late Charles E. Pickle — told me that he had lost or destroyed his stenographic notes many years ago.

The testimony must have been confusing to a jury of laymen, unskilled in accounting or banking methods. O. Henry's trial began on February 15, 1898, just a little over six months after his wife's death. The courtroom in which he was tried was on the second floor of the old Federal Court Building, on the northeast corner of West Sixth Street and Colorado Street, now called O. Henry Hall and used for administrative offices by The University of Texas. As a young lawyer, I tried many cases in this courtroom, and so for posterity I have made a diagram of the way it used to look. The trial judge was T. S. Maxey, the Virginia-educated presiding judge for the Western District of Texas, who held court in Austin twice a year in February and July. Will's attorneys were R. Hamilton Ward and Ashby James; the district attorney was R. U. Culberson, and his assistant was Duval West. D. H. Hart was the deputy clerk; Charley Pickle, the court reporter.

The twelve jurors were these: W. H. Barr, the foreman, from Sprinkle in Travis County; Hugh McClure, from Oatmanville, in Travis County; L. H. Washington, a black man, a minister from Giddings; S. B. Mallett, from Burnet; Christopher Bigon, from Giddings; J. A. Caspar, from Maysfield in Milam County; Mark Patterson, of Taylor's Gin in Burnet County; T. H. Lipscomb, from Independence, Washington County; W. H. Wren, of Lampasas County; Joe Bryson, from Leander in Williamson County; Charles Anders, of Schulenberg in Fayette County; and — the lone Austinite on the jury — Marion D. Townley, editor and publisher of the *Southern Republican*. Margaret was never brought to the courtroom, for Will would never bring himself to capitalize on his heartbreaking loss. Instead, he sat there quietly, hands often clasped behind his head. Will Porter said that as soon as he saw the jury, he knew they they would never understand the complexities of the case. On February 17, 1898, the jurors returned a verdict of guilty, the original verdict signed by Barr as foreman erroneously spelling *defendant* as *defendent!*

Will wrote his mother-in-law this letter after the trial.

> Right here I want to state solemnly to you that in spite of the jury's verdict I am absolutely innocent of wrongdoing in that bank matter, except so far as foolishly keeping a position that I could not successfully fill. Any intelligent person who heard the evidence presented knows that I should have been acquitted. After I saw the jury I had very little hopes of their understanding enough of the technical matters presented to be fair. I am naturally crushed by the result. . . . I would have a few of my friends still believe that there is some good in me.

To understand what happened to Will Porter, one must know something of banking styles in nineteenth-century Texas. Edmunds Travis, an excellent historian and newspaperman — once part-owner of the *Austin Statesman* — wrote several informative articles about O. Henry which were published in the old *Bunker's Texas Monthly.* This is his analysis of Will's problems in the bank:

> . . . he had entered upon a career for which he was fitted neither by temperament nor training. He had too much job, even for a banker. And he was no banker. . . . He had to receive deposits, cash checks and drafts, and keep books on the side. To make matters worse, the bank was conducted along decidedly informal lines. It had begun as an institution devoted largely to stockmen's accounts, and its ways were the ways of the Old West. Overdrafts were allowed generously, and in the case of the officials of the bank, the formality of checking was often dispensed with. A slip in the cash drawer or a word to the teller accounted for many withdrawals of cash. Such practice added to the burdens of an employee who would have been overburdened without them.

Dr. Marilyn McAdams Sibley confirms this view in her splendid biography of George W. Brackenridge (1973). "If the San Antonio National Bank represented Brackenridge's success," she says, the First National Bank of Austin "marked his failure." The bank opened April 11, 1874, but George Brackenridge, himself an astute businessman, unfortunately left the management of the First National Bank of Austin to his brothers, Tom and Bob. Tom became the president of the bank and Bob, its cashier. Tom raised registered Jersey bulls and bronze turkeys on his farm south of Austin; Bob, an M.D., was involved in church work and the improvement of hospital care. (Brackenridge Hospital in Austin was later named for him.) Tom was a retired Confederate major and devoted a great deal of time to the Confederate Home. He even ran for governor! Mrs. Sibley writes that these activities

> left little time for the First National, and its affairs reflected as much. A parade of bank examiners testified to the brothers' unfitness for their jobs at the bank. They were "honest," the examiners reported; there was "not the slightest suggestion of criminality"; they enjoyed a "good reputation" in Austin. But there was little else of a complimentary nature that could be said of them except that they did business in a handsome building at a convenient location. They were "thoroughly incompetent"; they used "very poor business methods"; their bank suffered "continued and sustained losses"; the only real banker in the family was brother George in San Antonio and for some strange reason he paid little heed to the Austin operation. "Why they are continued in charge is beyond me," commented one examiner. . . . (Sibley, *Southwestern Historical Quarterly*, 74 (April 1971), 483–484.)

Then the brothers discovered that the bookkeeper, J. M. Thornton, Bob Brackenridge's nephew, had embezzled or "borrowed" some funds he could not repay. The Brackenridges solved this — not by prosecuting Thornton — but by dismissing him from his post and levying an assessment on the stockholders. When a bank examiner questioned the discrepancies and the coverup, Tom Brackenridge asked him to keep it quiet.

Will Porter entered the bank scene solely because his Land Office job had evaporated with a change of commissioners. Athol said that Will was afraid to take time off for lunch, the bank was so poorly run. It is difficult for the modern reader to imagine the situation Will Porter had to cope with, since today we are so accustomed to very large institutions with many employees, machines, and computers.

In 1893 George Brackenridge sold the bank to Frank Hamilton and James R. Johnson of the private banking house of James H. Raymond and Company. Tom and Bob and Will Porter continued in the same posts they had held before, but Will had begun publishing *The Rolling Stone* and was looking forward to a time when he could get into a field closer to his natural interests.

The comptroller of the currency in Washington at this time began to pressure federal banks to correct laxities in their banking methods, so that when Mr. "Nettlewick-Gray" came to inspect the newly purchased bank in the fall of 1894, he felt himself under a mandate to expose any and all irregularities. He cited fifty instances of such irregularities, totaling $5,654.20, and named the teller, Will Porter, as the probable culprit. The new owner, Frank Hamilton, testified before the grand jury on Porter's behalf, saying that he may have indeed made mistakes but was definitely not a thief and should not be prosecuted as one. The bank examiner was furious when he learned the grand jury had no-billed Porter and that furthermore J. M. Thornton was the foreman of that grand jury! The very same Thornton who had earlier been involved in irregular banking practices at the very same bank!

Gray wrote a heated letter to the comptroller in Washington, pointed a finger at District Attorney Culberson for his lenience, and in every way set out to "get his man." This time he was successful in bringing Will Porter to trial, with the results already related. The prosecution dropped all of the charges but two, totaling $854.08, and they had amended a fatal flaw in the original indictment, alleging embezzlement of funds on November 12, 1895, though Porter was not working at the bank on that date, but was living in Houston and working on the Houston *Post.*

The prosecution could never prove that Will Porter actually had possession of any monies taken from bank funds — only that there were undisputed mixups and flaws in bookkeeping for which he was responsible. Years later, when he was a retired judge in San Antonio, Duval West told a reporter that he believed Will Porter was the victim of the banking practices of the day and innocent of intentional misappropriation of funds.

Will Porter's case was appealed by Ward and James, a prominent firm of capable Austin lawyers, to the Circuit Court of Appeals at New Orleans. The judgment of the trial court was affirmed by the appellate court on December 13, 1898, though for months Porter had written his family that he hoped for a reversal of the decision.

Almost all scholars agree that what made it difficult for the jury to acquit Will Porter was the fact, proved at trial, that he had skipped the trial first set for July 6, 1896. This made Porter look guilty whether he was or not, and a jury has the right to consider flight, at least in part, as an admission of guilt. O. Henry himself said that his flight was a fatal error. "I am like Lord Jim," he said, "because we both made one fateful mistake at the supreme crisis of our lives, a mistake from which we could not recover."

O. Henry wrote three stories which describe the casual banking practices he had witnessed; in them he never appeared to lose his sense of balance and humor, and he never seemed to be accusing any persons or person. These are "Friends in San Rosario," "A Call Loan," and "The Guardian of the Accolade."

His case was almost won in higher court on the point that the lower court had refused to submit the issue of whether Will Porter was actually a fugitive from justice. But, when it was discovered that the record did not disclose that Porter's attorneys had requested a charge on this issue at the trial, the judge writing the opinion of the appellate court was compelled to affirm the case. In the opinion it was stated that

> an entirely different case would be presented if the plaintiff in error had requested the trial judge to submit the question of flight to the jury, and if, upon the judge's refusal to do so, the point had been duly preserved for review by us. . . . If this statement were sustained by the record, a serious question would be presented; but we find nothing in the bills of exception to sustain the statement.

There are numerous aspects of Will Porter's trial, then, to bear in mind as one tries to assess his guilt or innocence. Certainly F. B. Gray was correct in finding not a few irregularities in the books. Most assuredly Will Porter received a fair trial, and Culberson and West were reluctant to prosecute him. There is no question that many persons testified to his good character and that his life shows that at no other time was he ever accused of unethical or dishonest acts. Any fairminded student of his case would acknowledge that he worked in a bank just taken over by new owners from men who had no talent for running a bank. The grand jury at first no-billed Porter and the bank's new owner befriended him. Yet the trial jury found him guilty. Three factors sent Will Porter to prison: the chaos of the bank records from years past; the comptroller's decision to crack down on Texas banks and prevent a repetition of the Thornton case; and the question mark attached to his innocence because he fled to Honduras to avoid trial in July 1896.

The final judgment on the guilt or innocence of William S. Porter is written in Vol. 91, *Federal Reporter,* at page 494, but the final judgment on Will Porter of Austin was written by O. Henry in his story, "The Roads We Take," published in the New York *World* for August 7, 1904.

> It was an accident my comin' West. I was walkin along the road with my clothes in a bundle. . . . I came to a place one evenin' where the road forked and I didn't know which fork to take. I studied about it for half an hour and then took the left-hand. . . . I've often wondered if I wouldn't have turned out different if I'd took the other road. . . .

Oh, I reckon you'd have ended up about the same. It ain't the roads we take; it's what's inside of us that makes us turn out the way we do.

There are many in Austin who think "ole" Will Porter turned out "right good."

[II]

The Imprisoned Splendor

Jenny Lind Porter

William Sidney Porter was born in Greensboro; O. Henry, in Columbus. Will's parents were Dr. Algernon Sidney and Mary Jane Swaim Porter; O. Henry was the child of *Necessity* and *Invention*. Will married and had two children; O. Henry begot nearly 300 mind children, the short stories. Porter was buried in Asheville; O. Henry is his sole survivor.

My concern here is not his guilt nor his innocence but what he did with the "time to write" he found in prison. Other men before him had written their hearts out in dungeons: St. Paul, Galileo, Sir Thomas More, John Bunyan, John Donne, Cervantes, Napoleon, Touissaint L'Ouverture, Dostoevsky. Sir Walter Raleigh wrote a history of mankind during his thirteen years in prison. Daniel Defoe's writing talent got him both in and out of jail; he was locked up because of a satire and released because of a ballad. Leigh Hunt took his wife and enormous brood of children with him to Horsemonger Lane Jail, where he installed books, busts, venetian blinds, and a piano. He was there for calling the Prince Regent, among other unflattering things, "a fat Adonis of fifty." Thoreau spent a day in jail for nonpayment of his poll tax.

A picture of O. Henry as he looked upon entering prison showed all the defeat and strain of the past two years. He was now prisoner No. 30664, five feet seven, with blue eyes, chestnut brown hair, broad shoulders, and a mustache. Death had claimed his mother, his father, his grandmother Ruth, his Aunt Lina, his infant son, and, only seven months before the trial, his young wife, Athol. He had lost his home, his job, and his reputation. In 1898 no one would have pointed his way if you had asked, "Where is the new master of the American short story?"

In the next ten years O. Henry furnished a surprise ending for young Will Porter's tragedy. Will was first assigned the duties of night clerk in the prison pharmacy, working from five at night to five in the morning. Things quieted down around midnight, and he was free to read and think. Gradually a synthesis of his forces allowed the "imprisoned splendor" within him to escape, so that in thirty-nine months he was able to produce twelve, perhaps thirteen, stories. These were sent to a contact in New Orleans, who then mailed them on to New York publishers. The author was now "O. Henry," a pseudonym probably adopted from the abbreviated name of a French pharmacist, Etienne Ossian Henry, though some of the stories were signed Sidney Porter or Olivier Henry. As a matter of fact, Will Porter employed twelve pseudonyms for his writing, and several years elapsed before he used "O. Henry" exclusively.

The stories explored his past, stabilized his present, and forecast his future. The indolent convict in his cell, the stoic guard on his rounds, how little they knew of this quiet man who sat scribbling at his desk beyond the pharmacy rail; beaten, hurt, and humiliated, it is true, but working again and writing as he had never written before. From Columbus the beacon light of his mind swept across the pear flats of the Frio bottom, illumined the excelsiored interior of a freight train bearing a hobo to New Orleans, played over the red tile roofs and adobe walls of Trujillo, pierced the shadows of Alamo Plaza, and returned to join the soft blue haze of the Blue Ridge Mountains.

> A death blow is a life blow to some,
> Who till they died, did not alive become.
> — Emily Dickinson

Out of the depths of Will Porter's despair came O. Henry.

A little notebook he kept in prison lists the stories in the order in which he sent them out.

The first story Will Porter wrote in prison and the first to which he signed the name, "O. Henry," was "Whistling Dick's Christmas Stocking" (*McClure's,* December 1899). Will Porter wrote his last column for the Houston *Post* on June 22, 1896, and shortly thereafter caught a train for New Orleans. Having skipped his trial, he was now "Shirley Worth," living in a room near the famed restaurant of Mme. Louis Begué and seeking anonymity in the great port city. Lonely and believing that a pardon or a dismissal of his case was only a matter of time, he must have found comfort in the beauty of old New Orleans.

How many weeks or months he spent there, we cannot say, but anyone who knows New Orleans will recognize the verisimilitude of O. Henry's descriptions, his perfect command of the colors, sounds, and fragrances which define its charm. The soft mélange of dialect is here, the clang of trolley, the whistle of a far-off train. The Negroes sing as they unload great ships with their burden of bananas and cocoanut and work in the fields of sugarcane and rice. The markets blaze with flowers. The squares, parks, levees, and boulevards are faithfully remembered.

Where Whistling Dick walks, Will Porter himself had walked, and what Whistling Dick hears and sees, Will Porter himself had heard and seen. It is a story brought to life through appeal to our senses. He entices us with the aroma of fresh bread in the French market; he repels us with the mildewed, briny stench of old tarpaulins. His genius attunes our ears to the tiniest sounds: the vicious soprano of a mosquito, the oily gurgle of the river, the hoarse croaking of frogs along the levee. When Whistling Dick picks up the girl's black silk stocking, our fingertips become his, stroking its delicacy.

Whistling Dick is the grand hobo, tramp, nomad, and pícaro of literature, noble though impecunious, high-minded though double-dyed in sloth. Deep within him there is a harmony that answers to harmony; a love of beauty that identifies with loveliness; a humor and a music that compel us to love this ambling rogue. The theme of the story is Whistling Dick's one requirement in life, *freedom,* and its hero is the first of seven leading characters in the prison stories who balance their faults with a single, compassionate deed. Writing this story in prison out of his poet-musician's heart, O. Henry must have imagined the freedom that would be his one day, when he could walk out of the door and down the path as he chose. There is a secondary theme in the hero's preference for honor over illicit gain.

O. Henry is very much at ease and accurate in his descriptions of hoboes and hobo camps. Whistling Dick is addressed as "Jack," the traditional salutation for a hobo. Possibly Will Porter caught a freight train to New Orleans and lived for a time in the hobo camps to conceal his identity. Certainly Whistling Dick is not O. Henry's only hobo; there is Chicken Ruggles, of "The Passing of Black Eagle," who loses all interest in robbing a train when he catches a whiff of excelsior from an open box car. "Black Eagle sniffed at the witching smell as the returned wanderer smells of the rose that twines his boyhood's home."

When he returned to Austin from Honduras in January 1897, Will Porter tried to earn some money by writing. At this time he may have composed an early version of this story called "Whistling Sam's Christmas Stocking." I discovered it in the Alderman Library archives of The University of Virginia and surmised that it was a flawed first draft of "Whistling Dick." Since O. Henry destroyed much of his youthful output, this draft is important, for it permits us to assess the swift evolution of his genius. For instance, in the early version the dialects are of inferior quality: "See here," said the policeman, "You don't look so convicky as some; lemme give you a tip. After twelve today all you tramps are going to be run in. There's too many of you in town. Can you use the pointer in your business?" The story as we know it reads, "Der orders are to bull all der pums after sunrise. . . . It's der pest tip you efer had. I gif it to you because I pelief you are not so bad as der rest. Und because you can vistle 'Der Freischütz' bezzer dan I myself gan." Now the ordinary policeman of "Whistling Sam" has become the "Big Fritz" of "Whistling Dick," an individual down to his flat flask, love of music, and German dialect. Here is the beginning of O. Henry's eventual mastery of dialect, a skill born of his lifelong love affair with the dictionary, his musician's ear, and his personal experience. In Austin and Fredericksburg he had listened to many friends "gargling away at each other in pectoral German."

The plots of the two versions are the same, though in the first sketch the character of Whistling Dick is not fully rounded, the descriptions of New Orleans are lifeless, and the marvelous later ending, a real *tour de force,* is completely absent.

Missing, too, from "Whistling Sam" is a vital element of "Whistling Dick," the use of music to set the tone of the story and give overtone to its theme. O. Henry was a fine musician, who sang, played the violin, and learned both guitar and mandolin. Margaret said that when they were alone, her father would often seat himself at the piano and play and sing for her by the hour, sometimes in dialect. He liked classical music and attended concerts and opera performances in Austin at the old Millett Opera House, but he also loved ragtime, folk songs, Spanish ballads, and popular tunes. The very last words of his life came from a song, "Turn up the lights / I don't want to go home in the dark."

It was therefore quite natural for O. Henry to invest this tale with an apt musical symbolism. The plot of *Der Freischütz,* "The Freeshooter," (1830) by Carl Maria von Weber, affords numerous musical parallels with "Whistling Dick," while the famous "Intermezzo" from Pietro Mascagni's 1890 opera, *Cavalleria Rusticana,* has identical function in both opera and story, expressing the calm before the storm of an evil plot. The "Intermezzo" is a tranquil melody, usually played by the orchestra as an entr'acte before a deserted stage, but Whistling Dick's favorite air from the overture to *Der Freischütz,* doubtless the plaintive, haunting oboe solo, is animated in tempo and interrupted by sinister and mocking echoes. To hear this oboe solo is to hear Whistling Dick himself, with "the trill of mountain brooks, the staccato of green rushes above the chilly lagoons, the pipe of sleepy birds."

A true American story, with its New Orleans setting, its hoboes, and its dialects, "Whistling Dick's Christmas Stocking" is the best of the prison stories. It is obvious that O. Henry, who quotes from 136 authors in his stories, was familiar with the adventures of Figaro, the character of Fagan in Dickens' *Oliver Twist,* and the English picaresque novels. Yet the work is in no way derivative and remains an American classic. The craft is that of supreme genius, the road Whistling Dick travels after he steps off that freight car heading straight for the lighted windows of Bellemeade Plantation.

Another New Orleans story, "Blind Man's Holiday," (*Ainslee's,* 1905), is not listed in O. Henry's notebook because it was mailed out from Pittsburgh in 1901. Nevertheless, it merits some discussion here. Its theme is *the necessity of tolerance, the dangers of a hardened, cynical view of the world.* O. Henry's poem, "The Crucible," found on his desk after his death in 1910, expresses the same idea.

> Hard ye may be in the tumult,
> Red to your battle hilts,
> Blow give for blow in the foray,
> Cunningly ride in the tilts;
> But when the roaring is ended,
> Tenderly, unbeguiled,
> Turn to a woman a woman's
> Heart, and a child's to a child.

"Blind Man's Holiday" is the tale of an embezzler who has left his hometown to escape the disgrace of his trial. He comes from a family once named *Larsen* (Larceny?), but his present name is *Lorison* (*Loris* means clown or buffoon). In the story Lorison craves love, trust, and forgiveness but fails the test of these qualities in himself. Athol was surely the model for Norah, toiling unselfishly over her needlework, but the character and thoughts of Lorison interest us more. "From his point of perspective he saw himself an outcast from society, forever to be a shady skulker along that ragged edge of respectability."

He was not of this world. . . . He had dropped into a distinctly new orbit. The stroke of ill fortune had acted upon him, in effect, as a blow delivered upon the apex of a certain ingenious toy, the musical top, which, when thus buffeted while spinning, gives forth, with scarcely retarded motion, a complete change of key and chord.

Lorison is only in part Will Porter, yet the story provides valuable insight into Will's days in New Orleans, his feelings of isolation and disillusionment, and his recognition that he had undergone a "complete change of key and chord." O. Henry must have been very concerned lest he become bitter and skeptical, blind to the presence of goodness and reluctant to admit that purity and unselfishness exist.

The second and also the third of his stories written in prison are set in Texas and yield portraits of two longtime friends. The land commissioner of "Georgia's Ruling" (*Outlook,* June 30, 1900) is Dick Hall, and the ranger of "An Afternoon Miracle" *(Everybody's,* July 1902) is Lee Hall, Dick's brother. In her book, *Captain Lee Hall of Texas* (copyright 1940, by the University of Oklahoma Press), Dora Neill Raymond says that Dick Hall as land commissioner "learned much of the power of avaricious stockmen and of the vagaries of the law. Sidney Porter, his clerk [spent four years] in the pink, castle-like structure on the Capitol grounds where he studied men and manners in the Land Office. Perched high on his draftsman's stool, he watched a little world revolve beneath — a world where powerful land sharks triumphed with the aid of shyster lawyers."

A story O. Henry wrote in his Austin days, "Bexar Scrip No. 2692" (initially printed in *The Rolling Stone*) depicts such a land shark — an older man, named "Sharp," a churchgoer, a pillar of the community who tries to steal title to a widow's property. "He found a fatal defect in the title of the land as on file in Bexar Scrip No. 2692 and placed a new certificate upon the survey in his own name. . . . Then he wrote her a letter, offering her the choice of buying from him or vacating at once." Next Sharp attempts to remove both the file and the certificate of title from the Land Office building. The widow's son, Absalom Harris, shows up and confronts him, whereupon Sharp murders young Harris and buries both him and the incriminating file.

O. Henry begins his "Bexar Scrip" story in the Land Office with the case of the missing file, much as Hawthorne prefaces *The Scarlet Letter* with a description of the Custom-House where he worked and his discovery of the tattered scarlet letter.

Was there really a missing file, or did Will Porter imagine it all? Indeed, there was! The file for Bexar Scrip No. 2692, covering land in Tom Green County, was missing as early as 1883. The name Absalom Harris of course suggests King David in the Bible, so logically the name of the "2692" landowner should have been David Harris. This was not the name of the original landowner but an excellent choice, nonetheless, for David Harris was a prominent member of Stephen F. Austin's Old Three Hundred families and was granted a sitio in what is now Harris County in 1824 and a tract of land on the west side of the San Jacinto River in 1830. Harris's attorney was hardly a nonentity himself— William Barret Travis.

In the old General Land Office, Will Porter learned Texas history from primary sources in an archive without parallel.

Although Sharp is successful in his "Bexar Scrip" crime, the land commissioner in "Georgia's Ruling" defeats the land sharks. Dick Hall could hardly have objected to his portrait in this story. He emerges as the man he truly was, a person of great decency, integrity, and humanity; an administrator not easily intimidated; a memorable character. "He dressed in fine black, and there was a suggestion of Roman drapery in his long coat-skirts."

Richard Moore Hall, educated as a civil engineer, was born November 17, 1851, in Iredell County, North Carolina, and died November 18, 1927, in Houston. The son of Dr. and Mrs. James K. Hall, Dick arrived in Texas in 1872, served as county surveyor of Grayson County from 1875 to 1877, married Bettie Hughes in 1880, and ranched below Cotulla in La Salle County until 1884, when he moved to Florence in Williamson County. He was elected commissioner of the General Land Office in Texas (1887–1891) and then ran unsuccessfully against James Stephen Hogg for governor of Texas. Will Porter owed the Halls six of the happiest years of his life: the two years he lived in their home when he worked on their ranch, and the four years he spent in the Land Office.

O. Henry did not allow "Georgia's Ruling" to be published in book form while he lived. Some attribute this to the fact that it was such an intimate, revealing picture of Richard Moore Hall in his Land Office days. Most certainly state employees who worked closely with a public official were bound by high standards of ethics and etiquette. But in addition, this story touches upon Will Porter's secret territory of grief, and O. Henry was always prone to shelter his private life from public scrutiny.

The land commissioner of the story is a widower, yet Dick Hall's wife Betty was very much alive when Hall was land commissioner. She was alive at the time of Will's trial, in 1898, and she even contacted District Attorney Culberson on Porter's behalf. Dick and Betty Hall were the parents of two children, Mab and Don.

The widower of this story is thus O. Henry himself. It is he who looks out of the window of the Land Office and sees the cemetery to the east. It is his father's heart that aches for the baby he and Athol buried there in 1888. It is he who yearns for his little girl — not dead, but not to be seen again by him for years. It is the former draftsman who returns and sees once more the stoneflagged floors and plastered walls of this place where long ago he was so happy. *Ach, so!* It is O. Henry who recalls, as he writes this story, that directly across the street from this German castle was another stone building, the jail.

The theme of "Georgia's Ruling" is *love for a child and the power of that love to inspire and motivate the parent.* "He was a reserved man, and dignified almost to austerity, but the child had come below it all and rested upon his very heart, so that she scarcely missed the mother's love that had been taken away. There was a wonderful companionship between them, for she had many of his own ways, being thoughtful, and serious beyond her years." More than anything, O. Henry wanted to retain the love and respect of his child and to make her proud of him. He shielded her from knowledge of his imprisonment and mailed her loving, whimsical letters.

Margaret wrote the sequel to "Georgia's Ruling" twenty-three years later, in a special O. Henry issue of *The Mentor*, when she described his success as a father. He was, she said, "gentle, generous, gallant. . . . a rare companion — and a friend. The perfect friend."

The third story written in prison was "An Afternoon Miracle," a reworking of "The Miracle of Lava Canyon" (1897). The first version may be the better story of the two because it has an authentic setting in a western town, and its heroine, Dicey Reed, is a lovable, natural young girl. The only thing unnatural about her is her entire first name, Boadicea, for the bold Celtic queen who led the Iceni to battle against the Romans. In "An Afternoon Miracle" Dicey's counterpart is Miss Alvarita, an exotic snakecharmer. Both girls are described as strangers to fear. Dicey is not afraid of "snakes, dogs, spiders, gossips, and men," and Miss Alvarita appears in shows with a blue racer on either arm and Kuku, an eleven-foot Asian python, around her neck. "I never saw anything I was afraid of yet," says she. Each young lady attracts her man with the coy subterfuge of a century past: she conceals her confidence and bravery and prevails upon the hero to protect her — Dicey, from a "horrid lizard" and Alvarita, from a little caterpillar. In his ranch days, O. Henry had ample opportunity to see the courageous response of women to frontier conditions. George Wilkins Kendall of *Texan Santa-Fé Expedition* fame, tells how his wife, Adeline de Valcourt, coped with having to remove a rattlesnake that had coiled up around their French clock on the mantel.

The model for the hero in each tale is Lee (Red) Hall. He is the cool, blond sheriff of Lava Canyon, and he is the laconic border ranger, Bob Buckley. Lt. Sandridge of "The Caballero's Way" is also Lee Hall, "made of sunshine," "six feet two, blond as a Viking, dangerous as a machine gun." Will Porter never forgot this sun god of his youth, whom he had known in legend before he knew him in person. It is said that Lee Hall told Will Porter the tale of the jealous Blas, his Mexican sweetheart, and her ranger lover which inspired O. Henry's Cisco Kid masterpiece, "The Caballero's Way," a story known to millions through motion pictures and television. As a young ranchhand working on the 400,000-acre Dull-Hall ranch from 1882 to 1884, Will Porter saw firsthand the restraint and bravery with which Lee Hall handled fence cutters, cattle rustlers, and outlaws.

In his prison days, Will certainly needed *courage,* which is the theme of this story. He must often have thought of the wonderful control which "Red" Hall exhibited under pressure. Many spoke of Will Porter's calm demeanor when he was in prison and the quick courage with which he felled a giant Negro who was threatening the prison doctor, Dr. George W. Williard. "I was looking around for the guard when Sydney Porter, my drug clerk, went over his counter like a panther. All of his hundred and seventy or eighty pounds were behind the blow he sent into the Negro's jaw. The Negro came down on the floor like a ton of brick. Instantly Porter was behind his counter again. He did not utter a word."

In "An Afternoon Miracle" the ranger delivers "the good Saxon knockout blow. . . . and Garcia was down and out, with his head under a clump of prickly pear." Will could probably identify with the outwardly calm, inwardly tense Buckley, who tried to conceal his inner turmoil from others, "the horrible tightening of the chest," the "dry mouth."

"Money Maze" (*Ainslee's,* May 1901) and "Rouge et Noir" (*Ainslee's,* December 1901), the latter by "Olivier Henry," should be studied together, for they are drawn from Will Porter's 1896 Honduras experiences. "Rouge et Noir" derives its name from a gambling game played at a table that has two red and two black diamond-shaped marks on which bets are placed. It is furthermore the name of an 1830 novel of adventure by Stendhal, the pseudonym of a Frenchman named Henri-Marie Beyle (1783–1842). O. Henry may have read this novel, for we know that he read Dumas and Guy de Maupassant.

When Will Porter left New Orleans, he went on a fruit steamer to Honduras ("depths") in Central America. He may have worked on the New Orleans *Delta* or the *Picayune*, but he couldn't write for a newspaper in Trujillo or Puerto Cortés, and he wound up digging ditches and doing odd jobs, his fluency in Spanish a great asset. There seems to be little truth in Al Jennings's incredible yarn that he and his brother Frank and "Bill Porter" went from Honduras to Buenos Aires and Peru, and from there to Mexico City, San Diego, San Francisco, and back to San Antonio. We know for a fact that Will was gone from Austin only a little over six months and that Mrs. Roach wrote to Will in Honduras about Athol's weakened condition, causing him to leave Honduras and return home to Austin. Lollie Cave Wilson, an enduring family friend, writes in *Hard to Forget* that she received three letters from Will postmarked Honduras, one of these from Trujillo and one from Puerto Cortés.

The theme of "Money Maze" is *the incompetence of the guardians of the law,* while the theme of "Rouge et Noir" is the vagaries of fortune, where *life is a game of chance* with unpredictable, sudden gains and losses. It must have been great fun for O. Henry to write the comical "Money Maze," about a bank president absconding with a bag of money, innocent daughter in tow. Thus the exiled Dante hurled his enemies into hell — on paper. Mr. J. Churchill Wahrfield, the president-embezzler, and his daughter are chased by detective Shorty Flynn, who apprehends the wrong couple, President Miraflores and his opera-singer girlfriend, Julia Gordon, also equipped with a stolen bag of gold. The bank president shoots himself, and the *presidente* and his girl escape with their bag of loot intact.

O. Henry later wrote other stories about bankers, including one who tiptoes into the family bank at midnight and puts something out of the vault into his big old valise. It turns out to be merely two quarts of "silk-velvet bourbon," but the family retainer, Uncle Bushrod, first thinks it is money, and he is worried about a stain on the family honor of Mr. Robert Weymouth, the president of the bank, and Mr. William Weymouth, the cashier. "Lawd! Lawd!" says Uncle Bushrod, "Scan'lous sights upon dis yearth when de Weymouth fambly done turn out robbers and 'bezzlers!" This story, "A Guardian of the Accolade," should be read with two other bank stories by O. Henry, "Friends in San Rosario" and "A Call Loan."

The banana republic setting for both "Money Maze" and "Rouge et Noir" is Honduras. Its history goes back to Columbus, who claimed this land for the King of Spain in 1502, and to Hernando Cortés, who founded Puerto Cortés in 1525. In all, O. Henry wrote eight stories laid in Central America, and these form the basis of his first and only novel, *Cabbages and Kings* (1904). It was Witter Bynner (whom O. Henry called "Bitter Wynter") who hit upon the idea of changing some names and blending the eight stories into a single narrative. Not long after this, O. Henry gave Witter Bynner the manuscript copies of "A Fog in Santone" and "Blind Man's Holiday," but Doubleday's Harry Peyton Steger blocked Witter Bynner's plan to publish them in a volume Bynner called *Two Women*. Where the manuscript of "A Fog in Santone" had been in the seventy-nine years since Bynner received it as a gift from O. Henry until it turned up again in 1983 remains a mystery.

Malcolm D. McLean of Robertson's Colony fame has written a lively article about O. Henry in Honduras which tracks the writer in Trujillo and Puerto Cortés. Dr. McLean flew from Tegucigalpa to Trujillo to visit this "formidable border of tropical jungle topped by the overweening Cordilleras" and to see with an historian's eyes the truth or falsity of O. Henry's Honduras. Even the passage of sixty years could not obliterate the fact that O. Henry gave a truthful picture of the land and its people. There were the palm-thatched huts of the Caribs, a hotel reminiscent of the Hotel de los Estranjeros, the *fiestas* and *bailes*, the town at the sea-edge "like a little pearl in an emerald band." There were the "dinky little mud houses, grass over your shoetops in the street," and the "fearful mountains and streams."

The northern coastline where O. Henry landed stretches some 400 miles along the Caribbean Sea. O. Henry describes a fruit steamer chartered by the New Orleans fruit trade, lying out to sea with half-naked Caribs unloading her piles of bananas. What was the town like? "Grass huts, 'dobes, five or six two-story houses, population half-breeds, Caribs and blackamoors." The town also boasted of an American colony, glad that there was no extradition treaty with Honduras: "two defaulting bank presidents, one short county treasurer, four manslayers, and a widow — arsenic, I believe was the suspicion."

O. Henry displays his knowledge of Honduran exports in his summing up of Mackenzie as a "banana king, a rubber prince, a sarsaparilla, indigo, and mahogany baron." The Honduras O. Henry knew had large coffee farms and banana plantations and dealt in sugar, cattle, hardwoods, and cotton. He correctly describes the climate (rainy from May to October) and the mixed racial inheritance of the people. "Los Indios, looking like prehistoric stone idols, come down from the mountains to peddle their handiwork in the streets."

"Pasa was descended from the proudest Spanish families in the country."

He was also familiar with the history of this "volatile" republic, racked by revolutions and wars since it lay between Guatemala, Salvador, and Nicaragua. Honduras declared its independence from Spain and joined the Central American Federation. Under Francisco Marazán the Liberals achieved many reforms, but the Conservatives opposed him. In 1838 the Federation dissolved, and Honduras became an independent nation. Nevertheless, Liberals and Conservatives fought for control, and neighboring countries constantly interfered, resulting in a succession of rulers and revolutions from 1883 to 1903. In "Rouge et Noir," for instance, old Presidente Zarilla is in power one minute and out the next, having lost in the "game of chance" which was Central American politics. Such a president may be buried with "military dishonors."

These two stories reveal new facets of O. Henry's genius and herald the return of his rollicking sense of humor. He even authors a little sly joke on himself! Detective Flynn urges the man he takes to be Wahrfield the banker to "go back and take your medicine like a man. They'll only give you a five, or, maybe, a seven spot, and they'll send you to one of the reform pens where you will only have to keep books,* or feed the warden's chickens."

The prison notebook lists "No Story" (*Metropolitan,* June 1909), but "The Point of the Story" (*Redbook,* November 1903, as by Sidney Porter), is doubtless the original version. "No Story" is set in New York, whereas "The Point of the Story" remains close to the Austin experience. The theme of both stories fits the thinking of a normal young man like O. Henry, shut up in prison and deprived of feminine companionship: *No nice girl can be expected to marry a reprobate or a man with a past.* The setting of each story is a newspaper office, but where "No Story" refers to Long Island and quotes a Cohan song, "The Point of the Story" names the ingenue "Miss Rosa"** and alludes to a "Miss Ella Pease." In both stories the men in the newspaper office are continually asking for advances or borrowing from each other. Writing of the shaky finances of a young newspaperman may have brought to mind the Pease name, for Will Porter once wrote Miss Julia Pease and asked for a loan to underwrite his news-

---

* O. Henry's second job in prison.

** This probably derives from the name of Lollie Cave Wilson's sister. [cf. "Miss Rosa" in "A Fog in Santone."] When O. Henry named the boss "McArdle" he may have been thinking of the famous Texas historical painter, Henry Arthur McArdle of San Antonio (1836–1907).

paper, *The Rolling Stone*. Former Governor Elisha M. Pease had died in 1883, but Miss Julia and her mother continued to live at "Woodlawn," the stately family residence designed by Abner Cook which became, in recent years, the home of Governor and Mrs. Allan Shivers. We do not know if Will got his loan, but a famous contemporary did — Elisabet Ney, the sculptress. She hitched up her skirts and her buggy, sped over to "Woodlawn," and charmed them all. She even got them to serve her a vegetarian diet. Whether Will Porter ever met the eccentric artist or not, history doesn't say, but he did dance with her friend, Nannie Huddle, wife of William Henry Huddle, the historical painter whose "Surrender of Santa Anna" hangs in the Texas State Capitol. Nannie was herself a painter, and her hands served as the model for the hands of Elizabet Ney's "Lady Macbeth."

O. Henry's fears that no fine woman would ever love him, once he was out of prison, proved groundless. In 1946 Sara Coleman Porter told Judge Trueman O'Quinn about a conversation she had with O. Henry before they were married. They had gone for a ride in a carriage in Central Park, and O. Henry asked if she had any shadows in her past. Thinking his question related to morals, Sara replied, "Indeed not!" "Then I must tell you of my own," he said, and he proceeded to tell her the truth about himself and to explain he thought she had a right to know and also the right to change her mind about marrying him, if she wished. Happily, Sara did not change her mind. On November 27, 1907, she married William Sidney Porter, by then famous as O. Henry. The newspapers considered the elegant wedding "Quite a Story":

> The marriage took place last night at 8 o'clock at the home of the bride's brother, James Sloan Coleman, Sr., on Victoria Road, the Rev. Dr. R. F. Campbell officiating. Promptly at the appointed hour Mr. Porter entered the drawing room with his best man, Gilman Hall of New York City, editor of *Everybody's* Magazine. Then came Mrs. James Coleman, sister-in-law of the bride. . . . Palms, fern, southern smilax, and white chrysanthemums decorated the drawing room. The dining room was a veritable bower of pink flowers and greenery. An orchestra played throughout the evening, and a buffet supper was served to some sixty to seventy guests.
>
> The bride wore a white lace gown with an interlining of white chiffon and taffeta, made in princess style, the bottom of the skirt designed in bow knots outlined with seed pearls, while the whole gown was embroidered in pearls. The conventional veil was done away with instead of which a white aigrette was worn. She carried

a shower bouquet of lilies of the valley. [Greensboro *Daily News*,
September 14, 1969]

Sara told Judge O'Quinn that the two and a half years they had together were the happiest years of her life, and in her book, *Wind of
Destiny* (1916), she said of her husband, "the man was greater than
the author."

"A Fog in Santone" (*Cosmopolitan*, 1912) and "The Enchanted
Kiss" (*Metropolitan*, February 1904) are San Antonio stories. Like
"Whistling Dick," they preserve the spirit of a unique American city
and set O. Henry on his way to becoming a noted laureate of cities,
the author of stories wherein a city itself almost speaks.

In Austin Will Porter printed his short-lived newspaper, *The
Rolling Stone*, in the old Bruegherhof building on the southeast corner
of Tenth and Congress, but he handled his street sales and circulation and did his writing and artwork in upstairs quarters next to the
southwest corner of Ninth and Congress. Then in January of 1895,
Will attempted to increase sales by opening a San Antonio office at
903 South Presa Street and acquiring a partner in an Englishman
named Henry Ryder-Taylor. Naturally, he made frequent trips to
San Antonio.

Joseph Gallegly of Rice University has written an interesting
book on San Antonio and its environs in the days of O. Henry —
From Alamo Plaza to Jack Harris' Saloon. He believes that the setting for
"A Fog in Santone" was Scholz's Palm Garden.

> At Scholz's. . . . patrons rolled high dice to settle the score for
> drinks and rang for service a new-fangled contraption called an
> electric bell. There was an exquisite combination string and brass
> band to entertain guests while they sat at card tables in the semi-
> privacy of stalls or played at billiards in the large gameroom. In
> stall or in parlor, under brilliant incandescent lights, in this lovely
> center, with its setting of oleanders, palms, and cacti, the careworn
> visitor could recreate himself with the same degree of lavish ele-
> gance as that furnished in the patio of the Menger Hotel.

If Walter and "Miss Rosa" were not seated in the Palm Garden, Dr. Gallegly believes the Harnish and Baer Restaurant, with its
banana trees and fine beer, is another possibility. O. Henry knew all
of this area very well; in "Seats of the Haughty," for example, Lu-
cullus Polk and Solomon Mills order a round of drinks at the Menger Bar.

Like Walter Goodall of Memphis, Will Porter had come to
Texas from a southern state at age nineteen to cure a suspected tubercular condition. In those days, the country around Uvalde and

San Antonio attracted thousands of tubercular patients to the "Purest atmosphere, sir, on earth." Will had been Athol's daily attendant in the last half year of her life, and all of this personal experience lies behind his realistic accounts of the disease. "On the red streams of Hemorrhagia a few souls drifted away, leaving behind pathetic heaps, white and chill as the fog itself." The power and the pathos of his description made this a hard story to sell.

A melancholy Spanish quatrain sets the mood for the story, where a young, unhappy prostitute encourages Goodall to live and get well and then puts his powdered morphine in her own drink. In *The Complete Writings of O. Henry*, XII, the quatrain reads:

> En las tardes sombrillos del invierro
> En el prado a marar me reclino,
> Y maldigo mi fausto destino,
> Una vida la mas infeliz.

No proofreader nor editor had ever caught the errors which rob this stanza of its meaning. Fortunately, I was able to consult O. Henry's original manuscript and found that what he wrote was this:

> En las tardes sombrillos del *invierno*   (winter)
> En el prado á *llorar* me reclino,   (to weep)
> Y maldigo mi fausto destino—
> Una vida la más infeliz.

Dr. Miguel González-Gerth of The University of Texas and I agreed that this was likely part of a Spanish song which Will Porter had heard someone sing and that he simply recorded what he *thought* he had heard. His ear had missed the elision of "mi infausto" (my unlucky) and interpreted "sombrías" (shadowy) as "sombrillos." Therefore the stanza in its correct form should read:

> En las tardes sombrías del invierno
> En el prado á llorar me reclino,
> Y maldigo mi infausto destino—
> Una vida la más infeliz.

At last I could translate it into English verse and imagine Will Porter singing it and accompanying himself on the guitar.

> In the shadowy evenings of winter
> I fall to the earth and I weep,
> And I curse the sad fate I was born to,
> The unhappy lot I must keep.

There is no question that O. Henry considered killing himself. The proof may be found on some small sheets of dark cream paper now in the Humanities Research Center of The University of Texas. On May 18, 1898, Will Porter wrote to Mrs. Roach:

> I have tried to reconcile myself to remaining here for a time, but am about at the end of my endurance. There is absolutely not one thing in life at present or in prospect that makes it of value. I have decided to wait until the New Orleans court decides the appeal. . . . I can stand any kind of hardships or privations on the outside, but I am utterly unable to continue the life I lead here. I know all the arguments that could be advanced as to why I should endure it, but I have reached the limit of endurance. . . . It will be better for every one else and a thousand times better for me to end the trouble instead of dragging it out longer.

Gradually, he regained hope and left behind "the shadowy evenings of winter," the probable thought of using the "more than enough" white powder he could easily have obtained from the prison pharmacy where he worked. "A Fog in Santone" is O. Henry's suicide story, and it must have given him emotional catharsis to put it on paper. Clearly, the theme of "A Fog in Santone" is *the consideration and the rejection of suicide.* Without condemning those who took that route, O. Henry turned his face toward life. There are many literary references in this story — to Shakespeare's *Twelfth Night* and *Hamlet,* to Tennyson's "Crossing the Bar," to the *Rubáiyát* of Omar Khayyám, but none is more touching than his allusion to a line from Edgar Allan Poe's "The Raven" — "respite and nepenthe, from the memories of Lenore." The lost Lenore was of course Poe's wife, Virginia Clemm, who died of tuberculosis when she was very young, like Athol Estes Porter.

"The Enchanted Kiss" has for its theme *a man's frustrations in reaching his goal in life,* and the tendency to ascribe one's failures to fate. At the outset of the story we are introduced to the hero, a shy young drug clerk (shades of Will Porter) named Tansey who dreams of a kiss from his adored Miss Katie Peek. In prison, O. Henry must often have dreamed of love and affection and the symbol of love, a kiss. Tansey's slender frame enclosed the "passion of Romeo, the gloom of Lara, the romance of D'Artagnan, and the desperate inspiration of Melnotte." A romantic young man indeed, part Shakespeare's Romeo and akin to Byron's Lara, Dumas' D'Artagnan, and Bulwer-Lytton's Melnotte! But his proper kinsman is Ferdinand, of Shakespeare's *The Tempest,* for "The Enchanted Kiss" from beginning to end is subtly attuned to Shakespeare's dramatic romance and full of beautiful, sustained echoes from this play. Katie's father is "a very queer fish, and according to repute, not of the freshest."

In *The Tempest* Trinculo sees Caliban and says, "What have we here? a man or a fish? Dead or alive? A fish, he smells like a fish; a very ancient and fish-like smell; a kind of not of the newest Poor-John." Tansey listens to the "goblin music that still follow'd." "Afraid? . . . Nay! nor of these apparitions, nor of that spectral singing that always pursued him." *The Tempest* reads, "Where should this music be? I' the air or th'earth? / It sounds no more. . . . Thence I have follow'd it." "Art thou afeard?" says Caliban.

> Be not afeard. The isle is full of noises,
> Sounds and sweet airs, that give delight and hurt not.
> Sometimes a thousand twangling instruments
> Will hum about mine ears, and sometimes voices. . . .

Ariel's song, "Full fathom five thy father lies," which ends "Hark, now I hear them — Ding-dong, bell" is comically turned into "When you hear them bells go tingalingling."

Miss Katie really likes Tansey, and the young couple sometimes play cribbage, as Ferdinand and Miranda play chess in *The Tempest.* One night after work, Tansey has two drinks of absinthe and wanders through the misty, winding streets of San Antonio as lost and bewildered as Ferdinand shipwrecked on Prospero's island. Scenes and characters appear and fade; Tansey is challenged, jostled, threatened, tempted, and ever at the end of every dream sequence Miss Katie awaits him, with a kiss. He wonders if fate leads him to Miss Katie's arms.

Nonetheless, when he returns to the boarding house and Miss Katie gives him an opportunity, he does not kiss her. It is Tansey who aborts his opportunity, not fate.

"The Enchanted Kiss" is a story more of atmosphere than of plot, but it brings us a masterful portrait of San Antonio. There is also a dream vision of the siege of the Alamo, a magic sentence or two that summon a troop of spectral horsemen to their ancient charge. One recalls Will Porter's drawing of the Alamo and also an amusing poem he wrote in "Charge of the Light Brigade" rhythm allowing the Mexicans their revenge upon the Texans — the invention of the tamale.

"A Blackjack Bargainer" (*Munsey's*, August 1901, as by Sydney Porter) returns to the southern mountains of O. Henry's youth — pokeberry, elder, sassafras, and sumac country. "Whistling Dick" and "A Blackjack Bargainer" alike represent O. Henry's maturing command of plotting, tempo, unity, and condensation.

The theme of this story is *the good that resides in the worst of us.* It is the same theme found in "A Chaparral Christmas Gift," the "spot

of good somewhere in everybody." Yancey Goree is a gambler like
Lorison and a drunkard like Clay. What this fallen aristocrat really
likes is a good card game, and he will do anything to support his
folly. Again we encounter O. Henry the humorist, a joyful man writing joyfullly, blending the groans and chuckles of this sad and funny
world. Yancey Goree does the unthinkable: he sells his family feud to
a yellow-fanged old mountaineer named Pike Garvey. "That's two
hundred dollars, Mr. Goree, what you would call a f'ar price for a
feud that's been 'lowed to run down like yourn hev." Yet when
Garvey is about to shoot Yancey's cousin, Colonel Abner Coltrane,
Yancey takes the bullet himself and, dying, murmurs, "Good
friend."

We notice that Pike Garvey is an expert marksman, like
O. Henry: "I kin hit a squirrel's eye at a hundred yard." Pike gets
all dressed up to come into town and we see that one detail of his
generally ludicrous apparel represents something O. Henry himself
liked, a pair of fine yellow kid gloves. Perhaps O. Henry was thinking of Robert Browning's fondness for yellow leather gloves.

"Hygeia at the Solito" (*Everybody's*, February 1903) is laid in
Texas and depicts a cocky little prizefighter-jockey named Cricket
McGuire who recovers from tuberculosis on the Curtis Raidler
ranch south of San Antonio. Cricket has come to Texas for the February 1896 prizefight between Bob Fitzsimmons and Peter Maher,
staged across the border from Langtry because the legislature had
ruled that prizefights were illegal in Texas. Bat Masterson took the
gate receipts for this actual, historic fight which disappointed everyone because Fitzsimmons knocked Maher out in ninety-five seconds
of the first round. The stranded Cricket goes home with Raidler on
the International and Great Northern Railway, which ran from San
Antonio through Cotulla to Laredo. Cricket is cured, as Will Porter
himself was cured, by life on the ranch below Cotulla: the fresh,
clean, dry air, the simple food, a daily routine where one lived and
slept close to the earth. In his observations on the Texas stories of
O. Henry, Judge O'Quinn has reminded us that when the cure for
tuberculosis was ultimately found in 1943, it came from the soil, the
discovery of Selman Abraham Waksman, a soil microbiologist.

The theme of this story is *the healing power of nature;* Hygeia was
the Greek goddess of health. Like Wordsworth, who found that he
was greatly renewed by mentally revisiting "spots of time" when he
lived close to nature in the English Lake District, O. Henry drew
upon his memories of Texas ranch country for healing and strength.

The recuperating Will used to lie on a cot under a hackberry
tree near Dick Hall's ranch house, drinking water from a cool red

jar, studying his dictionary, and reading. After a long bull snake fell on the black cook's ironing board, the cook ran off and Will became her substitute. He soon became accustomed to working with camp staples, the corn, beans, bacon, potatoes, flour, and onions from which came biscuits, corn bread, flapjacks, and stew. Will especially liked corn bread and steak and onions, and in "The Pimienta Pancakes" he writes about pancakes that are "golden sunshine. . . . honey-browned by the ambrosial fires of Epicurus."

On the ranch, young Will Porter had become a man, booted, spurred and sombreroed. He had learned about the rivalry between the cattlemen and the "pink-eyed snoozers," the sheepmen. He had absorbed the stories of Texas outlaws, Ben Thompson, King Fisher, Sam Bass, and John Wesley Hardin. The Halls gave Will a never-to-be-forgotten rough education in Texas ranch life. Twenty years later he poured all of this knowledge into more than forty Texas stories. In prison O. Henry put one foot in the stirrup again and gazed across the Rio Grande. "Hygeia at the Solito" was the first of his Texas ranch stories, the first in a long series of works which described the land of paisano and prickly pear, rattlesnakes and rangers, corrals and cactus, six-shooters and saddles, saloons and sagebrush, lassoes and longhorns, bluebonnets and bandits. O. Henry would always love Texas.

"The Duplicity of Hargraves" (*Junior Munsey*, February 1902) is the tale of a pompous old Southern major whose dress, speech, prejudices, and idiosyncrasies are imitated by an actor-friend. When the major joins a theatre audience and sees himself portrayed in all his "absurd grandiloquence" (though his lovable characteristics are represented, too), he is outraged. Hargraves tries to assure him that neither insult nor ridicule was intended, that an actor's aim was the perfect expression of a character. The theme of this story is very likely *tolerance* and the need for us to "see ourselves as ithers see us."

As O. Henry wrote these stories, many of which pictured characters from widely separated regions with their dialects and customs, he was like Hargraves, objective and nonjudgmental, an artist in search of the truth. William Lyon Phelps said, "The essential truthfulness of his art is what gave his work immediate recognition." The English critic A. St. John Adcock wrote of O. Henry: "You come to think of his men and women less as characters he has drawn than as people he has known, he writes of them with such familiar acquaintance, and makes them so vividly actual to you."

Dr. Alphonso Smith, professor of English at The University of Virginia and O. Henry's friend and biographer, stated that Washington Irving *legendized* the short story; Poe *standardized* the short story; Hawthorne *allegorized* the short story; Bret Harte *localized* the short story; and O. Henry *humanized* the short story.

"The Marionettes" (*Black Cat,* April 1902) has a title and a theme perhaps explained by a sketch Will Porter once wrote for the Houston *Post:*

> Life is neither tragedy nor comedy. It is a mingling of both. High above us omnipotent hands pull the strings that choke our laughter into sobs and cause strange sounds of mirth to break in upon our deepest grief. We are marionettes that dance and cry, scarce at our own wills; and at the end, the flaring lights are out, we are laid to rest in our wooden boxes, and down comes the dark night to cover the scene of our brief triumph.

"The Marionettes" is the story of a physician* who by day is a perfectly respectable citizen, devoted to his family and practice. At night, however, he is a burglar. One evening he has just pocketed his share of a three-man burglary ($830)** and is proceeding homeward when a frantic servant, seeing his black leather medicine case, calls him into a home to attend her employer. Soon the mysterious stranger pulls the strings of his marionettes, and the husband and wife, who have never seen him before, receive death and life through his hands. This is one of three O. Henry stories in which a wife abuser is murdered; the others are "A Municipal Report" and "A Departmental Case." O. Henry knew the writings of Bob Ingersoll, who often voiced the opinion that only the most depraved of men will strike a woman. "A doctor-burglar!" says the husband. "I never yet struck a woman," replies Dr. James.

The themes of the stories which O. Henry wrote in prison are these: love of freedom; love of a child and the power of that love to inspire and motivate the parent to good works; the necessity of remaining courageous; the incompetence of the guardians of the law and the uneven administration of justice; the game of chance which is life; the unreasonable expectation that a nice girl would marry a man with a past; the consideration and rejection of suicide; man's frustrations in reaching his goals and the folly of ascribing one's failures to fate; the good that resides in the worst of us; the healing power of nature; tolerance; and in *The Marionettes, the mystery of life, where unseen forces are at work.*

The twelve stories which embody these themes tell us a great

---

* The son of a physician, O. Henry was himself a licensed pharmacist. He also learned a great deal from working with the prison doctors — hence, his knowledge of medicine, revealed in the accurate details of this story.

** Curiously like the sum Porter was alleged to have embezzled.

deal about O. Henry's personal and artistic growth. In them we find the precursor of Jimmy Valentine, the safecracker O. Henry made world famous, and the first of the "Southern Colonels" of O. Henry, a kinsman of those in "A Municipal Report" and "Hostages to Momus." Here is his first Texas ranch story, and here are two stories which grew into his first and only novel, *Cabbages and Kings*. We witness his gradual control of several dialects, the revival of his sense of humor, and the solid evidence of his growing command of story structure. Many of the stories have the surprise ending we associate with his name. Three establish him as the writer of stories in which a city is almost part of the cast of characters.

There are no stories strictly about banks among the twelve, though later on he wrote three, each one an objective and sometimes humorous depiction of the casual banking practices prevalent in Texas in the 1890s. A remarkable man, William Sidney Porter!

In prison and afterward he did not indulge in self-vilification, preaching, moralizing, blaming others, nor justifying himself. Rather he set out, with intelligence and discipline, to challenge failure, to rebuild his shattered world, to make the acquaintance of his higher self, and to unlock the imprisoned splendors of his creative imagination. When Will Porter arrived in Ohio, April 25, 1898, he had lost his legal trial. When he left Columbus on July 24, 1901, he had won the trial of his character and had begun an amazing career.

What Whistling Dick was whistling. *This is the passage from the Overture to Carl Maria von Weber's* Der Freischütz *which O. Henry himself must have loved and which his character, Whistling Dick, was doubtless whistling. It is the most famous melody in this work. Notice the B-natural is here, showing the accuracy of O. Henry's every detail.*

[III]

The Twelve
Prison Stories

Whistling Dick's Christmas Stocking

It was with much caution that Whistling Dick slid back the door of the box car, for Article 5716, City Ordinances, authorized (perhaps unconstitutionally) arrest on suspicion, and he was familiar of old with this ordinance. So, before climbing out, he surveyed the field with all the care of a good general.

He saw no change since his last visit to this big, alms-giving, long-suffering city of the South, the cold-weather paradise of the tramps. The levee where his freight car stood was pimpled with dark bulks of merchandise. The breeze reeked with the well-remembered, sickening smell of the old tarpaulins that covered bales and barrels. The dun river slipped along among the shipping with an oily gurgle. Far down toward Chalmette he could see the great bend in the stream outlined by the row of electric lights. Across the river Algiers lay, a long, irregular blot, made darker by the dawn which lightened

First published in *McClure's Magazine* for December 1899, as by O. Henry, the first story by William Sidney Porter written under the pen name "O. Henry." Although Porter used other pen names occasionally for the next few years, the pen name O. Henry within the next decade became the name by which he was universally recognized.

Nineteenth of twenty-two stories in *Roads of Destiny,* published by Doubleday, Page & Company, New York, 1909.

the sky beyond. An industrious tug or two, coming for some early sailing-ship, gave a few appalling toots, that seemed to be the signal for breaking day. The Italian luggers were creeping nearer their landing, laden with early vegetables and shellfish. A vague roar, subterranean in quality, from dray wheels and street cars, began to make itself heard and felt; and the ferryboats, the Mary Anns of water craft, stirred sullenly to their menial morning tasks.

Whistling Dick's red head popped suddenly back into the car. A sight too imposing and magnificent for his gaze had been added to the scene. A vast, incomparable policeman rounded a pile of rice sacks and stood within twenty yards of the car. The daily miracle of the dawn, now being performed above Algiers, received the flattering attention of this specimen of municipal official splendor. He gazed with unbiased dignity at the faintly glowing colors until, at last, he turned to them his broad back, as if convinced that legal interference was not needed, and the sunrise might proceed unchecked. So he turned his face to the rice bags, and drawing a flat flask from an inside pocket, he placed it to his lips and regarded the firmament.

Whistling Dick, professional tramp, possessed a half friendly acquaintance with this officer. They both loved music. Still, he did not care, under the present circumstances, to renew the acquaintance. There is a difference between meeting a policeman upon a lonely street corner and whistling a few operatic airs with him, and being caught by him crawling out of a freight car. So Dick waited, as even a New Orleans policeman must move on some time — perhaps it is a retributive law of nature — and before long "Big Fritz" majestically disappeared between the trains of cars.

Whistling Dick waited as long as his judgment advised, and then slid swiftly to the ground. Assuming as far as possible the air of an honest laborer who seeks his daily toil, he moved across the network of railway lines, with the intention of making his way by quiet Girod Street to a certain bench in La Fayette Square, where, according to appointment, he hoped to rejoin a pal known as "Slick," this adventurous pilgrim having preceded him by one day, in a cattle car into which a loose slat had enticed him.

As Whistling Dick picked his way where night still lingered among the big, reeking, musty warehouses, he gave way to the habit that had won for him his title. Subdued, yet clear, with each note as true and liquid as a bobolink's, his whistle tinkled about the dim, cold mountains of brick like drops of rain falling into a hidden pool. He followed an air, but it swam mistily into a swirling current of improvisation. You could cull out the trill of mountain brooks, the staccato of green rushes shivering above chilly lagoons, the pipe of sleepy birds.

Rounding a corner, the whistler collided with a mountain of blue and brass.

"So," observed the mountain calmly, "you are alreaty pack. Und dere vill not pe frost before two veeks yet! Und you haf forgotten how to vistle. Dere was a valse note in dot last bar."

"Watcher know about it?" said Whistling Dick, with tentative familiarity; "you wit yer little Cherman-band nixcumrous chunes. Watcher know about music? Pick yer ears, and listen agin. Here's de way I whistled it — see?"

He puckered his lips, but the big policeman held up his hand.

"Shtop," he said, "und learn der right way. Und learn also dot a rolling shtone gan't vistle for a cent."

Big Fritz's heavy mustache rounded into a circle, and from its depths came a sound deep and mellow as that from a flute. He repeated a few bars of the air the tramp had been whistling. The rendition was cold, but correct, and he emphasized the note he had taken exception to.

"Dot p is p natural, und not p vlat. Py der vay, you petter pe glad I meet you. Von hour later, and I vould haf to put you in a gage to vistle mit der chail pirds. Der orders are to bull all der pums afder sunrise."

"To which?"

"To bull der pums — eferybody mitout fisible means. Dirty days is der price, or fifteen tollars."

"Is dat straight, or a game you givin' me?"

"It's der pest tip you efer had. I gif it to you pecause I pelief you are not so bad as der rest. Und pecause you gan vistle 'Die Freischutz' bezzer dan I myself gan. Don't run aginst any more bolicemans aroundt der corners, but go avay vrom town a few tays. Goot-pye."

So Madame Orleans had at last grown weary of the strange and ruffled brood that came yearly to nestle beneath her charitable pinions.

After the big policeman had departed, Whistling Dick stood for an irresolute minute, feeling all the outraged indignation of a delinquent tenant who is ordered to vacate his premises. He had pictured to himself a day of dreamful ease when he should have joined his pal; a day of lounging on the wharf, munching the bananas and cocoanuts scattered in unloading the fruit streamers; and then a feast along the free-Lunch counters from which the easy-going owners were too good natured or too generous to drive him away, and afterward a pipe in one of the little flowery parks and a snooze in some shady corner of the wharf. But here was a stern order to exile, and one that he knew must be obeyed. So, with a wary eye open for the gleam of brass buttons, he began his retreat toward a rural refuge. A few days in the country need not necessarily prove disastrous. Beyond the possibility of a slight nip of frost, there was no formidable evil to be looked for.

However, it was with a depressed spirit that Whistling Dick passed the old French market on his chosen route down the river. For safety's sake, he still presented to the world his portrayal of the part of the worthy artisan on his way to labor. A stall-keeper in the market, undeceived, hailed him by the generic name of his ilk, and "Jack" halted, taken by surprise. The vendor, melted by this proof of his own acuteness, bestowed a foot of Frankfurter and half a loaf, and thus the problem of breakfast was solved.

When the streets, from topographical reasons, began to shun the river bank, the exile mounted to the top of the levee, and on its well-trodden path pursued his way. The suburban eye regarded him with cold suspicion. Individuals reflected the stern spirit of the city's heartless edict. He missed the seclusion of the crowded town and the safety he could always find in the multitude.

At Chalmette, six miles upon his desultory way, there suddenly menaced him a vast and bewildering industry. A new port was being established; the dock was being built, compresses were going up; picks and shovels and barrows struck at him like serpents from every side. An arrogant foreman bore down upon him, estimating his muscles with the eye of a recruiting sergeant. Brown men and black men all about him were toiling away. He fled in terror.

By noon he had reached the country of the plantations, the great, sad, silent levels bordering the mighty river. He overlooked fields of sugar-cane so vast that their farthest limits melted into the sky. The sugar-making season was well advanced, and the cutters were at work; the wagons creaked drearily after them; the negro teamsters inspired the mules to greater speed with mellow and sonorous imprecations. Dark green groves, blurred by the blue of distance, showed where the plantation houses stood. The tall chimneys of the sugar-mills caught the eye miles distant, like lighthouses at sea.

At a certain point Whistling Dick's unerring nose caught the scent of frying fish. Like a pointer to a quail, he made his way down the levee side straight to the camp of a credulous and ancient fisherman, whom he charmed with song and story, so that he dined like an admiral, and then like a philosopher annihilated the worst three hours of the day by a nap under the trees.

When he awoke and again continued his hegira, a frosty sparkle in the air had succeeded the drowsy warmth of the day, and as this portent of a chilly night translated itself to the brain of Sir Peregrine, he lengthened his stride and bethought him of shelter. He traveled a road that faithfully followed the convolutions of the levee, running along its base, but whither he knew not. Bushes and rank grass crowded it to the wheel ruts, and out of this ambuscade the pests of the lowlands swarmed after him, humming a keen, vicious soprano. And as the night grew nearer, although colder, the whine of the mosquitos became a greedy, petulant snarl that shut out all other sounds. To his right, against the heavens, he saw a green light moving, and, accompanying it, the masts and funnels of a big incoming steamer, moving as upon a screen at a magic-lantern show. And there were mysterious marshes at his left, out of which came queer gurgling cries and a choked croaking. The whistling vagrant struck up a merry warble to offset these melancholy influences, and it is likely that never before, since Pan himself jigged it on his reeds, had such sounds been heard in those depressing solitudes.

A distant clatter in the rear quickly developed into the swift beat of horses' hoofs, and Whistling Dick stepped aside into the dew-wet grass to clear the track. Turning his head, he saw approaching a fine team of stylish grays drawing a double surrey. A stout man with a white mustache occupied the front seat, giving all his attention to the rigid lines in his hands. Behind him sat a placid, middle-aged lady and a brilliant looking girl hardly arrived at young ladyhood. The lap-robe had slipped partly from the knees of the gentleman driving, and Whistling Dick saw two stout canvas bags between his feet — bags such as, while loafing in cities, he had seen warily transferred between express wagons and bank doors. The remaining space in the vehicle was filled with parcels of various sizes and shapes.

As the surrey swept even with the side-tracked tramp, the bright-eyed girl, seized by some merry, madcap impulse, leaned out toward him with a sweet, dazzling smile, and cried, "Mer-ry Christmas!" in a shrill, plaintive treble.

Such a thing had not often happened to Whistling Dick, and he felt handicapped in devising the correct response. But lacking time for reflection, he let his instinct decide, and snatching off his battered derby, he rapidly extended it at arm's length, and drew it back with a continuous motion, and shouted a loud, but ceremonious, "Ah, there!" after the flying surrey.

The sudden movement of the girl had caused one of the parcels to become unwrapped, and something limp and black fell from it into the road. The tramp picked it up, and found it to be a new black silk stocking, long and fine and slender. It crunched crisply, and yet with a luxurious softness, between his fingers.

"Ther bloomin' little skeezicks!" said Whistling Dick, with a broad grin bisecting his freckled face. "W'ot do yer think of dat, now! Mer-ry Chris-mus! Sounded like a cuckoo clock, dat's what she did. Dem guys is swells, too, betcher life, an' der old 'un stacks dem sacks of dough down under his trotters like dey was common as dried apples. Been shoppin' for Chrismus, and de kid's lost one of her new socks w'ot she was goin' to hold up Santy wid. De bloomin' little skeezicks! Wit'her 'Mer-ry Chris-mus!' W'ot d'yer t'ink! Same as to say, 'Hello, Jack, how goes it?' and as swell as Fift'Av'noo, and as easy as a blowout in Cincinnat."

Whistling Dick folded the stocking carefully, and stuffed it into his pocket.

It was nearly two hours later when he came upon signs of habitation. The buildings of an extensive plantation were brought into view by a turn in the road. He easily selected the planter's residence in a large square building with two wings, with numerous good-sized, well-lighted windows, and broad verandas running around its full extent. It was set upon a smooth lawn, which was faintly lit by the far-reaching rays of the lamps within. A noble grove surrounded it, and old-fashioned shrubbery grew thickly about the walks and fences. The quarters of the hands and the mill buildings were situated at a distance in the rear.

The road was now enclosed on each side by a fence, and presently, as Whistling Dick drew nearer the houses, he suddenly stopped and sniffed the air.

"If dere ain't a hobo stew cookin' somewhere in dis immediate precinct," he said to himself, "me nose has quit tellin' de trut."

Without hesitation he climbed the fence to windward. He found himself in an apparently disused lot, where piles of old bricks were stacked, and rejected, decaying lumber. In a corner he saw the faint glow of a fire that had become little more than a bed of living coals, and he thought he could see some dim human forms sitting or lying about it. He drew nearer, and by the light of a little blaze that suddenly fired up he saw plainly the fat figure of a ragged man in an old brown sweater and cap.

"Dat man," said Whistling Dick to himself softly, "is a dead ringer for Boston Harry. I'll try him wit de high sign."

He whistled one or two bars of a rag-time melody, and the air was immediately taken up, and then quickly ended with a peculiar run. The first whistler walked confidently up to the fire. The fat man looked up, and spake in a loud, asthmatic wheeze:

"Gents, the unexpected, but welcome, addition to our circle is Mr. Whistling Dick, an old friend of mine for whom I fully vouches. The waiter will lay another cover at once. Mr. W. D. will join us at supper, during which function he will enlighten us in regard to the circumstances that give us the pleasure of his company."

"Chewin' de stuffin' out'n de dictionary, as usual, Boston," said Whistling Dick; "but t'anks all de same for de invitashun. I guess I finds meself here about de same way as yous guys. A cop gimme de tip dis mornin'. Yous workin' on dis farm?"

"A guest," said Boston sternly, "shouldn't never insult his entertainers until he's filled up wid grub. 'Taint good business sense. Workin'! — but I will restrain myself. We five — me, Deaf Pete, Blinky, Goggles, and Indiana Tom — got put onto this scheme of Noo Orleans to work visiting gentlemen upon her dirty streets, and we hit the road last evening just as the tender hues of twilight had flopped down upon the daisies and things. Blinky, pass the empty oyster-can at your left to the empty gentleman at your right."

For the next ten minutes the gang of roadsters paid their undivided attention to the supper. In an old five-gallon kerosene can they had cooked a stew of potatoes, meat, and onions, which they partook of from smaller cans they had found scattered about the vacant lot.

Whistling Dick had known Boston Harry of old, and knew him to be one of the shrewdest and most successful of his brotherhood. He looked like a prosperous stock-drover or a solid merchant from some country village. He was stout and hale, with a ruddy, always smoothly shaven face. His clothes were strong and neat, and he gave special attention to the care of his decent-appearing shoes. During the past ten years he had acquired a record for working a larger number of successfully managed confidence games than any of his acquaintances, and he had not a day's work to be counted against him. It was rumored among his associates that he had saved a considerable amount of money. The four other men were fair specimens of the slinking, ill-clad, noisome genus who carry their labels of "suspicious" in plain view.

After the bottom of the large can had been scraped, and pipes lit at the coals, two of the men called Boston aside and spake with him lowly and mysteriously. He nodded decisively, and then said aloud to Whistling Dick:

"Listen, sonny, to some plain talky-talk. We five are on a lay. I've guaranteed you to be square, and you're to come in on the profits equal with the boys, and you've got to help. Two hundred hands on this plantation are expecting to be paid a week's wages to-mor-

row morning. To-morrow's Christmas, and they want to lay off.
Says the Boss: 'Work from five to nine in the morning to get a train
load of sugar off, and I'll pay every man cash down for the week, and
a day extra.' They say: 'Hooray for the boss! It goes.' He drives to
Noo Orleans to-day, and fetches back the cold dollars. Two thousand and seventy-four fifty is the amount. I got the figures from a
man who talks too much, who got 'em from the book-keeper. The
boss of this plantation thinks he's going to pay this wealth to the
hands. He's got it down wrong; he's going to pay it to us. It's going
to stay in the leisure class, where it belongs. Now, half of this haul
goes to me, and the other half the rest of you may divide. Why the
difference? I represent brains. It's my scheme. Here's the way we're
going to get it. There's some company at supper in the house, but
they'll leave about nine. They've just happened in for an hour or so.
If they don't go pretty soon, we'll work the scheme anyhow. We
want all night to get away good with the dollars. They're heavy.
About nine o'clock Deaf Pete and Blinky'll go down the road about
a quarter beyond the house, and set fire to a big cane-field there that
the cutters haven't touched yet. The wind's just right to have it roar-
ing in two minutes. The alarm'll be given, and every man Jack about
the place will be down there in ten minutes, fighting fire. That'll
leave the money sacks and the women alone in the house for us to
handle. You've heard cane burn? Well, there's mighty few women
can screech loud enough to be heard above its crackling. The thing's
dead safe. The only danger is in being caught before we can get far
enough away with the money. Now, if you — ''

"Boston," interrupted Whistling Dick, rising to his feet, "t'anks
for de grub yous fellers has give me, but I'll be movin' on now."

"What do you mean?" asked Boston, also rising.

"W'y, you can count me outer dis deal. You outer know dat.
I'm on de bum all right enough, but dat other t'ing don't go wit' me.
Burglary is no good. I'll say good-night and many t'anks fer — ''

Whistling Dick had moved away a few steps as he spoke, but he
stopped very suddenly. Boston had covered him with a short re-
volver of roomy caliber.

"Take your seat," said the tramp leader. "I'd feel mighty proud
of myself if I let you go and spoil the game. You'll stick right in this
camp until we finish the job. The end of that brick pile is your limit.
You go two inches beyond that, and I'll have to shoot. Better take it
easy, now."

"It's my way of doin'," said Whistling Dick. "Easy goes. You
can depress de muzzle of dat twelve-incher, and run 'er back on the
trucks. I remains, as de newspape's say, 'in yer midst.' ''

"All right," said Boston, lowering his piece, as the other returned and took his seat again on a projecting plank in a pile of timber. "Don't try to leave; that's all. I wouldn't miss this chance even if I had to shoot an old acquaintance to make it go. I don't want to hurt anybody specially, but this thousand dollars I'm going to get will fix me for fair. I'm going to drop the road, and start a saloon in a little town I know about. I'm tired of being kicked around."

Boston Harry took from his pocket a cheap silver watch, and held it near the fire.

"It's a quarter to nine," he said. "Pete, you and Blinky start. Go down the road past the house, and fire the cane in a dozen places. Then strike for the levee, and come back on it, instead of the road, so you wont meet anybody. By the time you get back the men will all be striking out for the fire, and we'll break for the house and collar the dollars. Everybody cough up what matches he's got."

The two surly tramps made a collection of all the matches in the party, Whistling Dick contributing his quota with propitiatory alacrity, and then they departed in the dim starlight in the direction of the road.

Of the three remaining vagrants, two, Goggles and Indiana Tom, reclined lazily upon convenient lumber and regarded Whistling Dick with undisguised disfavor. Boston, observing that the dissenting recruit was disposed to remain peaceably, relaxed a little in his vigilance. Whistling Dick arose presently and strolled leisurely up and down, keeping carefully within the territory assigned him.

"Dis planter chap," he said, pausing before Boston Harry, "w'ot makes yer t'ink he's got de tin in de house wit'im?"

"I'm advised of the facts in the case," said Boston. "He drove to Noo Orleans and got it, I say, to-day. Want to change your mind and come in?"

"Naw, I was just askin'. Wot kind o' team did de boss drive?"

"Pair of grays."

"Double surrey?"

"Yep."

"Women folks along?"

"Wife and kid. Say, what morning paper are you trying to pump news for?"

"I was just conversin' to pass de time away. I guess dat team passed me in de road dis evenin'. Dat's all."

"As Whistling Dick put his hands into his pockets and continued his curtailed beat up and down by the fire, he felt the silk stocking he had picked up in the road.

"Ther bloomin' little skeezicks!" he muttered, with a grin.

As he walked up and down he could see, through a sort of natural opening or lane among the trees, the planter's residence some two hundred yards distant. The side of the house toward him exhibited spacious, well-lighted windows through which a soft radiance streamed, illuminating the broad veranda and some extent of the lawn beneath.

"What's that you said?" asked Boston, sharply.

"Oh, nuttin' 't all," said Whistling Dick, lounging carelessly, and kicking meditatively at a little stone on the ground.

"Just as easy," continued the warbling vagrant softly to himself, "an' sociable an' swell an' sassy, wit' her 'Mer-ry Chris-mus,' — wot d'yer t'ink, now!"

Dinner, three hours late, was being served in the Bellemeade plantation dining-room.

The dining-room and all its appurtenances spoke of an old *régime* that was here continued rather than suggested to the memory. The plate was rich to the extent that its age and quaintness alone saved it from being showy; there were interesting names signed in the corners of the pictures on the walls; the viands were of the kind that bring a shine into the eyes of *gourmets*. The service was swift, silent, lavish, as in the days when the waiters were assets like the plate. The names by which the planter's family and their visitors addressed one another were historic in the annals of two nations. Their manners and conversation had that most difficult kind of ease — the kind that still preserves punctilio. The planter himself seemed to be the dynamo that generated the larger portion of the gayety and wit. The younger ones at the board found it more than difficult to turn back upon him his guns of raillery and banter. It is true, the young men attempted to storm his works repeatedly, incited by the hope of gaining the approbation of their fair companions; but even when they sped a well-aimed shaft, the planter forced them to feel defeat by the tremendous discomfiting thunder of the laughter with which he accompanied his retorts. At the head of the table, serene, matronly, benevolent, reigned the mistress of the house, placing here and there the right smile, the right word, the encouraging glance.

The talk of the party was too desultory, too evanescent to follow, but at last they came to the subject of the tramp nuisance, one that had of late vexed the plantations for many miles around. The planter seized the occasion to direct his good-natured fire of raillery at the mistress, accusing her of encouraging the plague. "They swarm up and down the river every winter," he said. "They overrun New Orleans, and we catch the surplus, which is generally the worst part. And, a day or two ago, Madame Nouveau Orleans, suddenly discovering that she can't go shopping without brushing her skirts against great rows of the vagabonds sunning themselves on the banquettes, says to the police: 'Catch 'em all,' and the police catch a dozen or two, and the remaining three or four thousand overflow up and down the levees, and Madame there" — pointing tragically with the carving-knife at her — "feeds them. They won't work; they defy my overseers, and they make friends with my dogs; and you, Madame, feed them before my eyes, and intimidate me when I would interfere. Tell us, please, how many to-day did you thus incite to future laziness and depredation?"

"Six, I think," said Madame, with a reflective smile; "but you know two of them offered to work, for you heard them yourself."

The planter's disconcerting laugh rang out again.

"Yes, at their own trades. And one was an artificial flower-maker, and the other was a glass-blower. Oh, they were looking for work! Not a hand would they consent to lift to labor of any other kind."

"And another one," continued the soft-hearted mistress, "used quite good language. It was really extraordinary for one of his class. And he carried a watch. And had lived in Boston. I don't believe they are all bad. They have always seemed to me to rather lack development. I always look upon them as children with whom wisdom has remained at a standstill while dirt and whiskers have continued to grow. We passed one this evening as we were driving home who had a face as good as it was incompetent. He was whistling the intermezzo from 'Cavalleria,' and blowing the spirit of Mascagni himself into it."

A bright-eyed young girl who sat at the left of the mistress leaned over, and said in a confidential undertone:

"I wonder, mamma, if that tramp we passed on the road found my stocking, and do you think he will hang it up to-night? Now I can hang up but one. Do you know why I wanted a new pair of silk stockings when I have plenty? Well, old Aunt Judy says, if you hang up two that have never been worn, Santa Claus will fill one with good things, and Monsieur Pambé will place in the other payment for all the words you have spoken — good or bad — on the day before Christmas. That's why I've been unusually nice and polite to every one to-day. Monsieur Pambé, you know, is a witch gentleman; he — "

The words of the young girl were interrupted by a startling thing.

Like the wraith of some burned-out shooting star, a black streak came crashing through the window-pane upon the table, where it shivered into fragments a dozen pieces of crystal and china ware, and then glanced between the heads of the guests to the wall, imprinting therein a deep, round indentation, at which, to-day, the visitor to Bellemeade marvels as he gazes upon it and listens to this tale as it is told.

The women screamed in many keys, and the men sprang to their feet, and would have laid their hands upon their swords had not the verities of chronology forbidden.

The planter was the first to act; he sprang to the intruding missile, and held it up to view.

"By Jupiter!" he cried. "A meteoric shower of hosiery! Has communication at last been established with Mars?"

"I should say — ahem! — Venus," ventured a young gentleman visitor, looking hopefully for approbation toward the unresponsive young lady visitors.

The planter held at arm's length the unceremonious visitor — a long, dangling, black stocking. "She's loaded," he announced.

As he spoke he reversed the stocking, holding it by the toe, and down from it dropped a roundish stone, wrapped about by a piece of yellowish paper. "Now for the first interstellar message of the century," he cried; and nodding to the company, who had crowded about him, he adjusted his glasses with provoking deliberation, and examined it closely. When he finished, he had changed from the jolly host to the practical, decisive man of business. He immediately struck a bell, and said to the silent-footed mulatto man who responded: "Go and tell Mr. Wesley to get Reeves and Maurice and about ten stout hands they can rely upon, and come to the hall door at once. Tell him to have the men arm themselves, and bring plenty of ropes and plow lines. Tell him to hurry." And then he read aloud from the paper these words:

TO THE GENT OF DE HOUS.

Dere is 5 tuff hobose xcept meself in de vaken lot near de rode war de old brick piles is. Dey got me stuck up wid a gun see and I takes dis means of comunikaten 2 of der lads is gone down to set fire to de cain field below de hous and when yous fellers goes to turn de hoes on it de hole gang is goin to rob de hous of de money yoo got to pay off wit say git a move on ye say de kid dropt dis sock in der rode tel her mery crismus de same as she told me. Ketch de bums down de rode first and den sen a relefe core to get me out of soke yores truly

WHISTLEN DICK.

There was some quiet, but rapid, maneuvering at Bellemeade during the ensuing half hour, which ended in five disgusted and sullen tramps being captured, and locked securely in an outhouse pending the coming of the morning and retribution. For another result, the visiting young gentlemen had secured the unqualified worship of the visiting young ladies by their distinguished and heroic conduct. For still another, behold Whistling Dick, the hero, seated at the planter's table, feasting upon viands his experience had never before included, and waited upon by admiring femininity in shapes of such beauty and "swellness" that even his ever-full mouth could scarcely prevent him from whistling. He was made to disclose in detail his adventure with the evil gang of Boston Harry, and how he cunningly wrote the note and wrapped it around the stone and placed it in the toe of the stocking, and, watching his chance, sent it silently, with a wonderful centrifugal momentum, like a comet, at one of the big lighted windows of the dining-room.

The planter vowed that the wanderer should wander no more; that his was a goodness and an honesty that should be rewarded, and that a debt of gratitude had been made that must be paid; for had he not saved them from a doubtless imminent loss, and, maybe, a greater calamity? He assured Whistling Dick that he might consider himself a charge upon the honor of Bellemeade; that a position suited to his powers would be found for him at once, and hinted that the way would be heartily smoothed for him to rise to as high places of emolument and trust as the plantation afforded.

But now, they said, he must be weary, and the immediate thing to consider was rest and sleep. So the mistress spoke to a servant, and Whistling Dick was conducted to a room in the wing of the house occupied by the servants. To this room, in a few minutes, was brought a portable tin bathtub filled with water, which was placed on a piece of oiled cloth upon the floor. Here the vagrant was left to pass the night.

By the light of a candle he examined the room. A bed, with the covers neatly turned back, revealed snowy pillows and sheets. A worn, but clean, red carpet covered the floor. There was a dresser with a beveled mirror, a washstand with a flowered bowl and pitchers; the two or three chairs were softly upholstered. A little table held books, papers, and a day-old cluster of roses in a jar. There were towels on a rack and soap in a white dish.

Whistling Dick set his candle on a chair, and placed his hat carefully under the table. After satisfying what we must suppose to have been his curiosity by a sober scrutiny, he removed his coat, folded it, and laid it upon the floor, near the wall, as far as possible from the unused bathtub. Taking his coat for a pillow, he stretched himself luxuriously upon the carpet.

The tale of the historian is often disappointing; and if the historian be a workman who has an eye for effect and proportion, he has temptations to inaccuracy. For results fail to adjust themselves logically, and evince the most profound indifference toward artistic consequence. But here we are at the mercy of facts, and the unities — whatever they may be — must be crushed beneath an impotent conclusion.

When, on Christmas morning, the first streaks of dawn broke above the marshes, Whistling Dick awoke, and reached instinctively for his hat. Then he remembered that the skirts of Fortune had swept him into their folds on the night previous, and he went to the window and raised it, to let the fresh breath of the morning cool his brow and fix the yet dream-like memory of his good luck within his brain.

As he stood there, certain dread and ominous sounds pierced the fearful hollow of his ear.

The force of plantation workers, eager to complete the shortened task allotted them, were all astir. The mighty din of the ogre Labor shook the earth, and the poor tattered and forever disguised Prince in Search of his Fortune held tight to the window sill even in the enchanted castle, and trembled.

Already from the bosom of the mill came the thunder of rolling barrels of sugar, and (prison-like sound) there was a great rattling of chains as the mules were harried with stimulant imprecations to their places by the wagon tongues. A little vicious "dummy" engine, with a train of flat cars in tow, stewed and fumed on the plantation tap of the narrow-gauge railroad, and a toiling, hurrying, hallooing stream of workers were dimly seen in the half darkness loading the train with the weekly output of sugar. Here was a poem; an epic — nay, a tragedy — with Work! the curse of the world, for its theme.

The December air was frosty, but the sweat broke out upon Whistling Dick's face. He thrust his head out of the window, and looked down. Fifteen feet below him, against the wall of the house, he could make out that a border of flowers grew, and by that token he overhung a bed of soft earth.

Softly as a burglar goes, he clambered out upon the sill, lowered himself until he hung by his hands alone, and then dropped safely. No one seemed to be about upon this side of the house. He dodged low, and skimmed swiftly across the yard to the low fence. It was an easy matter to vault this, for a terror urged him such as lifts the gazelle over the thorn bush when the lion pursues. A crush through the dew-drenched weeds on the roadside, a clutching, slippery rush up the grassy side of the levee to the footpath at the summit, and — he was free!

The east was blushing and brightening. The wind, himself a vagrant rover, saluted his brother upon the cheek. Some wild geese, high above, gave cry. A rabbit skipped along the path before him, free to turn to the right or to the left as his mood should send him. The river slid past, and certainly no one could tell the ultimate abiding place of its waters.

A small, ruffled, brown-breasted bird, sitting upon a dogwood sapling, began a soft, throaty, tender little piping in praise of the dew which entices foolish worms from their holes; but suddenly he stopped, and sat with his head turned sidewise, listening.

From the path along the levee there burst forth a jubilant, stirring, buoyant, thrilling whistle, loud and keen and clear as the cleanest notes of the piccolo. The soaring sound rippled and trilled and arpeggioed as the songs of wild birds do not; but it had a wild free grace that, in a way, reminded the small brown bird of something familiar, but exactly what he could not tell. There was in it the bird call, or *reveille*, that all birds know; but a great waste of lavish, unmeaning things that art had added and arranged, besides, and that were quite puzzling and strange; and the little brown bird sat with his head on one side until the sound died away in the distance.

The little bird did not know that the part of that strange warbling that he understood was just what kept the warbler without his breakfast that morning; but he knew very well that the part he did not understand did not concern him, so he gave a little flutter of his wings and swooped down like a brown bullet upon a big fat worm that was wriggling on the levee path.

NOTES AND COMMENTS

Bellemeade, the name of the sugar plantation mansion in this story, doubtless comes from Greensboro, North Carolina, where young Will Porter lived only two blocks from the Tate mansion, named Bellemeade. There, as boys, Will and his friend Tom Tate often played about the Tate mansion, originally built by Henry Humphreys Tate in 1867 on Bellemeade Street. The Tate mansion has been demolished, but Bellemeade remains a prominent thoroughfare in Greensboro.

For review of literary evaluation and additional notes and comments related to "Whistling Dick's Christmas Stocking," reference is made to Dr. Porter's essay, Part II, "The Imprisoned Splendor," *ante,* pp.22–25.

Georgia's Ruling

If you should chance to visit the General Land Office, step into
the draughtsmen's room and ask to be shown the map of Salado
County. A leisurely German — possibly old Kampfer himself —
will bring it to you. It will be four feet square, on heavy drawing-
cloth. The lettering and the figures will be beautifully clear and dis-
tinct. The title will be in splendid, undecipherable German text, ornamented with classic Teutonic designs — very likely Ceres or Po-
mona leaning against the initial letters with cornucopias venting
grapes and wieners. You must tell him that this is not the map you
wish to see; that he will kindly bring you its official predecessor. He
will then say, "Ach, so!" and bring out a map half the size of the
first, dim, old, tattered, and faded.

By looking carefully near its northwest corner you will presently
come upon the worn contours of Chiquito River, and, maybe, if your
eyes are good, discern the silent witness of this story.

The Commissioner of the Land Office was of the old style; his
antique courtesy was too formal for his day. He dressed in fine

First published in *Outlook* Magazine for June 30, 1900, as by O. Henry.

Twenty-second of twenty-four stories in *Whirligigs,* published by Doubleday,
Page, & Company, New York, in 1910.

black, and there was a suggestion of Roman drapery in his long coat-skirts. His collars were "undetached" (blame haberdashery for the word); his tie was a narrow, funereal strip, tied in the same knot as were his shoe-strings. His gray hair was a trifle too long behind, but he kept it smooth and orderly. His face was clean-shaven, like the old statesmen's. Most people thought it a stern face, but when its official expression was off, a few had seen altogether a different countenance. Especially tender and gentle it had appeared to those who were about him during the last illness of his only child.

The Commissioner had been a widower for years, and his life, outside his official duties, had been so devoted to little Georgia that people spoke of it as a touching and admirable thing. He was a reserved man, and dignified almost to austerity, but the child had come below it all and rested upon his very heart, so that she scarcely missed the mother's love that had been taken away. There was a wonderful companionship between them, for she had many of his own ways, being thoughtful and serious beyond her years.

One day, while she was lying with the fever burning brightly in her cheeks, she said, suddenly:

"Papa, I wish I could do something good for a whole lot of children!"

"What would you like to do, dear?" asked the Commissioner. "Give them a party?"

"Oh, I don't mean those kind. I mean poor children who haven't homes, and aren't loved and cared for as I am. I tell you what, Papa!"

"What, my own child?"

"If I shouldn't get well, I'll leave them you — not *give* you, but just lend you, for you must come to mamma and me when you die too. If you can find time, wouldn't you do something to help them, if I ask you, Papa?"

"Hush, hush, dear, dear child," said the Commissioner, holding her hot little hand against his cheek; "you'll get well real soon, and you and I will see what we can do for them together."

But in whatsoever paths of benevolence, thus vaguely premeditated, that the Commissioner might tread, he was not to have the company of his beloved. That night the little frail body grew suddenly too tired to struggle further, and Georgia's exit was made from the great stage when she had scarcely begun to speak her little piece before the footlights. But there must be a stage manager who understands. She had given the cue to the one who was to speak after her.

A week after she was laid away, the Commissioner reappeared

at the Office, a little more courteous, a little paler and sterner, with the black frock-coat hanging a little more loosely from his tall figure.

His desk was piled with work that had accumulated during the four heartbreaking weeks of his absence. His chief clerk had done what he could, but there were questions of law, of fine judicial decisions to be made concerning the issue of patents, the marketing and leasing of school lands, the classification into grazing, agricultural, watered, and timbered, of new tracts to be opened to settlers.

The Commissioner went to work silently and obstinately, putting back his grief as far as possible, forcing his mind to attack the complicated and important business of his office. On the second day after his return he called the porter, pointed to a leather-covered chair that stood near his own, and ordered it removed to a lumber-room at the top of the building. In that chair Georgia would always sit when she came to the Office for him of afternoons.

As time passed, the Commissioner seemed to grow more silent, solitary, and reserved. A new phase of mind developed in him. He could not endure the presence of a child. Often when a clattering youngster belonging to one of the clerks would come chattering into the big business-room adjoining his little apartment, the Commissioner would steal softly and close the door. He would always cross the street to avoid meeting the school-children when they came dancing along in happy groups upon the sidewalk, and his firm mouth would close into a mere line.

It was nearly three months after the rains had washed the last dead flower-petals from the mound above little Georgia when the "land-shark" firm of Hamlin and Avery filed papers upon what they considered the "fattest" vacancy of the year.

It should not be supposed that all who were termed "land-sharks" deserved the name. Many of them were reputable men of good business character. Some of them could walk into the most august councils of the State and say: "Gentlemen, we would like to have this, and that, and matters go thus." But, next to a three years' drought and the boll-worm, the Actual Settler hated the Land-shark. The land-shark haunted the Land Office, where all the land records were kept, and hunted "vacancies" — that is, tracts of unappropriated public domain, generally invisible upon the official maps, but actually existing "upon the ground." The law entitled any one possessing certain State scrip to file by virtue of same upon any land not previously legally appropriated. Most of the scrip was now in the hands of the land-sharks. Thus, at the cost of a few hundred dollars, they often secured lands worth as many thousands. Naturally, the search for "vacancies" was lively.

But often — very often — the land they thus secured, though legally "unappropriated," would be occupied by happy and contented settlers, who had labored for years to build up their homes, only to discover that their titles were worthless, and to receive peremptory notice to quit. Thus came about the bitter and not unjustifiable hatred felt by the toiling settlers toward the shrewd and seldom merciful speculators who so often turned them forth destitute and homeless from their fruitless labors. The history of the State teems with their antagonism. Mr. Land-shark seldom showed his face on "locations" from which he should have to eject the unfortunate victims of a monstrously tangled land system, but let his emissaries do the work. There was lead in every cabin, molded into balls for him; many of his brothers had enriched the grass with their blood. The fault of it all lay far back.

When the State was young, she felt the need of attracting newcomers, and of rewarding those pioneers already within her borders. Year after year she issued land scrip — Headrights, Bounties, Veteran Donations, Confederates; and to railroads, irrigation companies, colonies, and tillers of the soil galore. All required of the grantee was that he or it should have the scrip properly surveyed upon the public domain by the county or district surveyor, and the land thus appropriated became the property of him or it, or his or its heirs and assigns, forever.

In those days — and here is where the trouble began — the State's domain was practically inexhaustible, and the old surveyors, with princely — yea, even Western American — liberality, gave good measure and overflowing. Often the jovial man of metes and bounds would dispense altogether with the tripod and chain. Mounted on a pony that could cover something near a "vara" at a step, with a pocket compass to direct his course, he would trot out a survey by counting the beat of his pony's hoofs, mark his corners, and write out his field notes with the complacency produced by an act of duty well performed. Sometimes — and who could blame the surveyor? — when the pony was "feeling his oats," he might step a little higher and farther, and in that case the beneficiary of the scrip might get a thousand or two more acres in his survey than the scrip called for. But look at the boundless leagues the State had to spare! However, no one ever had to complain of the pony understepping. Nearly every old survey in the State contained an excess of land.

In later years, when the State became more populous, and land values increased, this careless work entailed incalculable trouble, endless litigation, a period of riotous land-grabbing, and no little bloodshed. The land-sharks voraciously attacked these excesses in

the old surveys, and filed upon such portions with new scrip as unappropriated public domain. Wherever the identifications of the old
tracts were vague, and the corners were not to be clearly established,
the Land Office would recognize the newer locations as valid, and
issue title to the locators. Here was the greatest hardship to be
found. These old surveys, taken from the pick of the land, were already nearly all occupied by unsuspecting and peaceful settlers, and
thus their titles were demolished, and the choice was placed before
them either to buy their land over at a double price or to vacate it,
with their families and personal belongings, immediately. Land locators sprang up by hundreds. The country was held up and
searched for "vacancies" at the point of a compass. Hundreds of
thousands of dollars' worth of splendid acres were wrested from
their innocent purchasers and holders. There began a vast hegira of
evicted settlers in tattered wagons; going nowhere, cursing injustice,
stunned, purposeless, homeless, hopeless. Their children began to
look up to them for bread, and cry.

It was in consequence of these conditions that Hamlin and
Avery had filed upon a strip of land about a mile wide and three
miles long, comprising about two thousand acres, it being the excess
over complement of the Elias Denny three-league survey on Chiquito River, in one of the middle-western counties. This two-thou-
sand-acre body of land was asserted by them to be vacant land, and
improperly considered a part of the Denny survey. They based this
assertion and their claim upon the land upon the demonstrated facts
that the beginning corner of the Denny survey was plainly identified; that its field notes called to run west 5,760 varas, and then
called for Chiquito River; thence it ran south, with the meanders —
and so on — and that the Chiquito River was, on the ground, fully a
mile farther west from the point reached by course and distance. To
sum up: there were two thousand acres of vacant land between the
Denny survey proper and Chiquito River.

One sweltering day in July the Commissioner called for the papers in connection with this new location. They were brought, and
heaped, a foot deep, upon his desk — field notes, statements,
sketches, affidavits, connecting lines — documents of every description that shrewdness and money could call to the aid of Hamlin and
Avery.

The firm was pressing the Commissioner to issue a patent upon
their location. They possessed inside information concerning a new
railroad that would probably pass somewhere near this land.

The General Land Office was very still while the Commissioner
was delving into the heart of the mass of evidence. The pigeons

could be heard on the roof of the old, castle-like building, cooing and
fretting. The clerks were droning everywhere, scarcely pretending to
earn their salaries. Each little sound echoed hollow and loud from
the bare, stone-flagged floors, the plastered walls, and the iron-
joisted ceiling. The impalpable, perpetual limestone dust that never
settled, whitened a long streamer of sunlight that pierced the tattered window-awning.

It seemed that Hamlin and Avery had builded well. The Denny
survey was carelessly made, even for a careless period. Its beginning
corner was identical with that of a well-defined old Spanish grant,
but its other calls were sinfully vague. The field notes contained no
other object that survived — no tree, no natural object save Chiquito
River, and it was a mile wrong there. According to precedent, the
Office would be justified in giving it its complement by course and
distance, and considering the remainder vacant instead of a mere excess.

The Actual Settler was besieging the Office with wild protests
in re. Having the nose of a pointer and the eye of a hawk for the land-
shark, he had observed his myrmidons running the lines upon his
ground. Making inquiries, he learned that the spoiler had attacked
his home, and he left the plow in the furrow and took his pen in
hand.

One of the protests the Commissioner read twice. It was from a
woman, a widow, the granddaughter of Elias Denny himself. She
told how her grandfather had sold most of the survey years before at
a trivial price — land that was now a principality in extent and
value. Her mother had also sold a part, and she herself had succeeded to this western portion, along the Chiquito River. Much of it
she had been forced to part with in order to live, and now she owned
only about three hundred acres, on which she had her home. Her
letter wound up rather pathetically:

"I've got eight children, the oldest fifteen years. I work all day
and half the night to till what little land I can and keep us in clothes
and books. I teach my children too. My neighbors is all poor and has
big families. The drouth kills the crops every two or three years and
then we has hard times to get enough to eat. There is ten families on
this land what the land-sharks is trying to rob us of, and all of them
got titles from me. I sold to them cheap, and they aint paid out yet,
but part of them is, and if their land should be took from them I
would die. My grandfather was an honest man, and he helped to
build up this State, and he taught his children to be honest, and how
could I make it up to them who bought from me? Mr. Commissioner, if you let them land-sharks take the roof from over my chil-

dren and the little from them as they has to live on, whoever again
calls this State great or its government just will have a lie in their
mouths."

The Commissioner laid this letter aside with a sigh. Many,
many such letters he had received. He had never been hurt by them,
nor had he ever felt that they appealed to him personally. He was
but the State's servant, and must follow its laws. And yet, somehow,
this reflection did not always eliminate a certain responsible feeling
that hung upon him. Of all the State's officers he was supremest in
his department, not even excepting the Governor. Broad, general
land laws he followed, it was true, but he had a wide latitude in particular ramifications. Rather than law, what he followed was Rulings; Office Rulings and precedents. In the complicated and new
questions that were being engendered by the State's development
the Commissioner's ruling was rarely appealed from. Even the
courts sustained it when its equity was apparent.

The Commissioner stepped to the door and spoke to a clerk in
the other room — spoke as he always did, as if he were addressing a
prince of the blood:

"Mr. Weldon, will you be kind enough to ask Mr. Ashe, the
State school land appraiser, to please come to my office as soon as
convenient?"

Ashe came quickly from the big table where he was arranging
his reports.

"Mr. Ashe," said the Commissioner, "you worked along the Chiquito River, in Salado County, during your last trip, I believe. Do you
remember anything of the Elias Denny three-league survey?"

"Yes, sir, I do," the blunt, breezy surveyor answered. "I
crossed it on my way to Block H, on the north side of it. The road
runs with the Chiquito River, along the valley. The Denny survey
fronts three miles on the Chiquito."

"It is claimed," continued the Commissioner, "that it fails to
reach the river by as much as a mile."

The appraiser shrugged his shoulder. He was by birth and instinct an Actual Settler, and the natural foe of the land-shark.

"It has always been considered to extend to the river," he said,
dryly.

"But that is not the point I desired to discuss," said the Commissioner. "What kind of country is this valley portion of (let us say,
then) the Denny tract?"

The spirit of the Actual Settler beamed in Ashe's face.

"Beautiful," he said, with enthusiasm. "Valley as level as this
floor, with just a little swell on, like the sea, and rich as cream. Just

enough brakes to shelter the cattle in winter. Black loamy soil for six feet, and then clay. Holds water. A dozen nice little houses on it, with windmills and gardens. People pretty poor, I guess — too far from market — but comfortable. Never saw so many kids in my life."

"They raise flocks?" inquired the Commissioner.

"Ho, ho! I mean two-legged kids," laughed the surveyor; "two-legged, and bare-legged, and tow-headed."

"Children! oh, children!" mused the Commissioner, as though a new view had opened to him; "they raise children!"

"It's a lonesome country, Commissioner," said the surveyor. "Can you blame 'em?"

"I suppose," continued the Commissioner, slowly, as one carefully pursues deductions from a new, stupendous theory, "not all of them are tow-headed. It would not be unreasonable, Mr. Ashe, I conjecture, to believe that a portion of them have brown, or even black, hair."

"Brown and black, sure," said Ashe; "also red."

"No doubt," said the Commissioner. "Well, I thank you for your courtesy in informing me, Mr. Ashe. I will not detain you any longer from your duties."

Later, in the afternoon, came Hamlin and Avery, big, handsome, genial, sauntering men, clothed in white duck and low-cut shoes. They permeated the whole office with an aura of debonair prosperity. They passed among the clerks and left a wake of abbreviated given names and fat brown cigars.

These were the aristocracy of the land-sharks, who went in for big things. Full of serene confidence in themselves, there was no corporation, no syndicate, no railroad company or attorney-general, too big for them to tackle. The peculiar smoke of their rare, fat brown cigars was to be perceived in the sanctum of every department of State, in every committee-room of the Legislature, in every bank parlor and every private caucus-room in the State Capital. Always pleasant, never in a hurry, seeming to possess unlimited leisure, people wondered when they gave their attention to the many audacious enterprises in which they were known to be engaged.

By and by the two dropped carelessly into the Commissioner's room and reclined lazily in the big, leather-upholstered arm-chairs. They drawled a good-natured complaint of the weather, and Hamlin told the Commissioner an excellent story he had amassed that morning from the Secretary of State.

But the Commissioner knew why they were there. He had half promised to render a decision that day upon their location.

The chief clerk now brought in a batch of duplicate certificates for the Commissioner to sign. As he traced his sprawling signature, "Hollis Summerfield, Comr. Genl. Land Office," on each one, the chief clerk stood, deftly removing them and applying the blotter.

"I notice," said the chief clerk, "you've been going through that Salado County location. Kampfer is making a new map of Salado, and I believe is platting in that section of the county now."

"I will see it," said the Commissioner. A few moments later he went to the draughtsmen's room.

As he entered he saw five or six of the draughtsmen grouped about Kampfer's desk, gargling away at each other in pectoral German, and gazing at something thereupon. At the Commissioner's approach they scattered to their several places. Kampfer, a wizened little German, with long, frizzled ringlets and a watery eye, began to stammer forth some sort of an apology, the Commissioner thought for the congregation of his fellows about his desk.

"Never mind," said the Commissioner, "I wish to see the map you are making," and, passing around the old German, seated himself upon the high draughtsman's stool. Kampfer continued to break English in trying to explain.

"Herr Gommissioner, I assure you blenty sat I haf not it bremeditated — sat it wass — sat it itself make. Look you! from se field notes wass it blatted — bleace to observe se calls: South, 10° west 1,050 varas; south, 10° east 300 varas; south 100: south, 9; west, 200; south, 40° west 400 — und so on. Her Gommissioner, nefer would I have — "

The Commissioner raised one white hand, silently. Kampfer dropped his pipe and fled.

With a hand at each side of his face, and his elbows resting upon the desk, the Commissioner sat staring at the map which was spread and fastened there — staring at the sweet and living profile of little Georgia drawn thereupon — at her face, pensive, delicate, and infantile, outlined in a perfect likeness.

When his mind at length came to inquire into the reason of it, he saw that it must have been, as Kampfer had said, unpremeditated. The old draughtsman had been platting in the Elias Denny Survey, and Georgia's likeness, striking though it was, was formed by nothing more than the meanders of Chiquito River. Indeed, Kampfer's blotter, whereon his preliminary work was done, showed the laborious tracings of the calls and the countless pricks of the compasses. Then, over his faint penciling, Kampfer had drawn in India ink with a full, firm pen the similitude of Chiquito River, and forth had blossomed mysteriously the dainty, pathetic profile of the child.

The Commissioner sat for half an hour with his face in his hands, gazing downward, and none dared approach him. Then he arose and walked out. In the business office he paused long enough to ask that the Denny file be brought to his desk.

He found Hamlin and Avery still reclining in their chairs, apparently oblivious of business. They were lazily discussing summer opera, it being their habit — perhaps their pride also — to appear supernaturally indifferent whenever they stood with large interests imperiled. And they stood to win more on this stake than most people knew. They possessed inside information to the effect that a new railroad would, within a year, split this very Chiquito River valley and send land values ballooning all along its route. A dollar under thirty thousand profit on this location, if it should hold good, would be a loss to their expectations. So, while they chatted lightly and waited for the Commissioner to open the subject, there was a quick, sidelong sparkle in their eyes, evincing a desire to read their title clear to those fair acres on the Chiquito.

A clerk brought in the file. The Commissioner seated himself and wrote upon it in red ink. Then he rose to his feet and stood for a while looking straight out of the window. The Land Office capped the summit of a bold hill. The eyes of the Commissioner passed over the roofs of many houses set in a packing of deep green, the whole checkered by strips of blinding white streets. The horizon, where his gaze was focused, swelled to a fair wooded eminence flecked with faint dots of shining white. There was the cemetery, where lay many who were forgotten, and a few who had not lived in vain. And one lay there, occupying a very small space, whose childish heart had been large enough to desire, while near its last beats, good to others. The Commissioner's lips moved slightly as he whispered to himself: "It was her last will and testament, and I have neglected it so long!"

The big brown cigars of Hamlin and Avery were fireless, but they still gripped them between their teeth and waited, while they marveled at the absent expression upon the Commissioner's face.

By and by he spoke suddenly and promptly.

"Gentlemen, I have just indorsed the Elias Denny survey for patenting. This office will not regard your location upon a part of it as legal." He paused a moment, and then, extending his hand as those dear old-time ones used to do in debate, he enunciated the spirit of that Ruling that subsequently drove the land-sharks to the wall, and placed the seal of peace and security over the doors of ten thousand homes.

"And, furthermore," he continued, with a clear, soft light upon his face, "it may interest you to know that from this time on this Office will consider that when a survey of land made by virtue of a certificate granted by this State to the men who wrested it from the wilderness and the savage — made in good faith, settled in good faith, and left in good faith to their children or innocent purchasers — when such a survey, although overrunning its complement, shall call for any natural object visible to the eye of man, to that object it shall hold, and be good and valid. And the children of this State shall lie down to sleep at night, and rumors of disturbers of title shall not disquiet them. For," concluded the Commissioner, "of such is the Kingdom of Heaven."

In the silence that followed, a laugh floated up from the patent-room below. The man who carried down the Denny file was exhibiting it among the clerks.

"Look here," he said, delightedly, "the old man has forgotten his name. He's written 'Patent to original grantee,' and signed it 'Georgia Summerfield, Comr.' "

The speech of the Commissioner rebounded lightly from the impregnable Hamlin and Avery. They smiled, rose gracefully, spoke of the baseball team, and argued feelingly that quite a perceptible breeze had arisen from the east. They lit fresh fat brown cigars, and drifted courteously away. But later they made another tiger-spring for their quarry in the courts. But the courts, according to the reports in the papers, "coolly roasted them" (a remarkable performance, suggestive of liquid-air didoes), and sustained the Commissioner's Ruling.

And this Ruling itself grew to be a Precedent, and the Actual Settler framed it, and taught his children to spell from it, and there was sound sleep o' nights from the pines to the sage-brush, and from the chaparral to the great brown river of the north.

But I think, and I am sure the Commissioner never thought otherwise, that whether Kampfer was a snuffy old instrument of destiny, or whether the meanders of the Chiquito accidentally platted themselves into that memorable sweet profile or not, there was brought about "something good for a whole lot of children," and the result ought to be called "Georgia's Ruling."

NOTES AND COMMENTS

The Daughters of the Republic of Texas has printed a charming small booklet called *Stories of the Old Texas Land Office* containing a brief history of the Land Office, pictures, and two short stories by O. Henry which have their setting in that historic "Castle on the Rhine."

For review of literary evaluation and notes and comments related to "Georgia's Ruling," reference is made to Dr. Porter's essay, Part II, "The Imprisoned Splendor," *ante*, pp. 26–28.

An Afternoon Miracle

At the United States end of an international river bridge, four armed rangers sweltered in a little 'dobe hut, keeping a fairly faithful espionage upon the lagging trail of passengers from the Mexican side.

Bud Dawson, proprietor of the Top Notch saloon, had, on the evening previous, violently ejected from his premises one Leandro Garcia, for alleged violation of the Top Notch code of behavior. Garcia had mentioned twenty-four hours as a limit, by which time he would call and collect a plentiful indemnity for personal satisfaction.

This Mexican, although a tremendous braggart, was thoroughly courageous, and each side of the river respected him for one of these attributes. He and a following of similar bravoes were addicted to the pastime of retrieving towns from stagnation.

The day designated by Garcia for retribution was to be further signalized on the American side by a cattleman's convention, a bull fight, and an old settler's barbecue and picnic. Knowing the avenger to be a man of his word, and believing it prudent to court peace

First published in *Everybody's* Magazine for July 1902, as by O. Henry.

Eighth of nineteen stories in *Heart of the West,* published by McClure Company, New York, in 1907.

while three such gently social relaxations were in progress, Captain McNulty, of the ranger company stationed there, detailed his lieutenant and three men for duty at the end of the bridge. Their instructions were to prevent the invasion of Garcia, either alone or attended by his gang.

Travel was slight that sultry afternoon, and the rangers swore gently, and mopped their brows in their convenient but close quarters. For an hour no one had crossed save an old woman enveloped in a brown wrapper and a black mantilla, driving before her a burro loaded with kindling wood tied in small bundles for peddling. Then three shots were fired down the street, the sound coming clear and snappy through the still air.

The four rangers quickened from sprawling, symbolic figures of indolence to alert life, but only one rose to his feet. Three turned their eyes beseechingly but hopelessly upon the fourth, who had gotten nimbly up and was buckling his cartridge-belt around him. The three knew that Lieutenant Bob Buckley, in command, would allow no man of them the privilege of investigating a row when he himself might go.

The agile, broad-chested lieutenant, without a change of expression in his smooth, yellow-brown, melancholy face, shot the belt strap through the guard of the buckle, hefted his sixes in their holsters as a belle gives the finishing touches to her toilette, caught up his Winchester, and dived for the door. There he paused long enough to caution his comrades to maintain their watch upon the bridge, and then plunged into the broiling highway.

The three relapsed into resigned inertia and plaintive comment.

"I've heard of fellows," grumbled Broncho Leathers, "what was wedded to danger, but if Bob Buckley ain't committed bigamy with trouble, I'm a son of a gun."

"Peculiarness of Bob is," inserted the Nueces Kid, "he ain't had proper trainin'. He never learned how to git skeered. Now, a man ought to be skeered enough when he tackles a fuss to hanker after readin' his name on the list of survivors, anyway."

"Buckley," commented ranger No. 3, who was a misguided Eastern man, burdened with an education, "scraps in such a solemn manner, that I have been led to doubt its spontaneity. I'm not quite onto his system, but he fights, like Tybalt, by the book of arithmetic."

"I never heard," mentioned Broncho, "about any of Dibble's ways of mixin' scrappin' and cipherin'."

"Triggernometry?" suggested the Nueces infant.

"That's rather better than I hoped from you," nodded the Easterner, approvingly. "The other meaning is that Buckley never goes into a fight without giving away weight. He seems to dread taking the slightest advantage. That's quite close to foolhardiness when you are dealing with horse-thieves and fence-cutters who would ambush you any night, and shoot you in the back if they could. Buckley's too full of sand. He'll play Horatius and hold the bridge once too often some day."

"I'm on there," drawled the Kid; "I mind that bridge gang in the reader. Me, I go instructed for the other chap — Spurious Somebody — the one that fought and pulled his freight, to fight 'em on some other date."

"Anyway," summed up Broncho, "Bob's about the gamest man I ever see along the Rio Bravo. Great Sam Houston! If she gets any hotter she'll sizzle!" Broncho whacked at a scorpion with his four-pound Stetson felt, and the three watchers relapsed into comfortless silence.

How well Bob Buckley had kept his secret, since these men, for two years his side comrades in countless border raids and dangers, thus spake of him, not knowing that he was the most arrant physical coward in all that Rio Bravo country! Neither his friends nor his enemies had suspected him of aught else than the finest courage. It was purely a physical cowardice, and only by an extreme, grim effort of will had he forced his craven body to do the bravest deeds. Scourging himself always, as a monk whips his besetting sin, Buckley threw himself with apparent recklessness into every danger, with the hope of some day ridding himself of the despised affliction. But each successive test brought no relief, and the ranger's face, by nature adapted to cheerfulness and good humor, became set to the guise of gloomy melancholy. Thus, while the frontier admired his deeds, and his prowess was celebrated in print and by word of mouth in many camp-fires in the valley of the Bravo, his heart was sick within him. Only himself knew of the horrible tightening of the chest, the dry mouth, the weakening of the spine, the agony of the strung nerves — the never-failing symptoms of his shameful malady.

One mere boy in his company was wont to enter a fray with a leg perched flippantly about the horn of his saddle, a cigarette hanging from his lips, which emitted smoke and original slogans of clever invention. Buckley would have given a year's pay to have attained that devil-may-care method. Once the debonair youth said to him: "Buck, you go into a scrap like it was a funeral. Not," he added, with a complimentary wave of his tin cup, "but what it generally is."

Buckley's conscience was of the New England order with Western adjustments, and he continued to get his rebellious body into as many difficulties as possible; wherefore, on that sultry afternoon he chose to drive his own protesting limbs to investigation of that sudden alarm that had startled the peace and dignity of the State.

Two squares down the street stood the Top Notch saloon. Here Buckley came upon signs of recent upheaval. A few curious spectators pressed about its front entrance, grinding beneath their heels the fragments of a plate-glass window. Inside, Buckley found Bud Dawson utterly ignoring a bullet wound in his shoulder, while he feelingly wept at having to explain why he failed to drop the "blamed masquerooter" who shot him. At the entrance of the ranger, Bud turned appealingly to him for confirmation of the devastation he might have dealt.

"You know, Buck, I'd'a' plum got him, first rattle, if I'd thought a minute. Comin' a-masquerootin', playin' female till he got the drop, and turned loose. I never reached for a gun, thinkin' it was sure Chihuahua Betty, or Mrs. Atwater, or anyhow one of the Mayfield girls comin' a-gunnin', which they might, liable as not. I never thought of that blamed Garcia until — "

"Garcia!" snapped Buckley. "How did he get over here?"

Bud's bartender took the ranger by the arm and led him to the side door. There stood a patient gray burro cropping the grass along the gutter, with a load of kindling wood tied across its back. On the ground lay a black shawl and a voluminous brown dress.

"Masquerootin' in them things," called Bud, still resisting attempted ministrations to his wound. "Thought he was a lady till he give a yell and winged me."

"He went down this side street," said the bartender. "He was alone, and he'll hide out till night when his gang comes over. You ought to find him in that Mexican lay-out below the depot. He's got a girl down there — Pancha Sales."

"How was he armed?" asked Buckley.

"Two pearl-handled sixes, and a knife."

"Keep this for me, Billy," said the ranger, handing over his Winchester. Quixotic, perhaps, but it was Bob Buckley's way. Another man — and a braver one — might have raised a posse to accompany him. It was Buckley's rule to discard all preliminary advantage.

The Mexican had left behind him a wake of closed doors and an empty street, but now people were beginning to emerge from their places of refuge with assumed unconsciousness of anything having happened. Many citizens who knew the ranger, pointed out to him with alacrity the course of Garcia's retreat.

As Buckley swung along upon the trail he felt the beginning of the suffocating constriction about his throat, the cold sweat under the brim of his hat, the old, shameful, dreaded sinking of his heart as it went down, down, down in his bosom.

The morning train of the Mexican Central had that day been three hours late, thus failing to connect with the I, and G. N. on the other side of the river. Passengers for Los Estados Unidos grumblingly sought entertainment in the little swaggering mongrel town of two nations, for, until the morrow, no other train would come to rescue them. Grumblingly, because two days later would begin the great fair and races in San Antone. Consider that at that time San Antone was the hub of the wheel of Fortune, and the names of its spokes were Cattle, Wool, Faro, Running Horses, and Ozone. In those times cattlemen played at crack-loo on the sidewalks with double-eagles, and gentlemen backed their conception of the fortuitous card with stacks limited in height only by the interference of gravity. Wherefore, thither journeyed the sowers and the reapers — they who stampeded the dollars, and they who rounded them up. Especially did the caterers to the amusement of the people haste to San Antone. Two greatest shows on earth were already there, and dozens of smallest ones were on the way.

On a side track near the mean little 'dobe depot stood a private car, left there by the Mexican train that morning and doomed by an ineffectual schedule to ignobly await, amid squalid surroundings, connection with the next day's regular.

The car had been once a common daycoach, but those who had sat in it and cringed to the conductor's hatband slips would never have recognized it in its transformation. Paint and gilding and certain domestic touches had liberated it from any suspicion of public servitude. The whitest of lace curtains judiciously screened its windows. From its fore end drooped in the torrid air the flag of Mexico. From its rear projected the Stars and Stripes and a busy stove-pipe; the latter reenforcing in its suggestion of culinary comforts the general suggestion of privacy and ease. The beholder's eye, regarding its gorgeous sides, found interest to culminate in a single name in gold and blue letters extending almost its entire length — a single name, the audacious privilege of royalty and genius. Doubly, then, was this arrogant nomenclature here justified; for the name was that of "Alvarita, Queen of the Serpent Tribe." This, her car, was back from a triumphant tour of the principal Mexican cities, and now headed for San Antone, where, according to promissory advertisement, she would exhibit her "Marvellous Dominion and Fearless Control over Deadly and Venomous Serpents, Handling them with Ease as they Coil and Hiss to the Terror of Thousands of Tongue-tied Tremblers!"

One hundred in the shade kept the vicinity somewhat depeopled. This quarter of the town was a ragged edge; its denizens,
the bubbling froth of five nations; its architecture, tent, jacal, and
'dobe; its distractions; the hurdy-gurdy and the informal contribution to the sudden stranger's store of experience. Beyond this dis-
honorable fringe upon the town's jowl rose a dense mass of trees,
surmounting and filling a little hollow. Through this bickered a
small stream that perished down the sheer and disconcerting side of
the great canon of the Rio Bravo del Norte.

In this sordid spot was condemned to remain for certain hours
the impotent transport of the Queen of the Serpent Tribe.

The front door of the car was open. Its forward end was cur-
tained off into a small reception-room. Here the admiring and propitiatory reporters were wont to sit and transpose the music of Señorita Alvarita's talk into the more florid key of the press. A picture
of Abraham Lincoln hung against a wall; one of a cluster of school-
girls grouped upon stone steps was in another place; a third was
Easter lilies in a blood-red frame. A neat carpet was under foot. A
pitcher, sweating cold drops, and a glass stood upon a fragile stand.
In a willow rocker, reading a newspaper, sat Alvarita.

Spanish, you would say; Andalusian, or, better still, Basque;
that compound, like the diamond, of darkness and fire. Hair, the
shade of purple grapes viewed at midnight. Eyes, long, dusky, and
disquieting with their untroubled directness of gaze. Face, haughty
and bold, touched with a pretty insolence that gave it life. To hasten
conviction of her charm, but glance at the stacks of handbills in the
corner, green, and yellow, and white. Upon them you see an incompetent presentment of the señorita in her professional garb and pose.
Irresistible, in black lace and yellow ribbons, she faces you; a blue
racer is spiralled upon each bare arm; coiled twice about her waist
and once about her neck, his horrid head close to hers, you perceive
Kuku, the great eleven-foot Asian python.

A hand drew aside the curtain that partitioned the car, and a
middle-aged, faded woman holding a knife and a half-peeled potato
looked in and said:

"Alviry, are you right busy?"

"I'm reading the home paper, Ma. What do you think! that
pale, tow-headed Matilda Price got the most votes in the *News* for
the prettiest girl in Gallipo — *lees.*"

"Shuh! She wouldn't of done it if *you'd* been home, Alviry. Lord
knows, I hope we'll be there before fall's over. I'm tired gallopin'
round the world playin' we are dagoes, and givin' snake shows. But
that ain't what I wanted to say. That there biggest snake's gone

agin. I've looked all over the car and can't find him. He must have been gone an hour. I remember hearin' somethin' rustlin' along the floor, but I thought it was you."

"Oh, blame that old rascal!" exclaimed the Queen, throwing down her paper. "This is the third time he's got away. George never *will* fasten down the lid to his box properly. I do believe he's *afraid* of Kuku. Now I've got to go hunt him."

"Better hurry; somebody might hurt him."

The Queen's teeth showed in a gleaming, contemptuous smile. "No danger. When they see Kuku outside they simply scoot away and buy bromides. There's a crick over between here and the river. That old scamp'd swap his skin any time for a drink of running water. I guess I'll find him there, all right."

A few minutes later Alvarita stepped upon the forward platform, ready for her quest. Her handsome black skirt was shaped to the most recent proclamation of fashion. Her spotless shirt-waist gladdened the eye in that desert of sunshine, a swelling oasis, cool and fresh. A man's split-straw hat sat firmly upon her coiled, abundant hair. Beneath her serene, round, impudent chin a man's four-in-hand tie was jauntily knotted about a man's high, stiff collar. A parasol she carried, of white silk, and its fringe was lace, yellowly genuine.

I will grant Gallipolis as to her costume, but firmly to Seville or Valladolid I am held by her eyes; castanets, balconies, mantillas, serenades, ambuscades, escapades — all these their dark depths guaranteed.

"Ain't you afraid to go out alone, Alviry?" queried the Queen-mother anxiously. "There's so many rough people about. Mebbe you'd better — "

"I never saw anything I was afraid of yet, Ma. 'Specially people. And men in particular. Don't you fret. I'll trot along back as soon as I find that runaway scamp."

The dust lay thick upon the bare ground near the tracks. Alvarita's eye soon discovered the serrated trail of the escaped python. It led across the depot grounds and away down a smaller street in the direction of the little cañon, as predicted by her. A stillness and lack of excitement in the neighborhood encouraged the hope that, as yet, the inhabitants were unaware that so formidable a guest traversed their highways. The heat had driven them indoors, whence out-drifted occasional shrill laughs, or the depressing whine of a mal-treated concertina. In the shade a few Mexican children, like vivi-fied stolid idols in clay, stared from their play, visionstruck and silent, as Alvarita came and went. Here and there a woman peeped from a door and stood dumb, reduced to silence by the aspect of the white silk parasol.

A hundred yards and the limits of the town were passed; scattered chaparral succeeding, and then a noble grove, overflowing the bijou cañon. Through this a small bright stream meandered. Park-like it was, with a kind of cockney ruralness further endorsed by the waste papers and rifled tins of picnickers. Up this stream, and down it, among its pseudo-sylvan glades and depressions, wandered the bright and unruffled Alvarita. Once she saw evidence of the recreant reptile's progress in his distinctive trail across a spread of fine sand in the arroyo. The living water was bound to lure him; he could not be far away.

So sure was she of his immediate proximity that she perched herself to idle for a time in the curve of a great creeper that looped down from a giant water-elm. To reach this she climbed from the pathway a little distance up the side of a steep and rugged incline. Around her chaparral grew thick and high. A late-blooming ratama tree dispensed from its yellow petals a sweet and persistent odor. Adown the ravine rustled a sedative wind, melancholy with the taste of sodden, fallen leaves.

Alvarita removed her hat, and undoing the oppressive convolutions of her hair, began to slowly arrange it in two long, dusky plaits.

From the obscure depths of a thick clump of evergreen shrubs five feet away, two small jewel-bright eyes were steadfastly regarding her. Coiled there lay Kuku, the great python; Kuku, the magnificent, he of the plated muzzle, the grooved lips, the eleven-foot stretch of elegantly and brilliantly mottled skin. The great python was viewing his mistress without a sound or motion to disclose his presence. Perhaps the splendid truant forefelt his capture, but, screened by the foliage, thought to prolong the delight of his escapade. What pleasure it was, after the hot and dusty car, to lie thus, smelling the running water, and feeling the agreeable roughness of the earth and stones against his body! Soon, very soon the Queen would find him, and he, powerless as a worm in her audacious hands, would be returned to the dark chest in the narrow house that ran on wheels.

Alvarita heard a sudden crunching of the gravel below her. Turning her head she saw a big, swarthy Mexican, with a daring and evil expression, contemplating her with an ominous, dull eye.

"What do you want?" she asked as sharply as five hairpins between her lips would permit, continuing to plait her hair, and looking him over with placid contempt. The Mexican continued to gaze at her, and showed his teeth in a white, jagged smile.

"I no hurt-y you, Señorita," he said.

"You bet you won't," answered the Queen, shaking back one finished, massive plait. "But don't you think you'd better move on?"

"Not hurt-y you — no. But maybeso take one *beso* — one li'l kees, you call him."

The man smiled again, and set his foot to ascend the slope. Alvarita leaned swiftly and picked up a stone the size of a cocoanut.

"Vamoose, quick," she ordered peremptorily, "you *coon!*"

The red of insult burned through the Mexican's dark skin.

"*Hidalgo, yo!*" he shot between his fangs. "I am not neg-r-ro! *Diabla bonita,* for that you shall pay me."

He made two quick upward steps this time, but the stone, hurled by no weak arm, struck him square in the chest. He staggered back to the footway, swerved half around, and met another sight that drove all thoughts of the girl from his head. She turned her eyes to see what had diverted his interest. A man with red-brown, curling hair, and a melancholy, sunburned, smooth-shaven face was coming up the path, twenty yards away. Around the Mexican's waist was buckled a pistol belt with two empty scabbards. He had laid aside his sixes — possibly in the jacal of the fair Pancha — and had forgotten them when the passing of the fairer Alvarita had enticed him to her trail. His hands now flew instinctively to the scabbards, but finding the weapons gone, he spread his fingers outward with the eloquent, abjuring, deprecating Latin gesture, and stood like a rock. Seeing his plight, the newcomer unbuckled his own belt containing two revolvers, threw it upon the ground, and continued to advance.

"Splendid!" murmured Alvarita, with flashing eyes.

As Bob Buckley, according to the mad code of bravery that his sensitive conscience imposed upon his cowardly nerves, abandoned his guns and closed in upon his enemy, the old, inevitable nausea of abject fear wrung him. His breath whistled through his constricted air passages. His feet seemed like lumps of lead. His mouth was dry as dust. His heart, congested with blood, hurt his ribs as it thumped against them. The hot June day turned to moist November. And still he advanced, spurred by a mandatory pride that strained its uttermost against his weakling flesh.

The distance between the two men slowly lessened. The Mexican stood, immovable, waiting. When scarce five yards separated them, a little shower of loosened gravel rattled down from above to the ranger's feet. He glanced upward with instinctive caution. A pair of dark eyes, brilliantly soft, and fierily tender, encountered and held his own. The most fearful heart and the boldest one in all the Rio Bravo country exchanged a silent and inscrutable communication. Alvarita, still seated within her vine, leaned forward above the breast-high chaparral. One hand was laid across her bosom. One great dark braid curved forward over her shoulder. Her lips were parted; her face was lit with what seemed but wonder — great and absolute wonder. Her eyes lingered upon Buckley's. Let no one ask or presume to tell through what subtle medium the miracle was performed. As by a lightning flash two clouds will accomplish counterpoise and compensation of electric surcharge, so on that eye-glance the man received his complement of manhood, and the maid conceded what enriched her womanly grace by its loss.

The Mexican, suddenly stirring, ventilated his attitude of apathetic waiting by conjuring swiftly from his boot-leg a long knife. Buckley cast aside his hat, and laughed once aloud, like a happy schoolboy at a frolic. Then, empty-handed, he sprang nimbly, and Garcia met him without default.

So soon was the engagement ended that disappointment imposed upon the ranger's warlike ecstasy. Instead of dealing the traditional downward stroke, the Mexican lunged straight with his knife. Buckley took the precarious chance, and caught his wrist, fair and firm. Then he delivered the good Saxon knock-out blow — always so pathetically disastrous to the fistless Latin races — and Garcia was down and out, with his head under a clump of prickly pears. The ranger looked up again to the Queen of the Serpents.

Alvarita scrambled down to the path.

"I'm mighty glad I happened along when I did," said the ranger.

"He — he frightened me so!" cooed Alvarita.

They did not hear the long, low hiss of the python under the shrubs. Wiliest of the beasts, no doubt he was expressing the humiliation he felt at having so long dwelt in subjection to this trembling and coloring mistress of his whom he had deemed so strong and potent and fearsome.

Slowly, slowly they walked. The ranger regained his belt of weapons. With a fine timidity she begged the indulgence of fingering the great .45's with little "Ohs" and "Ahs" of new-born, delicious shyness.

The *cañoncito* was growing dusky. Beyond its terminus in the river bluff they could see the outer world yet suffused with the waning glory of sunset.

A scream — a piercing scream of fright from Alvarita. Back she cowered, and the ready, protecting arm of Buckley formed her refuge. What terror so dire as to thus beset the close of the reign of the never-before-daunted Queen?

Across the path there crawled a *caterpillar* — a horrid, fuzzy, two-inch caterpillar! Truly, Kuku, thou wert avenged. Thus abdicated the Queen of the Serpent Tribe — *viva la reina!*

NOTES AND COMMENTS

Will Porter had been working on the Houston *Post*, in Houston, about nine months when he received word that his trial in Austin was set for July 6, 1896. Porter spoke fluent Spanish and somehow conceived a plan to escape to Honduras and later get his wife Athol and daughter Margaret to join him in making Honduras their permanent home. The plan could not succeed because Athol's health would not permit her to undertake a life away from her mother's constant care in Austin.

After Porter had been in Honduras less than six months he received word from Athol's mother that Athol could not be expected to live much longer because of her condition as a victim of tuberculosis. Porter promptly returned to Austin, made new bond with the court's approval, and set about caring for Athol, who on July 25, 1897, breathed her last and was buried in Oakwood Cemetery at Austin.

Porter's trial had not been reset and he returned to writing as a freelancer. In this period, before going to trial the following February 15, in 1898, Will Porter wrote and sold to McClure's Syndicate a story titled "The Miracle of Lava Canyon" as by W. S. Porter. "An Afternoon Miracle" is a later version of the same plot and similar characters. A typescript of "The Miracle of Lava Canyon," with Porter's corrections in ink, is now in the O. Henry Collection of the Austin History Center, together with the desk at which Porter made the original draft of that story.

For review of literary evaluation and additional notes and comments related to "An Afternoon Miracle" and "The Miracle of Lava Canyon," reference is made to Dr. Porter's essay, Part II, "The Imprisoned Splendor," *ante*, at pp. 28–29.

Money Maze

They will tell you, in Anchuria, that President Miraflores of that volatile republic died by his own hand in the coast town of Cibolo. That he had reached thus far in flight from the inconveniences of an imminent revolution, and that a quarter of a million *pesos*, government funds, which he carried with him in an American leather valise as a souvenir of his tempestuous administration, were never afterward found.

For a *real*, a muchacho will show you his grave. It is back of the town, near a little bridge that spans a mango swamp. A plain slab of undressed pine stands at its head.

Some one has burned upon the headpiece, with a hot iron, this inscription:

RAMON ANGEL DE LAS CRUZES
Y MIRAFLORES,
PRESIDENTE DE LA REPUBLICA
DE ANCHURIA.

First published in *Ainslee's* magazine for May 1901, as by O. Henry.

This story was never republished in book form, but its title supplied the heading of Chapter VII of *Cabbages and Kings*, the first book by O. Henry, published by McClure, Phillips & Co., New York, in 1904.

QUE SEA SU JUEZ, DIOS.

It is characteristic of this buoyant people that they pursue no man beyond his grave. "Let God be his judge!" Even with that quarter of a million unfound they could not engrave upon his tombstone the sarcasm of "a good and great man gone to his reward."

An old half-breed Indian tends this grave with fidelity and the dawdling minuteness of inherited sloth. He chops down the weeds with his *machete,* plucks away ants and scorpions with his horny fingers, and sprinkles it daily with water from the plaza fountain.

To the guest, the people of Cibolo will relate the story of the tragic death of their old President; how he strove to fly with the public funds and Doña Julia Gordon, the young American opera singer, and how, being apprehended by members of the revolutionary party in this coast town, he shot himself through the head rather than give up the funds and, as follows, the Señorita Gordon. They will relate, further, that Doña Julia, her adventurous bark of fortune shoaled by the simultaneous loss of her distinguished admirer and the souvenir quarter million, dropped anchor on this stagnant coast, awaiting a rising tide. The tide was ready, in the form of a wealthy American resident — a banana king, a rubber prince, a sarsaparilla, indigo and mahogany baron. The señorita married this American one month after the ill-fated President was buried with military dishonors, and while the "Vivas" of the new administration were saluting Liberty and prospective spoils.

The house of the American is to be seen on a bald foot-hill of the Cordilleras near the town. It is a conglomerate structure of the finest woods, brick, glass, palm, thatch, adobe and bamboo. The natives speak of its interior with admiration — "figure-it-to-your-self" — there are floors polished like mirrors, hand-woven Indian rugs of silk fibre, tall glasses, musical instruments, and painted walls.

Of the American, Don Frank Mackenzie, and of his wife, they have nothing but good to say. Don Frank has lived among them for years, and has compelled their respect. His lady is easily queen of what social life the sober coast affords. The Commandante's wife, herself, who was of the proud Castilian family of Monteleon y Dolorosa de los Santos y Mendez, feels honored to unfold her napkin with olive-hued, ringed hands at the table of the Señora Mackenzie. Were you to refer — with your northern prejudices — to the vivacious past of Mrs. Mackenzie, when her gleeful abandon upon the comic opera stage captured the mature President's fancy, or to her part in that statesman's downfall and malfeasance, the Latin shrug of the shoulder would be your only answer and rebuttal. The native dames admired the beautiful American lady, and many of them envied her possession of the marriage certificate signed by the good Padre Espirition.

It would seem that the story is ended; that the close of a tragedy and the climax of a romance have covered the ground of interest, but, to the more curious reader it shall be some slight instruction to learn why the old Indian, Galvez, is secretly paid to keep green the grave of President Miraflores by one who never saw that statesman in life or death. Also, why Don Emilio Villanueva, Minister of Finance during the Miraflores administration, and close friend to the deceased President, should, after dining at Mackenzie's house during a short visit to the coast, make the following remark to a friend:

"F-f-f-f-t! I say it to you. Twenty times in the Capital, I have taken wine in the company of Doña Julia Gordon. As many times I have heard her sing like the *ruiseñor* that she was. *Por el cuerpo de Cristo* this Madame Mackenzie — *aunque una Señora muy agradable* — is no more Doña Julia Gordon than I, myself, am. *Figuraselo?*"

The threads of the events reach far, stretching across the sea. Following them out, it will also be made clear why Shorty Flynn of the Columbia Detective Bureau, New York, lost his job. Also why Dr. Angel, middle-aged, dark-featured *poseur* of the boulevards of Paris, smokes two-franc cigars.

Cibolo lay in its usual stupor. The Caribbean swished upon the sand beach, the parrots screamed in the range and ceiba trees, the palms were waving their limber fronds foolishly, like an awkward chorus at the prima donna's cue to enter.

Suddenly the town was full of excitement. A boy dashed down the grass-grown street, shrieking, *"Busca el Señor Mackenzie. Un telégrafo por él!"* Knots of women, ox-eyed, bare-armed, ecru-complexioned, gathered at corners and caroled plaintively to one another: *"Un telégrafo por Señor Mackenzie!"* The word spread swiftly. The Commandante, who was loyal to the Ins, and suspected Mackenzie's devotion to the Outs, hissed "Aha!" and wrote in his secret memorandum book, *"Julio el 10 — Vinó un telégrafo por Señor M."*

Informed by a dozen voluntary messengers, Señor Mackenzie emerged from some contiguity of shade, and proceeded toward the telegraph office. The ox-eyed women gazed at him with shy admiration, for his type drew them. He was big, blond and jauntily dressed in white linen and buckskin *zapatos*. His manner was bold, but kind, and humorous.

The dispatch was from Bob Engelhardt, a "Gringo" in the capital city, an ice manufacturer, a sworn revolutionist, and "good people." The wily Bob seemed to have circumvented successfully the

impossibility of sending a confidential message in either Spanish or
English. The result was the following literary gem:

> His nibs skedaddled yesterday per jack rabbit line with all the
> spondulicks in the pot, and the bunch of calico he's spoons on.
> She's a peach, easy. Our crowd in good shape, but the boodle is six
> figures short. We must have the swag the main guy scooped. You
> collar it. He's headed for the briny. You know what to do.

This remarkable screed conveyed the information to Mackenzie
that the President had decamped for the coast with the public
money, accompanied by the opera singer, Julia Gordon, his infatua-
tion for whom was the gossip of the republic.

Mackenzie pocketed his message and went to talk it over with
his friend and co-conspirator, Dr. Zavalla, a native politician of
much ingenuity. Mackenzie had taken up political intrigue as a matter of business. He was acute enough to wield a certain influence
among leading schemers, and prosperous enough to purchase the respect of the petty office-holders. His support was considered so far
useful to the revolutionary party that, if the wheel revolved, he stood
to win a twenty-year concession to thirty thousand manzanas of the
finest timber land along the coast.

By reference to the "jack rabbit line" in Bob's message, it was
understood that the head of the government, the swag and Julia had
taken the mule-back route to the coast. Indeed, no other route was
there. A week's trip it was — over fearful mountains and streams; a
jiggety-joggety journey; hot and ice-cold, and wet and dry.

The trail, after descending the mountains, turned to a trident,
the central prong ending at Cibolo. Another branched off to Coralio;
the third penetrated Alazan.

At Coralio was a harbor, and strict quarantine and clearing
regulations. The fugitives would never attempt to escape there. At
Cibolo or Alazan they might hope to board a tramp freighter or a
fruit steamer by the aid of a rowboat or sloop, as the vessels anchored half a mile from shore.

But Mackenzie and Zavalla sent horseback messengers up and
down the coast with warning to the local leaders of the Liberal
movement — to Benavidez at Coralio, and to Varras at Alazan — in-
structing them to patrol the water line, and to arrest the flying President at all hazards if he should show himself in their territory. After
these precautions there was nothing to do but cover the Cibolo district with lookouts and await results. The fugitives would, beyond a
doubt, move as secretly as possible, and endeavor to board a vessel
by stealth from some hiding-place on shore.

On the eighth day after the receipt of Engelhardt's message, the *Karlsefin*, Norwegian steamer, chartered by the New Orleans fruit trade, anchored off Cibolo, with three hoarse toots of her siren. Mackenzie stood on the beach with the crowd of idlers, watching everything without ostentation. He and Zavalla had stationed men faithful to the cause at intervals along the shore for a mile each way from the town, on the lookout for President Miraflores, of whom nothing had been seen or heard. The customs officers, in their red trousers and Panama hats, rowed out to the vessel and returned. The ship's gig landed her purser with his papers, and then took out the quarantine doctor with his umbrella and clinical thermometer. Next, a swarm of half-naked Caribs began to load the piles of bananas upon lighters, and row them out to the steamer.

About four o'clock in the afternoon a marine monster, unfamiliar in those waters, hove in sight; — a graceful steam yacht, painted white, clean-cut as a steel engraving, see-sawing the waves like a duck in a rain-barrel. A white boat, manned by a white-uniformed crew, came ashore, and a stocky-built man leaped upon the sands. He made his way toward Mackenzie, who was obviously the most conspicuously Anglo-Saxon figure present, and seemed to turn a disapproving eye on the rather motley congregation of native Anchurians. Mackenzie greeted him as men sprung from the Islands greet one another in alien lands.

Conversation developed that the newly-landed one was named Smith, and that he had come in a yacht. A meager biography truly, for the yacht was most apparent, and the Smith not beyond a reasonable guess before the revelation. Yet, to the eye of Mackenzie, who had seen several things, there was a discrepancy between Smith and his yacht. A bullet-headed man Smith was, with an oblique, dead eye, and the mustache of a cocktail mixer. Unless he had shifted costumes before leaving for shore, he had affronted the deck of his correct vessel in a pearl-gray derby, a checked suit, fancy vest and vaudeville neckwear. Men owning pleasure yachts generally harmonize with them better.

Smith looked business, but he was no advertiser. He commented upon the scenery, remarking upon its fidelity to the pictures in the geography, and then inquired for the U.S. Consul. They pointed out to him the starred and striped bunting hanging on a pole above the door of a squat adobe house, and Smith plowed his way through the sand thither, his haberdashery creating a discord against a background of tropical blues and greens.

Mackenzie smoked cigars and walked the shingle under the cocoanut palms. His nets were well spread. The roads were so few, the opportunities for embarkation so limited, the two or three probable points of exit so well guarded that it would be strange indeed if there should slip through the meshes so much of the country's dignity, romance and collateral.

Night came, and satisfied with the precautions taken, the American strolled back through the town. Oil lamps burned, a sickly yellow, at random corners. Though yet early, the ways were almost depeopled. A few inhabitants were at their monotonous diversions, dragging at whining concertinas, fingering the guitar or sadly drinking *anisada* in the cantinas. All the streets were by-streets; there were no thoroughfares. Mackenzie turned along one of them, and crouched swiftly in the shadow, for a tall, muffled man passed, carrying a heavy valise. A woman at his elbow seemed to hurry him on. They went rapidly, Mackenzie following, until they reached and entered *a posada* known as the "Hotel de los Estranjeros," a dreary hostelry greatly in disuse both by strangers and friends.

At that moment there came along one Estebán, a barber, an enemy to existing government, a jovial plotter against stagnation in any form. He greeted Mackenzie with flatulent importance.

"What think you, Don Frank! I have tonight shaved *la barba* — what you call the 'weeskers' of El Señor Presidente himself. Consider! He sent for me to come. In a *pobre casa* he awaited — a verree leetle house. I think he desired not to be known, but — *carajo!* — can you shave a man and not see his face? This gold piece he gave me, and said it was to be all quite still. I think, Don Frank, there is what you call one chip over the bug."

In a few words Mackenzie explained the state of affairs to Estebán. Knowing the man to be a partisan Liberal, he made him watch the house to see that no one left it, while he himself entered it at once.

He was an acquaintance of the *madama* who conducted the *posada*. He found her to be a woman with little curiosity.

"Ah! it is the Señor Mackenzee. Not often does he honor this unworthy house. *Que?* — bright eyes — at my age! *Vaya!* Señor Mackenzee. Guests in the house? Why not? Two, but just finished to arrive — a señor not quite old, and a señora of sufficient handsomeness. To their rooms they have ascended, not desiring the to-drink nor the to-eat. Two rooms — *numero nueve* and *numero diez*. The Señor Mackenzie desires to speak with them? *Como no?* It is well."

Mackenzie saw that the trigger of his American .038 was free from pocket lining, and ascended the dark stairway. A saffron light from a hanging lamp in the hallway above allowed him to select the gaudy numbers on the doors. He turned the knob of number nine, entered and closed the door behind him.

If that was Julia Gordon seated by the table in the poorly furnished room, report had done her charms no injustice. She rested her head upon one hand. Extreme fatigue was signified in every line of her figure, and upon her countenance a deep perplexity was written. Her eyes were gray irised, and of that mold that seems to have belonged to all the famous queens of hearts. Their whites were singularly clear and brilliant, concealed above the irises by horizontal lids, and showing a snowy line below them. Such eyes denote great nobility, passion, and, if you can conceive it, a most selfish generosity. She looked up, when the American entered, in surprised inquiry, but without fear.

Mackenzie took off his hat and seated himself coolly on the edge of the table by which she sat. He held a lighted cigar between his fingers. He took this course upon the theory that preliminaries would be squandered upon the Señorita Gordon.

"Good-evening," he said. "Now madam, let us come to business at once. I know who is in the next room, and what he carries in that valise. I am here to dictate terms of surrender."

The lady neither replied nor moved, but steadily regarded the cigar in Mackenzie's hand.

"We," continued the dictator, — "I speak for a considerable mass of the people — demand the return of stolen funds belonging to them. Our terms go very little farther than that. They are very simple. As an accredited spokesman, I promise that our interference will cease with their acceptance. It is on my personal responsibility that I add congratulations to the gentleman in number ten upon his taste in feminine charms."

Returning his cigar to his mouth, Mackenzie observed her, and saw that her eyes followed and rested upon it with icy and significant concentration. Apparently, she had not heard a word he had said. He understood, tossed the cigar out the window, and, with an amused laugh, slid from the table to his feet. The lady smiled.

"That is better," she said, clipping her words off neatly. "For a second lesson in good manners, you may now tell me by whom I am being insulted."

"I'm rather sorry there's not enough time for more lessons," said Mackenzie, regretfully. "Come, now; I appeal to your good sense. You have shown yourself, in more than one instance, to be quite aware of what is to your advantage. There is no mystery here. I am Frank Mackenzie, and I have come for the money. I entered this room at a venture. Had I entered the other I would have had it by now. The gentleman in number ten has betrayed a great trust. He has robbed his people of a large sum, which I am in time to prevent their losing. I do not say who that gentleman is, but if I should be forced to see him, and he should prove to be a certain high official of the republic, it would be my duty to arrest him. The house is guarded. I am offering you liberal terms. Bring me the valise containing the money, and we will call the affair ended."

The lady rose from her chair and stood for a moment, thinking deeply. "Do you live here, Mr. Mackenzie?" she asked, presently.

"Yes."

"And your authority for this intrusion?"

"I am an instrument of the republic. I was advised by wire concerning the movements of the — gentleman in number ten."

"I have a question or two to ask you. I think you are a man more apt to be truthful than — timid. What sort of place is this town?"

"This town? Oh, a banana town, as they run. Grass huts, 'dobes, five or six two-story houses — population half-breeds, Caribs and blackamoors. No sidewalks; no amusements. Rather unmoral. That's an off-hand sketch, of course."

"Are there any inducements, say in a business or social way, for one to reside here?"

"One," said Mackenzie, smiling. "There are no afternoon teas — and another — there's no extradition treaty."

"He told me," went on the lady, speaking as if to herself, and with a slight frown, "that there were towns on this coast of importance; that there was a pleasing social order — especially an American colony of cultured residents."

"There is an American colony," he continued, gazing at her in some wonder. "Two defaulting bank presidents, one short county treasurer, four manslayers, and a widow — arsenic, I believe, was the suspicion. I, myself, complete the colony, but, as yet, have not distinguished myself by any felony."

"Do not lose hope," returned the lady, dryly, "I see nothing in your actions tonight to guarantee you future obscurity. Some mistake has been made; I do not know just where. But *him* you shall not disturb. The journey has fatigued him so that he is fallen asleep, I think, in his clothes. You talk of stolen money! Remain where you are, and I will bring you that valise you covet so." She turned upon him a peculiar, searching look that ended in a quizzical smile. "It is a puzzling thing," she continued; "you force my door, and you follow your ruffianly behavior with the basest accusations, and yet" —

she paused a moment, as if to reconsider what she was about to say
— "and yet — I am sure there has been some mistake."

She took step toward the door that connected the two rooms,
but Mackenzie stopped her by a light touch upon her arm. I have
said before that women turned to look at him on the streets. He was
a kind they seem to admire, big, good-looking, and with an air of
kindly truculence. This woman was to be his fate, and he did not
know it; but he must have felt the first throes of destiny, for, of a sudden, the knowledge of what report named her turned bitter in his
throat.

"If there has been any mistake," he said hotly, "it was yours. I
do not blame that man who has lost his honor, his country, and is
about to lose the poor consolation of his stolen riches, as much as I
do you, for I can very well see how he was brought to it. By heavens,
I can understand and pity him. It is such women as you that strew
this degraded coast with wretched exiles, that drag — "

The lady interrupted him by a gesture.

"There is no need," she said, coldly, "to continue your insults.
I do not understand you, nor do I know what mad blunder you are
making, but if the inspection of the contents of a gentleman's port-
manteau will rid me of you, let us delay no longer."

She passed quickly and noiselessly into the other room, and returned with the heavy leather valise. Mackenzie set it upon the
table, and began to unfasten the straps. She stood by with an expression of infinite scorn and weariness.

The valise opened wide, and Mackenzie dragged out one or two
articles of closely folded clothing, exposing the bulk of the contents
— package after package of tightly packed American banknotes of
large denomination. Judging by the high figures written upon the
bands that bound them, the total must have reached into the
hundreds of thousands. Mackenzie saw, with surprise and a thrill of
pleasure that he wondered at, that the woman experienced an unmistakable shock. She gasped, and leaned heavily against the table.
She had been ignorant, then, that her companion had looted the
government treasury. But why, he angrily asked himself, should he
be so well pleased to find this wandering singer not so black as report painted her?

A noise in the other room startled them both. The door swung
open, and an elderly smooth-faced, dark complexioned man, half
dressed, hurried into the room.

The pictures of President Miraflores extant in Cibolo represented him as the possessor of a luxuriant and carefully tended sup-

ply of dark whiskers, but the barber Estebán's story had prepared Mackenzie's eye for the change.

The man stumbled into the light, his eyes heavy from weariness and sleep, but flashing with alarm.

"What does this mean?" he demanded, in excellent English, with a keen and perturbed look at the American — "robbery?"

"Very nearly," answered Mackenzie; "but I guess I'm in time to prevent it. This cash goes back to the people to whom it belongs." He thrust both hands into the pockets of his loose linen coat. The President's hand went quickly behind him.

"Don't draw," called Mackenzie, sharply. "I've got you covered from my pocket."

The lady advanced and laid one hand on the shoulder of the hesitating defaulter. She pointed with the other to the table. "Tell me the truth," she said. "Whose money is that?"

The man did not answer. He gave a deep, long-drawn sigh, leaned and kissed her on the forehead and stepped back into the other room and closed the door.

Mackenzie foresaw his purpose and jumped for the door, but the report of the pistol echoed as his hand touched the knob. A heavy fall followed, and some one struggled past him into the suicide's room.

A desolation, thought Mackenzie, greater than the loss of cavalier and gold must have been in the heart of the enchantress to have forced from her, in that moment, the cry of one turning to the only all-forgiving, all-comforting earthly consoler — to have made her call out from that dishonored and bloody room — "Oh, mother! mother!"

But there were shouts of alarm, and hurrying feet were coming up the stairs. Mackenzie had his duty to perform. Circumstances had made him custodian of the country's treasure. They who were coming might not possess his scruples. Swiftly closing the valise, he leaned far out the window and softly dropped it into a thick orange tree below.

They will tell you in Cibolo, as they told me, how the shot alarmed the town; how the upholders of the law came apace — the Commandante in a head-waiter's jacket and red slippers, with girded sword, the bare-footed policemen with clanking bayonets and indifferent mien.

They say that the countenance of the dead man was marred by the effects of the shot, but he was identified as the down-fallen President by both Mackenzie and the barber Estebán. The story of his flight from the capital being made public just then, no further confirmation was deemed necessary. So they buried him on the following day, and his grave is there.

They will relate to you how the revolutionary party (now come, without opposition, to be in power) sifted the town and raked the country to find the dead President's valise containing Anchuria's surplus capital, but without success, though aided by Señor Mackenzie himself.

You will hear how Mackenzie, like a tower of strength, shielded the Señorita Julia through those subsequent distressful days. And how his scruples as to her past career (if he had any) vanished, and her adventuresome waywardness (if she had any) disappeared, and they were wedded and were happy.

But they cannot tell you (as I shall) what became of the money that Mackenzie dropped into that orange tree. But that comes later; for it is now time to consider the wishes of those who desire to learn why Shorty Flynn lost his situation. It is deemed fit that Mr. Flynn tell his own story.

MR. FLYNN'S STORY.

The chief rang up headquarters and told me to come up-town quick to an address he gave. I went there, and found him in a private office with a lot of directors who were looking pretty fuzzy. They stated the case: The President of the Republic Loan and Trust Company had skipped with nearly a quarter of a million in cash, and an expert was digging up a further shortage in his accounts at the rate of a thousand a day. The directors wanted him back pretty bad, but they wanted the money worse. They said they needed it. They had traced the old gent to where he boarded a tramp fruit steamer bound for Central America, or somewhere, with a big gripsack and his daughter — all the family he had.

Not to mention all the talk we had, in six hours I was on board a steam yacht belonging to one of the directors, and hot on the trail of the fruit tub. I had a pretty good idea where the old boy would strike for. At that time we had a treaty with about every foreign country except Belgium, and that banana republic, Anchuria. There wasn't a photo of old Wahrfield to be had in New York — he had been foxy there — but I had his description, and besides, the lady with him would be almost a dead give-away.

In my time I've brought back some pretty high flyers from places where I couldn't legally touch them. It's done with a bluff. When they won't be bluffed, I jump on them to get back all the boodle I can. I've kidnapped one or two, but that's dangerous. The best way is to strike them as soon as possible after they land in a foreign place. Get your work in before they get acquainted; while they're homesick and rattled, and short on nerve.

We struck the monkey coast one afternoon about four. There was a ratty-looking steamer off shore taking on bananas. The monkeys were loading her up with big barges. It might be the one the old man had taken, and it might not. I went ashore to look around. The scenery was pretty good. I never saw any finer on the New York stage. I struck an American on shore, a big, cool chap, standing around with the monkeys. He showed me the Consul's office. The Consul was a Dutchman named Bruck, and he had his mitt out for further orders. He sized me up for an investor, and tried to sell me a cocoanut franchise, a gold mine, a mahogany graft with officials — already — bribed — coupon attachment, and an imitation diamond ring. He stood in with the monkeys and got a rake-off every time a trick was turned. I got what I wanted to know out of him. He said the fruiter loading was the *Karlsefin*, running to New Orleans, but took her last cargo to New York on account of an overstocked home market. Then I was sure my people were on board, as the Consul said no passengers had landed. Just then the quarantine doctor dropped in for a chat, and he said there was a gentleman and lady on the fruiter, and they would come ashore in a few hours, as soon as the gent recovered a little from a sea-sick spell. So, all that I had to do, then, was to wait.

After dark I walked around and investigated that town some, and it was enough to give you the lions. If a man could stay in New York and be honest, he'd better do it than to hit that monkey town with a million.

Dinky little mud houses; grass over your shoe tops in the streets; ladies in low-neck-and-short-sleeves walking round smoking cigars; tree frogs rattling on Boulevard A like a hose carriage going to a ten blow; big mountains dropping gravel in the back yards, and the sea licking the paint of in front — no, sir — a man had better be in God's country living on free lunch than there.

The main street ran along the beach, and I walked down it, and then turned up a kind of lane where the houses were made of poles and straw? I wanted to see what the monkeys did when they weren't climbing cocoanut trees. The very first shack I looked in, I saw my people. They must have come ashore while I was promenading. A man about fifty, smooth face, heavy eyebrows, dressed in black broadcloth, looking like he was just about to say: "Can any little boy in the Sunday school answer that?" He was freezing on to a grip that weighed like a dozen gold bricks; and a swell girl — a regular peach, with a Fifth Avenue cut, was sitting on a wooden chair. An old black woman was fixing some coffee and beans on a table. The light they had came from a lantern hung on a nail. I went and stood in the door, and they looked at me, and I said:

"Mr. Wahrfield, you are my prisoner. I hope, for the lady's sake, you will take the matter sensibly. You know why I want you."

"Who are you?" says the old gent.

"Flynn," says I, "of the Columbia Detective Bureau. Now, sir, let me give you some good advice. You go back and take your medicine like a man. They'll only give you a five, or, maybe, a seven spot, and they'll send you to one of the reform pens where you will only have to keep books, or feed the warden's chickens. Is this a country for a young lady like Miss Wahrfield to live in? You give up the cash and go back easy and I'll put in a good word for you. I'll give you five minutes to decide." I pulled out my watch and waited.

Then the young lady chipped in. I could see she was one of the genuine high steppers, the kind that christen battleships and open chrysanthemum shows.

"Come inside," she says. "Don't stand in the door and disturb the whole street with that suit of clothes. Now, what is it you want?"

"Three minutes gone," I said. "I'll tell you again while the other two tick off. Wanted, in New York, J. Churchill Wahrfield, President of the Republic Loan and Trust Company. Also the funds belonging to said Company, now in that grip, in the unlawful possession of said J. Churchill Wahrfield."

"Oh-h-h-h!" says she, as if she was thinking, "you want to take us back to New York?"

"To take Mr. Wahrfield. There's no charge against you, miss. There'll be no objection, of course, to your returning with your father."

Of a sudden the girl gave a tiny scream and grabbed the old boy around the neck. "Oh father, father!" she says, kind of contralto; "can this be true? Have you taken money that is not ours? Speak, father!" It made you shiver to hear the tremolo stop she put on her voice.

Old Loan and Trust looked pretty bughouse when she first grappled him, but she went on, whispering in his ear and patting his off shoulder till he stood still, but sweating a little.

She got him to one side and they talked together a minute, and then he put on some gold eyeglasses and walked up and handed me the grip.

"Mr. Detective," he says, talking a little broken, "I conclude to return with you. I have finished to discover that life on this desolate and displeased coast would be worse than to die, itself. I will go back and hurl myself upon the mercy of the Loan-Trust Company. Have you brought a sheep?"

"Sheep!" says I; "I haven't a single — "

"Ship," cut in the young lady. "Don't get funny. Father is of German birth, and doesn't speak perfect English. How did you come?"

The girl was all broke up. She had a handkerchief to her face, and kept saying every little bit: "Oh, father, father!" She walked up to me and laid her lily-white hand on the clothes that had pained her at first. I smelt a million violets. She was a lula. I told her I came in a private yacht.

"Mr. Flynn," she says. "Oh, take us away from this horrid country at once. Can you! Will you! Say you will."

"I'll try," I said, concealing the fact that I was dying to get them on salt water before they could change their mind.

One thing they both kicked against was going through the town to the boat landing. Said they dreaded publicity, and now that they were going to return, they had a hope that the thing might yet be kept out of the papers. They swore they wouldn't go unless I got them out to the yacht without any one knowing it, so I agreed to humor them.

The sailors who rowed me ashore were playing billiards in a bar-room near the water, waiting for orders, and I proposed to have them take the boat down the beach half a mile or so, and take us up there. How to get them word was the question, for I couldn't leave the grip with the prisoner, and I couldn't take it with me, not knowing but what the monkeys might stick me up.

The young lady says the old colored woman would take them a note. I sat down and wrote it, and gave it to the dame with plain directions what to do, and she grins like a baboon and shakes her head.

Then Mr. Wahrfield handed her a string of foreign dialect, and she nods her head and says, "See, Senor," maybe fifty times, and lights out with the note.

"Old Augusta only understands German," said Miss Wahrfield, smiling at me. "We stopped in her house to ask where we could find lodging, and she insisted upon our having coffee. She tells us she was raised in a German family in San Domingo."

"Very likely," I said. "But you can search me for German words, except *nix verstay* and *noch einst*. I would have called that 'See, senor,' French, though, on a gamble."

Well, we three made a sneak around the edge of town so as not to be seen. We got tangled in vines and ferns and the banana bushes and tropical scenery a good deal. The monkey suburbs was as wild as places in Central Park. We came out on the beach a good half mile below. A brown chap was lying asleep under a co-coanut tree, with a ten-foot musket beside him. Mr. Wahrfield takes up the gun and pitches it in the sea. "The coast is guarded," he says. "Rebellion and plots ripen like fruit." He pointed to the sleeping man, who never stirred. "Thus," he says. "they perform trusts. Children!"

I saw our boat coming, and I struck a match and lit a piece of newspaper to show them where we were. In thirty minutes we were on board the yacht.

The first thing, Mr. Wahrfield and his daughter and I took the grip into the owner's cabin, opened it up, and took an inventory. There was two hundred and sixty thousand dollars in U.S. treasury certificates and bonds, besides a lot of diamond jewelry and a couple of hundred Havana cigars. I gave the old man the cigars and a receipt for the rest of the lot, as agent for the company, and locked the stuff up in my private quarters.

I never had a pleasanter trip than that one. After we got to sea, the young lady turned out to be the jolliest ever. The very first time we sat down to dinner, and the steward filled her glass with champagne — that director's yacht was a regular floating Waldorf-Astoria — she winks at me and says: "What's the use to borrow trouble, Mr. Fly Cop? Here's hoping you may live to eat the hen that scratches on your grave." There was a piano on board, and she sat down to it and sung better than you give up two cases to hear plenty times. She knew about nine operas clear through. She was sure enough *bon ton* and swell. She wasn't one of the "among others present" kind; she belonged on the special mention list!

The old man, too, perked up amazingly on the way. He passed the cigars, and says to me once, quite chipper, out of a cloud of smoke: "Mr. Flynn, somehow I think the Loan-Trust Company will not give me that much trouble. Guard well the grip — valise of the money, Mr. Flynn, for that it must be returned to them that it belongs when we finish to arrive."

When we landed in New York I 'phoned to the chief to meet us in that directors' office. We got in a cab and went there. I carried the grip, and we walked in, and I was pleased to see that the chief had got together that same old crowd of moneybugs with pink faces and white vests to see us march in. I set the grip on the table. "There's the money," I said.

"And your prisoner?" said the chief.

I pointed to Mr. Wahrfield, and he stepped forward and says: "The honor of a word with you, sir, to explain."

He and the chief went into another room and stayed ten minutes? When they came back the chief looked as black as a ton of coal.

"Did this gentleman," he says to me. "have this valise in his possession when you first saw him?"

"He did," said I.

The chief took up the grip and handed it to the prisoner with a bow, and says to the director crowd: "Do any of you recognize this gentleman?"

They all shook their pink faces.

"Allow me to present," he goes on, "Senor Miraflores, President of the Republic of Anchuria. The senor has generously consented to overlook this outrageous blunder, on condition that we

undertake to secure him against the annoyance of public comment. It is a concession on his part to overlook an insult for which
he might claim international redress. I think we can gratefully
promise him secrecy in the matter."

They gave him a pink nod.

"Flynn," he says to me. "As a private detective you're
wasted. In a war, where kidnapping governments is in the rules,
you'd be invaluable. Come down to the office at eleven."

I knew what that meant.

"So that's the President of the monkeys," says I.

"Well, why couldn't he have said so?"

Wouldn't it jar you?

We are brought, at length, to the contemplation of one known
as Dr. Angel, a familiar figure among the foreign residents of the
French capital. A brilliant blonde, addressed as Mlle. Gordon, often
accompanies him in public. In cigars Dr. Angel is a connoisseur.
The brand he smokes costs two francs each. He smokes them because he can afford to do so.

It only remains to designate the ultimate fate of the respectable
sum of money in the valise which Frank Mackenzie dropped into the
orange tree. To that end, and to do justice to Mr. Mackenzie's taste
and honesty, the following extract from an article in a New York
newspaper may opportunely be appended.

"It will be remembered that some months ago, J. Churchill
Wahrfield. President of the Republic Loan and Trust Company of
this city, absconded with nearly a quarter of a million dollars of
the company's funds. Also, the sensational second act of this unusual financial drama, in which the entire missing sum was returned to the company, two weeks after Wahrfield's disappear-
ance, through the medium of New Orleans bankers.

"Yesterday the *dénouement* occurred in the shape of a draft for
$17,869.24, which was received by the treasurer of the company;
the amount being exactly identical with the published figures of
the remainder of Wahrfield's shortage, as was determined by the
expert accountant who examined the books.

"Of ex-President Wahrfield and his daughter, who left with
him, and who was a society belle, nothing has since been heard.
Chief Bayley of the Columbia Detective Bureau stated to-day, in
an interview, that he sent, at the time of the flight, an experienced
detective on a promising clue to the Central American coast, but
that he returned without a trace of the fugitives.

"Of course, the only tenable theory is that Wahrfield repented of his deed soon after his departure, and returned the stolen
funds. His shrewdness and financial ability must have caused For-

tune to knock a second time as his door, to have enabled him to so promptly liquidate the remainder of the deficit.

"Thus closes a most unique incident in the business world, and, as Wahrfield will hardly make himself and his whereabouts known to the public again, the mystery of the restitution will, doubtless, never be explained."

NOTES AND COMMENTS

This story, here reproduced as originally published in May 1901, probably was the longest short story O. Henry ever wrote. It supplied the principal plot for his only novel, *Cabbages and Kings,* when blended with seven other stories in some manner connected with Will Porter's few months in Honduras. In an article titled "A Decomposition of Cabbages and Kings," Paul S. Clarkson analyzed the making of the book in a well-documented dissertation, published in *American Literature* for May 1935.

The character of Uncle Bushrod in "The Guardian of the Accolade" (and possibly Uncle Caesar in "A Municipal Report" also) may have been based on that of Colonel E. M. House's butler and coachman, Allen Carthen. Colonel House gave Allen his elaborate uniform, replete with epaulettes, high hat with plume, and a sword. Allen wore this to weddings and funerals all over Austin, a sight which must have long remained in Will Porter's memory. See letters from Colonel House to Allen Carthen given by Judge O'Quinn to the Austin History Center.

For a review of literary evaluation and additional notes and comments related to "Money Maze," reference is made to Dr. Porter's essay, Part II, "The Imprisoned Splendor," *ante,* at pp. 29–32.

The Point of the Story

I sometimes made a few inferior sketches, illustrating the special articles I did for the paper, and naturally, I became hostilely familiar with the art department. That is how I became acquainted with Clay. Clay had something to do with the mechanical part of the business — he wore aprons, and his hands were stained with chemicals. He was a little fellow with a face full of curly, red beard like the coat of a red Irish setter. Drink was his passion, and the sword of dismissal hung always by a hair above his head.

One afternoon Clay came to my desk and stood, with the unmistakable air of the petitioner. I mutely invited the threatened disclosure.

"Old fellow," said he — he had no right to call me "old fellow" — "I'm in a squeeze, and I thought you might help me out."

Men on The Paper are brothers, despite the differences set up by whisky or the Saturday night envelope, so I slowly ran one hand into the pocket where nestled a crisp five dollar bill and five new sil-

First published in *Red Book* magazine for November 1903, as by O. Henry.

Under the title "No Story," a rewritten version of "The Point of the Story" became the twelfth of sixteen stories in *Options,* published by Harper & Brothers, New York and London, in 1909.

ver dollars that I had, an hour before, secured by means of abject sa-
laams before the business manager, as an advance on next week's
salary.

"No, sir," said Clay, raising a virtuous but trembling hand in
abnegation, "I don't want to borrow."

I tried to suppress a sigh of relief.

"But," said Clay, "I want five dollars."

I tried to reconcile his two statements with my experience with
men who worked on The Paper, but without success. "I've got a rattling good story for you," explained Clay — "one that ought to run
a column and a half, at least. Ordinarily, I would give you the tip for
nothing, old man, but I've been on a whizz — I'm dead broke, and
as you stand to clean up at least fifteen cartwheels on the turn, you
can afford to pay a V for the pointer. I'll return the five some day,"
continued Clay, "You may not believe it, but I will."

"What's the stunt?" I asked, mentally bidding farewell to the
five, for I had studied journalism apart from the colleges.

"It's a peach," said Clay, alluringly. "I just got onto it an hour
ago. It'll make a dandy story for the Sunday bedquilt. Treat it kind
of joshingly, you know, and top it off with a lot of sentimental rot,
and it'll make a hit. Now, listen. There's a girl just struck the town
looking for a fellow. She's from the country — one of those peaches-
and-cream, milk-and-roses, innocent, Maud Muller kind of sisters
that are as out of place in this town as a snow ball in Africa. I met
her a couple of blocks from the depot, and she told me her history as
pat as if I were her uncle Pete. She's come to a town of three million
people to find a fellow with the other end of a filopena — or some
such foolishness. There's a romance of some sort mixed up in the affair. She's going to marry George, and she skipped off to town to try
to find Hen without letting anybody know — d'you catch? It's a
great snap for a Sunday article. She'll talk you to a finish, and you
can work it up fine. Don't you see what a chance it is, Mr. Winslow,
for a corking good lot of Sunday drivel?

"Another thing is, she's got to be sent back home before her absence is discovered, or they'll begin to think things. And then she's liable to all kinds of predicaments in this city unless she's attended to. I
steered her to a boarding house where she's now in soak for dinner and
lodging, for I hadn't a cent and she hadn't either. You come down and
interview her, Mr. Winslow. You can get a lot of copy out of it — and
you don't know how handy five dollars would come to me."

"Now, Clay," said I, "you belong to the art department, and
therefore ought to have some imagination. Just imagine the look on
old McArdle's face if I were to hand in a batch of stuff about a coun-

try girl who had made a visit to town. Can't you conjure up a vision of my inevitable terminus? Country girls striking the city in the exuberance of their unsophisticatedness are as ipecac in the market."

Clay looked so woe-begone, so needy and depressed and impecunious and humbly supplicant that I relented. After all, the girl might be in crying need of some help beyond the insufficient power of the unstrung Clay. So, I paper-weighted my copy and declared myself ready to accompany him, with indisposition in my heart.

Clay made such a sordid and miserable figure when he had reported, ready for the journey, in his closely buttoned, dingy coat and battered hat, that I indulged myself to the extra expense of a cab. In this we proceeded to a quarter of the city designated by Clay — a street crowded with red brick houses of musty and insidious aspect. At one of these — a boarding house by its pseudo-hospitable exterior — we stopped. At the sound of the door bell Clay blanched, and shivered in his disreputable clothes. Long experience with formidable landladies had made him nervous even to stand upon their steps. When the signal was answered he thrust, with insinuating haste, a dollar, that he had secured from me in advance, into the hand of a heavy woman who opened the door. That was the amount for which the young woman from the country stood in pawn.

"The young lady," said the placated proprietress, in a bass voice, "is in the second floor parlor." Thither Clay and I ascended. A very pretty young lady, about nineteen, sat by a table. Traces of recent and not unbecoming grief marked her features. A piece of well-nibbled taffy candy lay convenient to her hand upon the table. At Clay's introduction I bowed, with genuine admiration and revived interest, to Miss Rosa Redfield. I could not repress a slight shudder as Clay labeled me as his "friend." To such depths is a man reduced when beauty and vanity and old clothes meet.

Tears yet stood in Miss Redfield's eyes. The consolations of taffy had battled losingly against loneliness. Her dewy, blue orbs looked upon Clay with hope and interest.

"Did you find him?" she asked, with all the engaging optimism of roseate youth.

Clay stood by the table like a contradiction of her solvent freshness and bloom. One hand was thrust into the bosom of his faded coat. His gingery whiskers masked his face almost to his eyes. I was sorry Clay had introduced me as his friend.

"No, I haven't found him," said he, "But I've brought Mr. Winslow, who will give you the same advice that I have."

The young lady looked at me, expectantly.

"If I were acquainted with the circumstances," I began, all at sea.

"Oh, dear me," said Miss Redfield, brightly, "It isn't as bad as that. There are no circumstances. I just came to the city to see if I could find Hen. I'm afraid I'm a terrible hayseed," she flashed with a dazzling, wet smile; "I thought I could find him. Ain't there directories you can look people up in? I met Mr. Clay accidentally and he brought me here. My, it's a great big town, Mr. Winslow! I didn't intend to come. I was riding over to spend the day with Ella Pease, and the train came along and stopped. I just tied old Pompey to a tree and slipped off my riding skirt and got on the cars. I had just enough money to pay the fare. I got to thinking of Hen, and I couldn't h-h-elp it."

The unashamed tears of frank youth fell from her eyes. Her head went down upon her arm, and she was shaken by the transitory grief of her self-stimulated sorrow. Suddenly she flashed out a rainy smile of rainbow promise.

"Won't George be mad when he finds out I came! But I don't care. If I could find Hen I wouldn't go back. Hen left Green Valley four years ago. I was to wait for him, and I did. We always went together. He wrote to me every week until about a year ago. Something must have happened to him. He wouldn't forget." Miss Rosa, in witness thereof dangled as the exhibit a bangle attached to a silver bracelet. "That's our promise keepsake. We cut a dime in two and each kept half of it."

"Miss Redfield," said Clay, "can you describe this young man, Hen — Martin, I believe you said his name was?"

"Of course I can. He had the nicest brown eyes, and wavy hair and a little curly mustache too cute for anything."

"Did he have," asked Clay, "a scar half an inch long on the left side of his chin?"

"Why, yes, he did. Didn't I mention that before? It was where I cut him with my scissors once when we were playing. Oh, you must have seen him, Mr. May — Clay. Where is he? Why hasn't he written to me?"

"I'm sorry to tell you, Miss Redfield," said Clay, nervously fingering his mat of red whiskers, "that Hen Martin is dead. He died about a year ago. I knew him pretty well. I've often heard him say he was going back to Green Valley as soon as he got prosperous enough. About a year ago he went to drinking, and he didn't amount to much. He knew he was a failure, and I guess that's why he stopped writing."

Again Miss Rosa turned to Niobe. She bowed her head and besprinkled her taffy with the overflow of grief. I sat, superfluous, wishing that I had not come, that Miss Rosa was not so pretty, and that I had never met Clay, who still stood by the table, squalid and melancholy, picking at the ragged binding of his coat. He began to speak again:

"In all of Hen Martin's folly and dissipation he never forgot Green Valley. That's where his heart was always. But he went down so low that at last he gave up hope. But he never forgot, and he asked to have that half of a silver dime that he always carried, buried with him."

Miss Rosa's sobs neared the hysterical, and I felt some heat at Clay for persisting in his theme. And then, suddenly, the belief seized me that the fellow was acting. In order to earn his five dollars and give me a run for my money he was working up this cheap melodrama. Perhaps he was even lying about having known the recreant Mr. Martin, and had created the story of his affecting but, to me, uninteresting demise. I thought it base and contemptible to thus turn to his profit the harmless escapade of the little country maiden. I resolved to discontinue all relations with that disreputable member of the art department.

"May I ask," said Clay, "if you l-l-like this gentleman you say you are engaged to?"

"George?" said Miss Rosa, rising from her tears like another charming lady from a larger body of salt water, "Of course I like George. He's awful good to me, and his father is going to give him a farm. He's a little poky, but — Oh, I guess I like George, but I got to thinking of H — H — H —"

"Come now, Miss Redfield," said Clay, rather authoritatively, successfully heading off another outburst of weeping, "let's talk about something else. The thing for you to do is to go back home as quick as you can, forget about this trip and marry George. You tell her so, Mr. Winslow."

At last I was to be of use. Clay sat down, with the air of an attorney resting his case. Miss Redfield looked at me expectantly. I coughed impressively and spake, as the oracle.

"Miss Redfield," I said, "it is an old saying that we seldom wed those whom we first love. Perhaps it is best so. Our youthful affections are often bestowed unworthily. This Mr. — er — Martin seems to have been one not likely to have made you happy. In time you will forget him. Mr. Clay advises you well. I can but endorse his recommendation that you return home as soon as possible. Marry Mr. — er — George if your heart so prompts you. He is, no doubt, a worthy young man — and the farm will be of use. As I said, time will lessen all griefs and soften all regrets, and the memory of Mr. Martin will gradually fade away, as it seems to should."

With the exception of the last phrase, which I felt was badly arranged, I thought my little speech quite neat and appropriate; and Miss Rosa appeared to be really calmed and restored by it. But it fell, wasted, upon the gloomy and disconsolate Clay. I liked the fellow less and less.

We three held a conference, and Miss Redfield was convinced that it behooved her to get back to Green Valley before her little journey should have become known. Also it was gently impressed upon her that it would be well to keep George in blissful ignorance of her visit to the city.

In half an hour she could board a train that would set her back again in Green Valley. Old Pompey, she was sure, would still be tied to his tree, and she could proceed to the home of Miss Pease. Thus no one would be the wiser concerning her deviation from the original programme of the day. To accomplish these ends we must move at once.

Miss Rosa was now quite in spirits again, and she looked so sweet and fresh in her dotted Swiss and sailor hat that I began to warm to the adventure, and was for providing bonbons and roses for the voyage, but Clay demonstrated that the schedule did not permit.

We left the house — Clay creeping warily down the stairs in his cautious boarding house manner — and hastened to the railroad station. It was necessary that I be of the party, for I was the good fairy; I was to pay the freight. Miss Rosa had brought no money along; and Clay and the most diminutive coin were strangers.

I paid three dollars for a ticket to Green Valley, and we placed the young lady aboard. When the train started she leaned from the window, while Clay and I trotted along the platform, receiving her pleasing and grateful adieus. Impartially she dealt them to each of us, and we saw her little handkerchief flying when the coach was afar.

Clay turned to me, stolidly, with a shifty, apprehensive look on his trampish countenance. I pulled out my five dollar bill and handed it to him, for I supposed that I owed it to him.

"Can you make a story out of it, Mr. Winslow," he asked, rather timidly, — "a column or so, anyhow — enough to pay you for what you are out?"

"Certainly not," I answered, "It isn't worth a paragraph. But I suppose we ought to be content. We've been able to help a nice little girl out of a scrape. Here's your money."

"No," said Clay; "the three dollars for the ticket and the dollar the landlady got comes out of my five. You might give me the other dollar; it'll get me drunk to-night."

I put a silver dollar in his hand. Clay was looking miserable and blue. I knew to how many schemes and inventions the slaves of drink are driven by their master, and I softened a little toward him.

"Ride back in a cab with me?" I offered.

"No, I'll walk. I'm very sorry, Mr. Winslow, that you can't see any copy in this business. You know, it seemed like a pretty strong situation to me."

"Oh, well," said I, "don't think any more of it. We've helped the little girl along, and we won't complain about the expense."

Clay unbuttoned his dingy coat to stow away his dollar in a safe place. I caught sight of a cheap, plated watch chain against his vest. Dangling from it, as a charm, was the half of a battered silver dime.

"What!" I exclaimed, catching hold of it.

"Yes," said Clay, dully, "That's right. My name's Henry Clay Martin."

NOTES AND COMMENTS

It is obvious that "The Point of the Story" was a story written by O. Henry at Columbus, probably a story having the background acquired by Will Porter during the nine months he had worked as a columnist and feature writer on the Houston *Post*. The notebook kept by Porter at Columbus listed "NO Story" but that title fits only the story published in *Metropolitan* magazine in June 1909, which has a background Will Porter could not have had prior to going to New York in 1902. As already noted, the story written at Columbus was published in *Red Book* magazine in November 1903, the story here produced.

For a review of literary evaluation and additional notes and comments related to "The Point of the Story," reference is made to Dr. Porter's essay, Part II, "The Imprisoned Splendor," *ante*, at pp. 32–34.

A Fog in Santone

The drug clerk looks sharply at the white face half concealed by the high-turned overcoat collar.

"I would rather not supply you," he says doubtfully. "I sold you a dozen morphia tablets less than an hour ago."

The customer smiles wanly. "The fault is in your crooked streets. I didn't intend to call upon you twice, but I guess I got tangled up. Excuse me."

He draws his collar higher, and moves out, slowly. He stops under an electric light at the corner, and juggles absorbedly with three or four little pasteboard boxes.

"Thirty-six," he announces to himself.

First published in *The Two Women*, a book comprising two stories by O. Henry, the manuscripts having been given by Will Porter to Witter Bynner in 1904 in appreciation for Bynner's help with *Cabbages and Kings*, Bynner's book published by Small, Maynard and Company, Boston, in 1910.

The second publication of this story, ostensibly the first, was republished in *Cosmopolitan* magazine for October 1912.

The third publication was as the seventh story in *Rolling Stones*, published by Doubleday, Page & Company, Garden City, New York, in 1912.

"More than plenty."

For, a gray mist had swooped upon Santone that night, an opaque terror that laid a hand to the throat of each of the city's guests. It was computed that three thousand invalids were hibernating in the town. They had come from by and wide, for here, among these contracted, river-sliced streets, the goddess Ozone has elected to linger.

Purest atmosphere, sir, on earth! You might think, from the river winding through our town, that we are malarial, but, no, sir! Repeated experiments made by both government and local experts prove that our air contains nothing deleterious — nothing but ozone, sir, pure ozone. Litmus paper tests made all along the river show — but you can read it all in the prospectuses; or the Santonian will recite it for you, word by word.

We may achieve climate, but weather is thrust upon us. Santone, then, cannot be blamed for this cold, gray fog that came and kissed the lips of the three thousand, and then delivered them to the cross. That night the tubercles, whose ravages hope holds in check, multiplied. The writhing fingers of the pale mist did not go thence bloodless. Many of the wooers of ozone capitulated with the enemy that night, turning their faces to the wall in that dumb, isolated apathy that so terrifies their watchers. On the red stream of Hemorrhagia a few souls drifted away, leaving behind pathetic heaps, white and chill as the fog itself. Two or three came to view this atmospheric wraith as the ghost of impossible joys, sent to whisper to them of the egregious folly it is to inhale breath into the lungs, only to exhale it again, and these used whatever came handy to their relief, pistols, gas or the beneficent muriate.

The purchaser of the morphia wanders into the fog, and, at length, finds himself upon a little iron bridge, one of the score or more in the heart of the city under which the small, tortuous river flows. He leans on the rail and gasps, for here the mist has concentrated, lying like a footpad to garrote such of the Three Thousand as creep that way. The iron bridge guys rattle to the strain of his cough, a mocking, phthisical rattle, seeming to say to him: "Clackety — clack! just a little rusty cold, sir, — but not from our river. Lit — mus paper all along the banks and nothing but ozone. Clack — et — y — clack!"

The morphia man at last recovers sufficiently to be aware of another overcoated man ten feet away, leaning on the rail, and just coming out of a paroxysm. There is a freemasonry among the Three Thousand that does away with formalities and introductions. A cough is your card; a hemorrhage a letter of credit. The morphia man, being nearer recovered, speaks first.

"Goodall: Memphis — pulmonary tuberculosis — guess last stages." The Three Thousand economize on words. Words are breath, and they need breath to write checks for the doctors.

"Hurd," gasps the other. "Hurd; of T'leder, T'leder, Ah-hia. Catarrhal bronkeetis. Name's Dennis, too — doctor says. Says I'll, — live four weeks if I — take care of myself. Got your walking papers yet?"

"My doctor," says Goodall, of Memphis, a little boastingly, "gives me three months."

"Oh," remarks the man from Toledo, filling up great gaps in his conversation with wheezes, "Damn the difference. What's months! Expect to — cut mine down to one week — and die in a hack — a four wheeler, not a cough. Be considerable moanin' of the bars when I put out to sea. I've patronized 'em — pretty freely since I struck my — present gait. Say, Goodall, of Memphis — if your doc has set your pegs so close — why don't you — get on a big spree and go — to the devil quick and easy — like I'm doing?"

"A spree!" says Goodall, as one who entertains a new idea, "I never did such a thing. I was thinking of another way, but —"

"Come on," invites the Ohioan, "and have some drinks. I've been at it — for two days, but the inf — ernal stuff won't bite like it used to. Goodall, of Memphis, what's your respiration?"

"Twenty-four."

"Daily — temperature?"

"Hundred and four."

"You can do it in two days. It'll take me a — week. Tank up, friend Goodall — have all the fun you can, then — off you go, in the middle of a jag, and s-s-save trouble and expense. I'm a s-son of a gun if this aint a health resort — for your whiskers! A Lake Erie fog'd get lost here in two minutes."

"You said something about a drink," says Goodall.

A few minutes later they line up at a glittering bar, and hang upon the arm rest. The bartender, blonde, heavy, well-groomed, sets out their drinks, instantly perceiving that he serves two of the Three Thousand. He observes that one is a middle-aged man, well dressed, with a lined and sunken face; the other a mere boy, who is chiefly eyes and overcoat. Disguising well the tedium begotten by many repetitions, the server of drinks begins to chant the sanitary saga of Santone. "Rather a moist night, gentlemen, for our town. A little fog from our river, but nothing to hurt. Repeated tests — "

"Damn your litmus papers," gasps Toledo, — "without any — personal offence intended. We've heard of 'em before. Let 'em turn red, white and blue. What we want is a repeated test of that — whiskey. Come again. I paid for the last round, Goodall, of Memphis."

The bottle oscillates from one to the other, continues to do so, and is not removed from the counter. The bartender sees two emaciated invalids dispose of enough Kentucky Belle to floor a dozen cowboys, without displaying any emotion save a sad and contemplative interest in the peregrinations of the bottle. So he is moved to manifest a solicitude as to the consequences.

"Not on your Uncle Mark Hanna," responds Toledo, "will we get drunk. We've been — vaccinated with whiskey and — cod liver oil. What would send you to the police station — only gives us a thirst. S-s-set out another bottle."

It is slow work trying to meet death by that route. Some quicker way must be found. They leave the saloon and plunge again into the mist. The sidewalks are mere flanges at the base of the houses; the street a cold ravine, the fog filling it like a freshet. Not far away is the Mexican quarter. Conducted as if by wires along the heavy air comes a guitar's tinkle, and the demoralizing voice of some señorita singing:

> *En las tardes sombrillos del invierno*
> *En el prado a llorar me reclino,*
> *Y maldigo mi fausto destino —*
> *Una vida la mas infeliz.*

The words of it they do not understand — neither Toledo nor Memphis, but words are the least important things in life. The music tears the breasts of the seekers after Nepenthe, inciting Toledo to remark:

"Those kids of mine — I wonder — By God, Mr. Goodall, of Memphis, we had too little of that whiskey! No slow music in mine, if you please. It makes you disremember to forget."

Hurd, of Toledo, here pulls out his watch, and says:

"I'm a son of a gun! Got an engagement for a hack ride out to San — Pedro Springs at eleven. Forgot it. A fellow from Noo York, and me, and the Castillo sisters at Rhinegelder's Garden. That Noo York chap's a lucky dog — Got one whole lung — good for a year yet. Plenty of money, too. He pays for everything. I can't afford — to miss the jamboree. Sorry you ain't going along. Good-by, Goodall, of Memphis."

He rounds the corner and shuffles away, casting off thus easily the ties of acquaintanceship as the moribund do, the season of dissolution being man's supreme hour of egoism and selfishness. But he turns and calls back through the fog to the other: "I say, Goodall, of

Memphis! If you get *there* before I do, tell 'em Hurd's a comin' too. Hurd, of T'leder, Ah-hia."

Thus Goodall's tempter deserts him. That youth, uncomplaining and uncaring, takes a spell at coughing, and, recovered, wanders desultorily on down the street, the name of which he neither knows nor recks. At a certain point he perceives swinging doors, and hears, filtering between them, a noise of wind and string instruments. Two men enter from the street as he arrives, and he follows them in. There is a kind of antechamber, plentifully set with palms and cactuses and oleanders. At little marble-topped tables some people sit, while soft-shod attendants bring beer. All is orderly, clean, melancholy — gay; of the German method of pleasure. At his right is the foot of a stairway. A man standing there holds out his hand. Goodall extends his, full of silver, and the man selects therefrom a coin. Goodall goes upstairs, and sees there two galleries extending along the sides of a concert hall which he now perceives to lie below and beyond the anteroom he had first entered. These galleries are divided into boxes or stalls which bestow, with the aid of hanging lace curtains, a certain privacy upon their occupants.

Passing, with aimless feet down the aisle contiguous to these saucy and discreet compartments, he is half checked by the sight, in one of them, of a young woman, alone, and seated in an attitude of reflection. This young woman becomes aware of his approach. A smile from her brings him to a standstill, and her subsequent invitation draws him, though hesitating, to the other chair in the box, a little table between them.

Goodall is only nineteen. There are some whom, when the terrible god Phthisis wishes to destroy he first makes beautiful; and the boy is one of these. His face is wax, and an awful pulchritude is born of the menacing flame in his cheeks. His eye reflects an unearthly vista engendered by the certainty of his doom. As it is forbidden man to guess accurately concerning his fate, it is inevitable that he shall tremble at the slightest lifting of the veil.

The young woman is well dressed, and exhibits a beauty of a distinctly feminine and tender sort; an Eve-like comeliness that seems scarcely predestined to fade.

It is immaterial, the steps by which the two mount to a certain plane of good understanding; they are short and few, as befits the occasion. A button against the wall of the partition is frequently disturbed, and a waiter comes and goes at its signal. Pensive Beauty would nothing of wine; two thick plaits of her blonde hair hang almost to the floor; she is a lineal descendant of the Loreley. So the waiter brings the brew; effervescent, icy, greenish-golden. The orchestra on the stage is playing "Oh, Rachel." The two youngsters have exchanged a good bit of information. She calls him "Walter," and he calls her "Miss Rosa."

Goodall's tongue is loosened, and he has told her everything about himself. About his home in Tennessee, the old pillared mansion under the oaks, the stables, the hunting; the friends he has; down to the chickens, and the box bushes bordering the walks. About his coming South for the climate, hoping to escape the hereditary foe of his family. All about his three months on a ranch; the deer hunts, the rattlers, and the rollicking in the cow camps. Then of his advent to Santone, where he has indirectly learned from a great specialist that his life's calendar probably contains but two more leaves. And then of this death-white, choking night which has come and strangled his fortitude, and sent him out to seek a port amid its depressing billows.

"My weekly letter from home failed to come," he told her, "and I was pretty blue. I knew I had to go before long, and I was tired of waiting. I went out and began morphine at every drug store where they would sell me a few tablets. I got thirty-six quarter-grains, and was going back to my room and take them, but I met a queer fellow on a bridge, who had a new idea."

Goodall fillips a little pasteboard box upon the table, "I put 'em all together in there."

Miss Rosa, being a woman, must raise the lid, and give a slight shiver at the innocent-looking triturates. "Horrid things! but, those little, white bits — they could never kill one!"

Indeed they could. Walter knew better. Nine grains of morphia! Why, half the amount might.

Miss Rosa demands to know about Mr. Hurd, of Toledo, and is told. She laughs like a delighted child. "What a funny fellow! But tell me more about your home and your sisters, Walter. I know enough about Texas and tarantulas and cowboys."

The theme is dear, just now, to his mood, and he lays before her the simple details of a true home; the little ties and endearments that so fill the exile's heart. Of his sisters, one, Alice, furnishes him a theme he loves to dwell upon.

"She is like you, Miss Rosa," he says. "Maybe not quite so pretty, but just as nice, and good, and —"

"There! Walter," says Miss Rosa sharply, "Now talk about something else."

But a shadow falls upon the wall outside, preceding a big, softly treading man, finely dressed, who pauses a second before the curtains and then passes on. Presently comes the waiter with a message: "Mr. Rolfe says —"

"Tell Rolfe I'm engaged."

"I don't know why it is," says Goodall, of Memphis, "but I don't feel as bad as I did. An hour ago I wanted to die, but since I've met you, Miss Rosa, I'd like, so much, to live."

The young woman whirls around the table, lays an arm behind his neck, and kisses him on the cheek.

"You must, dear boy," she says. "I know what was the matter. It was this miserable, foggy weather that has lowered your spirits and mine too — a little. But, look now!"

With a little spring she has drawn back the curtains. A window is in the wall, opposite, and lo! the mist is cleared away. The indulgent moon is out again, revoyaging the plumbless sky. Roof and parapet and spire are softly pearl enamelled. Twice, thrice the retrieved river flashes back, between the houses, the light of the firmament. A tonic day will dawn, sweet and prosperous.

"Talk of death, when the world is so beautiful!" says Miss Rosa, laying her hand on his shoulder. "Do something to please me, Walter. Go home to your rest, and say: 'I mean to get better,' and do it."

"If you ask it," says the boy, with a smile, "I will."

The waiter brings full glasses. Did they ring? No; but it is well. He may leave them. A farewell glass. Miss Rosa says: "To your better health, Walter." He says: "To our next meeting."

His eyes look no longer into the void, but gaze upon the antithesis of death. His foot is set in an undiscovered country tonight. He is obedient, ready to go. "Goodnight," she says.

"I never kissed a girl before," he confesses, "except my sisters."

"You didn't this time," she laughs; "I kissed you. — Goodnight."

"When shall I see you again?" he persists.

"You promised me to go home," she frowns, "and get well. Perhaps we shall meet again — soon. Goodnight." He hesitates, his hat in hand. She smiles broadly and kisses him once more, upon the forehead. She watches him far down the aisle, then sits again at the table.

The shadow falls once more against the wall. This time the big, softly stepping man parts the curtains and looks in. Miss Rosa's eye meets his, and, for half a minute they remain thus, silent, fighting a battle with that king of weapons. Presently the big man drops the curtains and passes on.

The orchestra ceases playing suddenly, and an important voice can be heard loudly talking in one of the boxes farther down the aisle. No doubt some citizen entertains there some visitor to the town, and Miss Rosa leans back in her chair and smiles at some of the words she catches:

"Purest atmosphere — in the world — litmus paper all along — nothing hurtful — our city — nothing but pure ozone."

The waiter returns for the tray and glasses. As he enters, the girl crushes a little empty pasteboard box in her hand, and throws it in a corner. She is stirring something in her glass with her hatpin.

"Why, Miss Rosa," says the waiter, with the civil familiarity he uses, — "Putting salt in your beer this early in the night!"

NOTES AND COMMENTS

O. Henry's use of the term Santone for the city of San Antonio shows clearly his familiarity with the Texas vernacular. Will Porter was personally familiar with San Antonio, having published his weekly newspaper in San Antonio, as well as in Austin, during the last few months of its publication in 1895. Will Porter's knowledge of the Spanish language enabled him to be "at home" in the city that was bilingual to a large extent.

Acquisition in recent months of the original manuscript of "A Fog in Santone" has enabled Dr. Porter, an accomplished Spanish scholar, to make an original contribution to understanding of the little song O. Henry set out in the story as he heard the song in Spanish.

For a review of literary evaluation and additional notes and comments related to "A Fog in Santone," reference is made to Dr. Porter's essay, Part II, "The Imprisoned Splendor," *ante*, pp. 34–36.

A Blackjack Bargainer

The most disreputable thing in Yancey Goree's law office was Goree himself, sprawled in his creaky old armchair. The rickety little office, built of red brick, was set flush with the street — the main street of the town of Bethel.

Bethel rested upon the foot hills of the Blue Ridge. Above it the mountains were piled to the sky. Far below it the turbid Catawba gleamed yellow along its disconsolate valley.

The June day was at its sultriest hour. Bethel dozed in the tepid shade. Trade was not. It was so still that Goree, reclining in his chair, distinctly heard the clicking of the chips in the grand jury room, where the "court house gang" was playing poker. From the open back door of the office a well worn path meandered across the grassy lot to the court house. The treading out of that path had cost Goree all he ever had — first an inheritance of a few thousand dollars, next the old family home, and, latterly, the last shreds of his self respect and manhood. The "gang" had cleaned him out. The broken gambler had turned drunkard and parasite; he had lived to see

First published in *Munsey's* magazine for August 1901, as by Sydney Porter.

Fifteenth of twenty-four stories in *Whirligigs,* published by Doubleday, Page & Company, New York, in 1910.

the day come when the men who had stripped him denied him a seat at the game. His word was no longer to be taken. The daily bout at cards had arranged itself accordingly, and to him was assigned the ignoble part of the onlooker. The sheriff, the county clerk, a sportive deputy, a gay attorney, and a chalk faced man hailing "from the valley," sat at table, and the sheared one was thus tacitly advised to go and grow more wool.

Soon wearying of his ostracism, Goree had departed for his office, muttering to himself as he unsteadily traversed the unlucky pathway. After a drink of corn whisky from a demijohn under his table, he had flung himself into his chair, staring, in a sort of maudlin apathy, out at the mountains immersed in the summer haze. The little white patch he saw away up on the side of Blackjack was Laurel, the village near which he had been born and bred. There, also, was the birthplace of the feud between the Gorees and the Coltranes. Now no direct heir of the Gorees survived except this plucked and singed bird of misfortune. To the Coltranes, also, but one male supporter was left — Colonel Abner Coltrane, a man of substance and standing, a member of the State Legislature, and a contemporary with Goree's father. The feud had been a typical one of the region; it had left a red record of hate, wrong, and slaughter.

But Yancey Goree was not thinking of feuds. His befuddled brain was hopelessly attacking the problem of the future maintenance of himself and his favorite follies. Of late, old friends of the family had seen to it that he had whereof to eat and a place to sleep, but whisky they would not buy for him, and he must have whisky. His law business was extinct; no case had been intrusted to him in two years. He had been a borrower and a sponge, and it seemed that if he fell no lower it would be from lack of opportunity. One more chance — he was saying to himself — if he had one more stake at the game, he thought he could win; but he had nothing left to sell, and his credit was more than exhausted.

He could not help smiling, even in his misery, as he thought of the man to whom, six months before, he had sold the old Goree homestead. There had come from "back yan' " in the mountains two of the strangest creatures, a man named Pike Garvey and his wife. "Back yan'," with a wave of the hand towards the hills, was understood among the mountaineers to designate the remotest fastnesses, the unplumbed gorges, the haunts of lawbreakers, the wolf's den, and the boudoir of the bear. In a cabin far up on Blackjack's shoulder, in the wildest part of these retreats, this odd couple had lived for twenty years. They had neither dogs nor children to mitigate the heavy silence of the hills. Pike Garvey was little known in the settlements, but all who had dealt with him pronounced him "crazy as a loon." He acknowledged no occupation save that of a squirrel hunter, but he "moonshined" occasionally by way of diversion. Once the "revenues" had dragged him from his lair, fighting silently and desperately like a terrier, and he had been sent to State's prison for two years. Released, he popped back into his hole like an angry weasel.

Fortune, passing over many anxious wooers, made a freakish flight into Blackjack's bosky pockets to smile upon Pike and his faithful partner.

One day a party of spectacled, knickerbockered, and altogether absurd prospectors invaded the vicinity of the Garveys' cabin. Pike lifted his squirrel rifle off the hooks and took a shot at them at long range on the chance of their being revenues. Happily he missed, and the unconscious agents of good luck drew nearer, disclosing their innocence of anything resembling law or justice. Later on, they offered the Garveys an enormous quantity of ready, green, crisp money for their thirty acre patch of cleared land, mentioning, as an excuse for such a mad action, some irrelevant and inadequate nonsense about a bed of mica underlying the said property.

When the Garveys became possessed of so many dollars that they faltered in computing them, the deficiencies of life on Blackjack began to grow prominent. Pike began to talk of new shoes, a hogshead of tobacco to set in the corner, a new lock to his rifle; and, leading Martella to a certain spot on the mountainside, he pointed out to her how a small cannon — doubtless a thing not beyond the scope of their fortune in price — might be planted so as to command and defend the sole accessible trail to the cabin, to the confusion of revenues and meddling strangers forever.

But Adam reckoned without his Eve. These things represented to him the applied power of wealth, but there slumbered in his dingy cabin an ambition that soared far above his primitive wants. Somewhere in Mrs. Garvey's bosom still survived a spot of femininity unstarved by twenty years of Blackjack. For so long a time the sounds in her ears had been the scalybarks dropping in the woods at noon, and the wolves singing among the rocks at night, and it was enough to have purged her of vanities. She had grown fat and sad and yellow and dull. But when the means came, she felt a rekindled desire to assume the perquisites of her sex — to sit at tea tables; to buy inutile things; to whitewash the hideous veracity of life with a little form and ceremony. So she coldly vetoed Pike's proposed system of fortifications, and announced that they would descend upon the world, and gyrate socially.

And thus, at length, it was decided, and the thing done. The village of Laurel was their compromise between Mrs. Garvey's preference for one of the large valley towns and Pike's hankering for primeval solitudes. Laurel yielded a halting round of feeble social distractions comportable with Martella's ambitions, and was not entirely without recommendation to Pike, its contiguity to the mountains presenting advantages for sudden retreat in case fashionable society should make it advisable.

Their descent upon Laurel had been coincident with Yancey Goree's feverish desire to convert property into cash, and they bought the old Goree homestead, paying four thousand dollars ready money into the spendthrift's shaking hands.

Thus it happened that while the disreputable last of the Gorees sprawled in his disreputable office, at the end of his row, spurned by the cronies whom he had gorged, strangers dwelt in the halls of his fathers.

A cloud of dust was rolling slowly up the parched street, with something traveling in the midst of it. A little breeze wafted the cloud to one side, and a new, brightly painted carryall, drawn by a slothful gray horse, became visible. The vehicle deflected from the middle of the street as it neared Goree's office, and stopped in the gutter directly in front of his door.

On the front seat sat a gaunt, tall man dressed in black broadcloth, his rigid hands incarcerated in yellow kid gloves. On the back seat was a lady who triumphed over the June heat. Her stout form was armored in a skin tight silk dress of the description known as "changeable," being a gorgeous combination of shifting hues. She sat erect, waving a much ornamented fan, with her eyes fixed stonily far down the street. However Martella Garvey's heart might be rejoicing at the pleasures of her new life, Blackjack had done his work with her exterior. He had carved her countenance to the image of emptiness and inanity; had imbued her with the stolidity of his crags, and the reserve of his hushed interiors. She always seemed to hear, whatever her surroundings were, the scalybarks falling and puttering down the mountainside. She could always hear the awful silences of Blackjack sounding through the stillest of nights.

Goree watched this solemn equipage, as it drove to his door, with only faint interest; but when the lank driver wrapped the reins about his whip, awkwardly descended, and stepped into the office, he rose unsteadily to receive him, recognizing Pike Garvey, the new, the transformed, the recently civilized.

The mountaineer took the chair Goree offered him. They who cast doubts upon Garvey's soundness of mind had a strong witness in the man's countenance. His face was too long, a dull saffron in hue, and immobile as a statue's. Pale blue, unwinking round eyes without lashes added to the singularity of his gruesome visage. Goree was at a loss to account for the visit.

"Everything all right at Laurel, Mr. Garvey?" he inquired.

"Everything all right, sir, and mighty pleased is Missis Garvey and me with the property. Missis Garvey likes yo' old place, and she likes the neighborhood. Society is what she 'lows she wants, and she is gettin' of it. The Rogerses, the Hapgoods, the Pratts, and the Troys hev been to see Missis Garvey, and she hev et meals to most of thar houses. The best folks hev axed her to differ'nt kinds of doin's. I cyan't say, Mr. Goree, that sech things suits me — fur me, give me them thar." Garvey's huge, yellow gloved hand flourished in the direction of the mountains. "That's whar I b'long, 'mongst the wild honey bees and the b'ars. But that ain't what I came fur to say, Mr. Goree. Thar's somethin' you got what me and Missis Garvey wants to buy."

"Buy!" echoed Goree. "From me?" Then he laughed harshly. "I reckon you are mistaken about that. I sold out to you, as you yourself expressed it, 'lock, stock, and barrel.' There isn't even a ramrod left to sell."

"You've got it; and we'uns want it. 'Take the money,' says Missis Garvey, 'and buy it, fa'r and squar'.' "

Goree shook his head. "The cubboard's bare," he said.

"We've riz," pursued the mountaineer, undeflected from his object, "a heap. We wuz pore as possums, and now we could hev folks to dinner every day. We been reco'nized, Missis Garvey says, by the best society. But there's somethin' we need we ain't got. She says it ought to been put in the 'ventory ov the sale, but it tain't thar. 'Take the money, then,' says she, 'and buy it fa'r and squar'.' "

"Out with it," said Goree, his racked nerves growing impatient.

Garvey threw his slouch hat upon the table, and leaned forward, fixing his unblinking eyes upon Goree's.

"There's a old feud," he said distinctly and slowly, " 'tween you'uns and the Coltranes."

Goree frowned ominously. To speak of his feud to a feudist is a serious breach of the mountain etiquette. The man from "back yan' " knew it as well as the lawyer did.

"No offense," he went on, "but purely in the way of business. Missis Garvey hev studied all about feuds. Most of the quality folks in the mountains hev 'em. The Settles and the Goforths, the Rankins and the Boyds, the Silers and the Galloways, hev all been cyarin' on feuds f'om twenty to a hunderd year. Yo' feud is twenty odd year old. The last man to drap was when yo' uncle, Jedge Paisley Goree, 'journed co't and shot Len Coltrane f'om the bench. Missis Garvey and me, we comes f'om the po' white trash. Nobody wouldn't pick a feud with we'uns, no mo'n with a fam'ly of tree toads. Quality people everywhar, says Missis Garvey, has feuds. We'uns ain't quality, but we're buyin' into it as fur as we can. 'Take the money, then,' says Missis Garvey, 'and buy Mr. Goree's feud, fa'r and squar'.' "

The squirrel hunter straightened a leg half across the room, drew a roll of bills from his pocket, and threw them on the table.

"Thar's two hundred dollars, Mr. Goree; what you would call a fa'r price for a feud that's been 'lowed to run down like yourn hev. Thar's only you left to cyar' on yo' side of it, and you'd make mighty po' killin'. I'll take it off yo' hands, and it'll set me and the Missis Garvey up among the quality. Thar's the money."

The little roll of currency on the table slowly untwisted itself, writhing and jumping as its folds relaxed. In the silence that followed Garvey's last speech the rattling of the poker chips in the court house could be plainly heard. Goree knew that the sheriff had just won a pot, for the subdued whoop with which he always greeted a victory floated across the square upon the crinkly heat waves. Beads of moisture stood on Goree's brow. Stooping, he drew the wicker covered demijohn from under his table, and filled a tumbler from it.

"A little corn liquor, Mr. Garvey? Of course you are joking about — what you spoke of. Opens quite a new market, doesn't it? Feuds, prime, two fifty to three. Feuds, slightly damaged — two hundred, I believe you said, Mr. Garvey?"

Goree laughed self consciously.

The mountaineer took the glass Goree handed him, and drank the whisky without a tremor of the lids of his staring eyes. The lawyer applauded the feat by a look of envious admiration. He poured his own drink, and took it like a drunkard, by gulps, and with shudders at the smell and taste.

"Two hunderd," repeated Garvey. "Thar's the money."

A sudden passion flared up in Goree's brain. He struck the table with his fist. One of the bills flipped over and touched his hand. He flinched as if something had stung him.

"Do you come to me," he shouted, "seriously with such a ridiculous, insulting, darned fool proposition?"

"It's fa'r and squar'," said the squirrel hunter, but he reached out his hand as if to take back the money; and then Goree knew that his own flurry of rage had not been from pride or resentment, but from anger at himself, knowing that he would set foot in the deeper depths that were being opened to him. He turned in an instant from an outraged gentleman to an anxious chafferer recommending his goods.

"Don't be in a hurry, Garvey," he said, his face crimson and his speech thick. "I accept your p-p-proposition, though it's dirt cheap at two hundred. A t-trade's all right when both p-purchaser and b-buyer are s-satisfied. Shall I w-wrap it up for you, Mr. Garvey?"

Garvey rose, and shook out his broadcloth. "Missis Garvey will be pleased. You air out of it, and it stands Coltrane and Garvey. Just a scrap ov writin', Mr. Goree, you bein' a lawyer, to show we traded."

Goree seized a sheet of paper and a pen. The money was clutched in his moist hand. Everything else suddenly seemed to grow trivial and light.

"Bill of sale, by all means. 'Right, title, and interest in and to' * * * 'forever warrant and —' No, Garvey, we'll have to leave out that 'defend,' " said Goree with a loud laugh. "You'll have to defend this title yourself."

The mountaineer received the amazing screed that the lawyer handed him, folded it with immense labor, and placed it carefully in his pocket.

Goree was standing near the window. "Step here." he said, raising his finger, "and I'll show you your recently purchased enemy. There he goes, down the other side of the street."

The mountaineer crooked his long frame to look through the window in the direction indicated by the other. Colonel Abner Coltrane, an erect, portly gentleman of about fifty, wearing the inevitable long, double breasted frock coat of the Southern lawmaker, and an old high silk hat, was passing on the opposite sidewalk. As Garvey looked, Goree glanced at his face. If there be such a thing as a yellow wolf, here was its counterpart. Garvey snarled as his unhuman eyes followed the moving figure, disclosing long, amber colored fangs.

"Is that him? Why, that's the man who sent me to the pen'tentiary once!"

"He used to be district attorney," said Goree carelessly. "And, by the way, he's a first class shot."

"I kin hit a squirrel's eye at a hunderd yard," said Garvey. "So that thar's Coltrane! I made a better trade than I was thinkin'. I'll take keer ov this feud, Mr. Goree, better'n you ever did!"

He moved towards the door, but lingered there, betraying a slight perplexity.

"Anything else today?" inquired Goree with frothy sarcasm.

"Any family traditions, ancestral ghosts, or skeletons in the closet? Prices as low as the lowest."

"Thar was another thing," replied the unmoved squirrel hunter, "that Missis Garvey was thinkin' of. 'Tain't so much in my line as t'other, but she wanted partic'lar that I should inquire, and ef you was willin', 'pay fur it,' she says, 'fa'r and square'.' Thar's a buryin' groun', as you know, Mr. Goree, in the yard of yo' old place, under the cedars. Them that lies thar is yo' folks what was killed by the Coltranes. The monyments has the names on 'em. Missis Garvey says a fam'ly buryin' groun' is a sho' sign of quality. She says ef we git the feud, thar's somethin' else ought to go with it. The names on them monyments is 'Goree,' but they can be changed to ourn by — "

"Go! Go!" screamed Goree, his face turning purple. He stretched out both hands towards the mountaineer, his fingers hooked and shaking. "Go, you ghoul! Even a Ch-Chinaman protects the g-graves of his ancestors — go!"

The squirrel hunter slouched out of the door to his carryall. While he was climbing over the wheel Goree was collecting, with feverish celerity, the money that had fallen from his hand to the floor. As the vehicle slowly turned about, the sheep, with a coat of newly grown wool, was hurrying, in indecent haste, along the path to the court house.

At three o'clock in the morning they brought him back to his office, shorn and unconscious. The sheriff, the sportive deputy, the county clerk, and the gay attorney carried him, the chalk faced man "from the valley" acting as escort.

"On the table," said one of them, and they deposited him there among the litter of his unprofitable books and papers.

"Yance thinks a lot of a pa'r of deuces when he's liquored up," sighed the sheriff reflectively.

"Too much," said the gay attorney. "A man has no business to play poker who drinks as much as he does. I wonder how much he dropped tonight."

"Close to two hundred. What I wonder is whar he got it. Yance ain't had a cent fur over a month, I know."

"Struck a client, maybe. Well, let's get home before daylight. He'll be all right when he wakes up, except for a sort of beehive feeling about the cranium."

The gang slipped away through the early morning twilight. The next eye to gaze upon the miserable Goree was the orb of day. He peered through the uncurtained window, first deluging the sleeper in a flood of faint gold, but soon pouring upon the mottled red of his flesh a searching white, summer heat. Goree stirred, half unconsciously, among the table's débris, and turned his face from the window. His movement dislodged a heavy law book, which crashed upon the floor. Opening his eyes, he saw, bending over him, a man in a black frock coat. Looking higher, he discovered a well worn silk hat, and, beneath it, the kindly, smooth face of Colonel Abner Coltrane.

A little uncertain of the outcome, the colonel waited for the other to make some sign of recognition. Not in twenty years had male members of these two families faced each other in peace. Goree's eyelids puckered as he strained his blurred sight towards his visitor, and then he smiled serenely.

"Have you brought Stella and Lucy over to play?" he said calmly.

"Do you know me, Yancey?" asked Coltrane.

"Of course I do. You brought me a whip with a whistle in the end."

So he had — twenty four years ago; when Yancey was six, and Yancey's father was his best friend.

Goree's eye wandered about the room. The colonel understood. "Lie still, and I'll bring you some," he said. There was a pump in the yard at the rear, and Goree closed his eyes, listening with rapture to the click of its handle and the bubbling of the falling stream. Coltrane brought a pitcher of the cool water, and held it for him to drink. Presently Goree sat up — a most forlorn object, his summer suit of flax soiled and crumpled, his discreditable head tousled and unsteady. He tried to wave one of his hands towards the colonel.

"Ex-excuse — everything, will you?" he said. "I must have drunk too much whisky last night, and gone to bed on the table." His brows knitted into a puzzled frown.

"Out with the boys a while?" asked Coltrane kindly.

"No, I went nowhere. I haven't had a dollar to spend in the last two months. Struck the demijohn too often, I reckon, as usual."

Colonel Coltrane touched him on the shoulder.

"A little while ago, Yancey," he began, "you asked me if I had brought Stella and Lucy over to play. You weren't quite awake then, and must have been dreaming you were a boy again. You are awake now, and I want you to listen to me. I have come from Stella and Lucy to their old playmate, and to my old friend's son. They know that I am going to bring you home with me, and you will find them as ready with a welcome as they were in the old days. I want you to come to my house and stay until you are yourself again, and as much longer as you will. We heard of your being down in the world, and in the midst of temptation, and we agreed that you should come over and play at our house once more. Will you come, my boy? Will you drop our old family trouble and come with me?"

"Trouble!" said Goree, opening his eyes wide. "There was never any trouble between us that I know of. I'm sure we've always been the best friends. But, good Lord, colonel, how could I go to your home as I am — a drunken wretch, a miserable, degraded spendthrift and gambler —"

He lurched from the table into his armchair, and began to weep maudlin tears, mingled with genuine drops of remorse and shame. Coltrane talked to him persistently and reasonably, reminding him of the simple mountain pleasures of which he had once been so fond, and insisting upon the genuineness of the invitation.

Finally he landed Goree by telling him he was counting upon his help in engineering the transportation of a large amount of felled timber from a high mountainside to a waterway. He knew that Goree had once invented a device for this purpose — a series of slides and chutes — upon which he had justly prided himself. In an instant the poor fellow, delighted at the idea of his being of use to any one, had paper spread upon the table, and was drawing rapid but piti-fully shaky lines in demonstration of what he could and would do.

The man was sickened of the husks; his prodigal heart was turning again towards the mountains. His mind was yet strangely clogged, and his thoughts and memories were returning to his brain one by one, like carrier pigeons over a stormy sea. But Coltrane was satisfied with the progress he had made.

Bethel received the surprise of its existence that afternoon when a Coltrane and a Goree rode amicably together through the town. Side by side they rode, out from the dusty streets and gaping towns-people, down across the creek bridge, and up towards the moun-tains. The prodigal had brushed and washed and combed himself to a more decent figure, but he was unsteady in the saddle, and he seemed to be deep in the contemplation of some vexing problem. Coltrane left him to his mood, relying upon the influence of changed surroundings to restore his equilibrium.

Once Goree was seized with a shaking fit, and almost came to a collapse. He had to dismount and rest at the side of the road. The colonel, foreseeing such a condition, had provided a small flask of whisky for the journey, but when it was offered to him Goree refused it almost with violence, declaring he would never touch it again. By and by he was recovered, and went quietly enough for a mile or two. Then he pulled up his horse suddenly, and said:

"I lost two hundred dollars last night, playing poker. Now, where did I get that money?"

"Take it easy, Yancey. The mountain air will soon clear it up. We'll go fishing, first thing, at the Pinnacle falls. The trout are jumping there like bullfrogs. We'll take Stella and Lucy along, and have a picnic on Eagle Rock. Have you forgotten how a hickory cured ham sandwich tastes, Yancey, to a hungry fisherman?"

Evidently the colonel did not believe the story of his lost wealth; so Goree retired again into brooding silence.

By late afternoon they had traveled ten of the twelve miles between Bethel and Laurel. Half a mile this side of Laurel lay the old Goree place; a mile or two beyond the village lived the Coltranes. The road was now steep and laborious, but the compensations were many. The tilted aisles of the forest were opulent with leaf and bird and bloom. The tonic air put to shame the pharmacopoeia. The glades were dark with mossy shade, and bright with shy rivulets winking from the ferns and laurels. On the lower side they viewed, framed in the near foliage, exquisite sketches of the far valley swooning in its opal haze.

Coltrane was pleased to see that his companion was yielding to the spell of the hills and woods. For now they had but to skirt the base of Painter's Cliff; to cross Elder Branch and mount the hill beyond, and Goree would have to face the squandered home of his fathers. Every rock he passed, every tree, every foot of the roadway, was familiar to him. Though he had forgotten the woods, they thrilled him like the music of "Home, Sweet Home."

They rounded the cliff, descended into Elder Branch, and paused there to let the horses drink and splash in the swift water. On the right was a rail fence that cornered there, and followed the road and stream. Inclosed by it was the old apple orchard of the home place; the house was yet concealed by the brow of the steep hill. Inside and along the fence, pokeberries, elders, sassafras, and sumac grew high and dense. At a rustle of their branches, both Goree and Coltrane glanced up, and saw a long, yellow, wolfish face above the fence, staring at them with pale, unwinking eyes. The head quickly disappeared; there was a violent swaying of the bushes, and an ungainly figure ran up through the apple orchard in the direction of the house, zigzagging among the trees.

"That's Garvey," said Coltrane; "the man you sold out to. There's no doubt but he's considerably cracked. I had to send him up for moonshining once, several years ago, in spite of the fact that I believed him irresponsible. Why, what's the matter, Yancey?"

Goree was wiping his forehead, and his face had lost its color.

"Do I look queer, too?" he asked, trying to smile. "I'm just remembering a few more things. Some of the alcohol has evaporated from my brain. I recollect now where I got that two hundred dollars."

"Don't think of it," said Coltrane cheerfully. "Later on we'll figure it all out together."

They rode out of the branch, and when they reached the foot of the hill Goree stopped again.

"Did you ever suspect I was a very vain kind of fellow, colonel?" he asked. "Sort of foolish proud about appearances?"

The colonel's eye refused to wander to the soiled, sagging suit of flax and the faded slouch hat.

"It seems to me," he replied, mystified, but humoring him, "I remember a young buck about twenty, with the tightest coat, the sleekest hair, and the prancingest saddle horse in the Blue Ridge."

"Right you are," said Goree eagerly. "And it's in me yet, though it don't show. Oh, I'm as vain as a turkey gobbler, and as proud as Lucifer. I'm going to ask you to indulge this weakness of mine in a little matter."

"Speak out, Yancey. We'll create you Duke of Laurel and Baron of Blue Ridge, if you choose; and you shall have a feather out of Stella's peacock's tail to wear in your hat."

"I'm in earnest. In a few minutes we'll pass the house up there on the hill where I was born, and where my people have lived for nearly a century. Strangers live there now — and look at me! I am about to show myself to them ragged and poverty stricken, a wastrel and a beggar. Colonel Coltrane, I'm ashamed to do it. I want you to let me wear your coat and hat until we are out of sight beyond. I know you think it a foolish pride, but I want to make as good a showing as I can when I pass the old place."

"Now, what does this mean?" said Coltrane to himself, as he compared his companion's sane looks and quiet demeanor with his strange request. But he was already unbuttoning the coat, assenting readily, as if the fancy were in no wise to be considered strange.

The coat and hat fitted Goree well. He buttoned the former about him with a look of satisfaction and dignity. He and Coltrane were nearly the same size — rather tall, portly, and erect. Twenty five years were between them, but in appearance they might have been brothers. Goree looked older than his age; his face was puffy and lined; the colonel had the smooth, fresh complexion of a temperate liver. He put on Goree's disreputable old flax coat and faded slouch hat.

"Now," said Goree, taking up the reins, "I'm all right. I want you to ride about ten feet in the rear as we go by, colonel, so that

they can get a good look at me. They'll see I'm no back number yet,
by any means. I guess I'll show up pretty well to them once more,
anyhow. Let's ride on."

He set out up the hill at a smart trot, the colonel following, as
he had been requested.

Goree sat straight in the saddle, with head erect, but his eyes
were turned to the right, sharply scanning every shrub and fence
and hiding place in the old homestead yard. Once he muttered to
himself, "Will the crazy fool try it, or did I dream half of it?"

It was when he came opposite the little family burying ground
that he saw what he had been looking for — a puff of white smoke,
coming from the thick cedars in one corner. He toppled so slowly to
the left that Coltrane had time to urge his horse to that side, and
catch him with one arm.

The squirrel hunter had not overpraised his aim. He had sent
the bullet where he intended, and where Goree had expected that it
would pass — through the breast of Colonel Abner Coltrane's black
frock coat.

Goree leaned heavily against Coltrane, but he did not fall. The
horses kept pace, side by side, and the colonel's arm kept him
steady. The little white houses of Laurel shone through the trees,
half a mile away. Goree reached out one hand and groped until it
rested upon Coltrane's fingers, which held his bridle.

"Good friend," he said, and that was all.

Thus did Yancey Goree, as he rode past his old home, make,
considering all things, the best showing that was in his power.

NOTES AND COMMENTS

"A Blackjack Bargainer" was one of at least seven stories O. Henry
wrote under the name Sydney Porter, a name Will Porter used profession-
ally in working with publishers and editors during his early years in New
York. It is noted that on two occasions he used the name Sidney Porter,
where the spelling of William Sidney Porter, as it appeared in the family
Bible, was used instead of Sydney, the spelling he adopted in New York.

For a review of literary evaluation and additional notes and comments
related to "A Blackjack Bargainer," reference is made to Dr. Porter's essay,
Part II, "The Imprisoned Splendor," *ante,* pp. 37–38.

The Enchanted Kiss

But a clerk in the Cut-Rate drug store was Samuel Tansey, yet his slender frame was a pad that enfolded the passion of Romeo, the gloom of Lara, the romance of D'Artagnan, and the desperate inspiration of Melnotte. Pity, then, that he had been denied expression, that he was doomed to the burden of utter timidity and diffidence, that Fate had set him tongue-tied and scarlet, before the muslin-clad angels whom he adored and vainly longed to rescue, clasp, comfort and subdue.

The clock's hands were pointing close upon the hour of ten while Tansey was playing billiards with a number of his friends. On alternate evenings he was released from duty at the store after seven o'clock. Even among his fellow-men Tansey was timorous and constrained. In his imagination he had done valiant deeds, and performed acts of distinguished gallantry; but in fact he was a sallow youth of twenty-three, with an over-modest demeanor and scant vocabulary.

When the clock struck ten, Tansey hastily laid down his cue

First published in *Metropolitan* magazine for February 1904, as by O. Henry.

Fifteenth of twenty-two stories in *Roads of Destiny,* published by Doubleday, Page & Company, New York, in 1909.

and struck sharply upon the show-case with a coin for the attendant to come and receive the pay for his score.

"What's your hurry, Tansey?" called one. "Got another engagement?"

"Tansey got an engagement!" echoed another. "Not on your life. Tansey's got to get home at ten by Mother Peek's orders."

"It's no such thing," chimed in a pale youth, taking a large cigar from his mouth; "Tansey's afraid to be late because Miss Katie might come down stairs to unlock the door, and kiss him in the hall."

This last delicate piece of raillery sent a fiery tingle into Tansey's blood, for the indictment was true — barring the kiss. That was a thing to dream of; to wildly hope for; but too remote and sacred a thing to think of lightly.

Casting a cold and contemptuous look at the speaker — a punishment commensurate with his own diffident spirit — Tansey left the room, descending the stairs into the street.

For two years he had silently adored Miss Peek, worshiping her from a spiritual distance through which her attractions took on stellar brightness and mystery. Mrs. Peek kept a few choice boarders, among whom was Tansey. The other young men romped with Katie, chased her with crickets in their fingers, and "jollied" her with an irreverent freedom that turned Tansey's heart into cold lead in his bosom. The signs of his adoration were few — a tremulous "Good morning," stealthy glances at her during meals, and occasionally (Oh, rapture!) a blushing, delirious game of cribbage with her in the parlor on some rare evening when a miraculous lack of engagement kept her at home. Kiss him in the hall! Aye, he feared it, but it was an ecstatic fear such as Elijah must have felt when the chariot lifted him into the unknown.

But to-night the gibes of his associates had stung him to a feeling of forward, lawless mutiny; a defiant, challenging, atavistic recklessness. Spirit of corsair, adventurer, lover, poet, bohemian, possessed him. The stars he saw above him seemed no more unattainable, no less high than the favor of Miss Peek or the fearsome sweetness of her delectable lips. His fate seemed to him strangely dramatic and pathetic, and to call for a solace consonant with its extremity. A saloon was near by, and to this he flitted, calling for absinthe — the tipple of the roué, the abandoned, the vainly sighing lover.

Once he drank of it, and again, and then again until he felt a strange, exalted sense of non-participation in worldly affairs pervade him. Tansey was no drinker; his consumption of three absinthe anisettes within almost as few minutes proclaimed his unproficiency in the art; Tansey was merely flooding with unproven liquor his sorrows; which record and tradition alleged to be drownable.

Coming out upon the sidewalk, he snapped his fingers defiantly in the direction of the Peek homestead, turned the other way, and voyaged, Columbus-like into the wilds of an enchanted street. Nor is the figure exorbitant, for, beyond his store the foot of Tansey had scarcely been set for years — store and boarding house; between these ports he was chartered to run, and contrary currents had rarely deflected his prow.

Tansey aimlessly protracted his walk, and, whether it was his unfamiliarity with the district, his recent accession of audacious errantry, or the sophistical whisper of a certain green-eyed fairy, he came at last to tread a shuttered, blank, and echoing thoroughfare, dark and unpeopled. And, suddenly, this way came to an end (as many streets do in the Spanish-built, archaic town of San Antone), butting its head against an imminent, high, brick wall. No — the street still lived! To the right and to the left it breathed through slender tubes of exit — narrow, somnolent ravines, cobble paved and unlighted. Accommodating a rise in the street to the right was reared a phantom flight of five luminous steps of limestones, flanked by a wall of the same height and of the same material.

Upon one of these steps Tansey seated himself and bethought him of his love, and how she might never know she was his love. And of Mother Peek, fat, vigilant and kind; not unpleased, Tansey thought, that he and Katie should play cribbage in the parlor together. For, the Cut-Rate had not cut his salary, which, sordidly speaking, ranked him star boarder at the Peek's. And he thought of Captain Peek, Katie's father, a man he dreaded and abhorred; a genteel loafer and spendthrift, battening upon the labor of his woman-folk; a very queer fish, and, according to repute, not of the freshest.

The night had turned chill and foggy. The heart of the town, with its noises, was left behind. Reflected from the high vapors, its distant lights were manifest in quivering, cone-shaped streamers, in questionable blushes of unnamed colors, in unstable, ghostly waves of far, electric flashes. Now that the darkness was become more friendly, the wall against which the street splintered developed a stone coping topped with an armature of spikes. Beyond it loomed what appeared to be the acute angles of mountain peaks, pierced here and there by little lambent parallelograms. Considering this vista, Tansey at length persuaded himself that the seeming mountains were, in fact, the convent of Santa Mercedes, with which ancient and bulky pile he was better familiar from different coigns of view. A pleasant noise of singing in his ears reinforced his opinion. High, sweet, holy carolling, far and harmonious and uprising, as of sanctified nuns at their responses. At what hour did the Sisters sing? He tried to think — was it six, eight, twelve? Tansey leaned his back against the limestone wall and wondered. Strange things followed. The air was full of white, fluttering pigeons that circled about, and settled upon the convent wall. The wall blossomed with a quantity of shining green eyes that blinked and peered at him from the solid masonry. A pink, classic nymph came from an excavation in the cavernous road and danced, barefoot and airy, upon the ragged flints. The sky was traversed by a company of beribboned cats, marching in stupendous, aerial procession. The noise of singing grew louder; an illumination of unseasonable fire-flies danced past, and strange whispers came out of the dark without meaning or excuse.

Without amazement Tansey took note of these phenomena. He was on some new plane of understanding, though his mind seemed to him clear and, indeed, happily tranquil.

A desire for movement and exploration seized him; he rose and turned into the black gash of street to his right. For a time the high wall formed one of its boundaries; but further on, two rows of black-windowed houses closed it in.

Here was the city's quarter once given over to the Spaniard. Here were still his forbidding abodes of concrete and adobe, standing cold and indomitable against the century. From the murky fissure, the eye saw, flung against the sky, the tangled filigree of his Moorish balconies. Through stone archways breaths of dead, vault-chilled air coughed upon him; his feet struck jingling iron rings in staples stone-buried for half a cycle. Along these paltry avenues had swaggered the arrogant Don, had caracoled and serenaded and blustered while the tomahawk and the pioneer's rifle were already uplifted to expel him from a continent. And Tansey, stumbling through his old-world dust, looked up, dark as it was, and saw Andalusian beauties glimmering on the balconies. Some of them were laughing and listening to the goblin music that still followed; others harked fearfully through the night, trying to catch the hoof beats of caballeros whose last echoes from those stones had died away a century ago. Those women were silent, but Tansey heard the jangle of horseless bridle-bits, the whirr of riderless rowels, and, now and then, a muttered malediction in a foreign tongue. But he was not frightened. Shadows, nor shadows of sounds could daunt him. Afraid? No. Afraid of Mother Peek? Afraid to face the girl of his heart? Afraid of tipsy Captain Peek? Nay! nor of these apparitions, nor of that spectral singing that always pursued him. Singing! He would show them! He lifted up a strong and untuneful voice:

"When you hear them bells go
tingalingling,"

serving notice upon those mysterious agencies that if it should come to a face-to-face encounter

"There'll be a hot time
In the old town
To-night!"

How long Tansey consumed in treading this haunted byway was not clear to him, but in time he emerged into a more commodious avenue. When within a few yards of the corner he perceived, through a window, that a small confectionery of mean appearance was set in the angle. His same glance that estimated its meagre equipment, its cheap soda-water fountain and stock of tobacco and sweets, took cognizance of Captain Peek within, lighting a cigar at a swinging gaslight.

As Tansey rounded the corner Captain Peek came out, and they met *vis-a-vis.* An exultant joy filled Tansey when he found himself sustaining the encounter with implicit courage. Peek, indeed! He raised his hand, and snapped his fingers loudly.

It was Peek himself who quailed guiltily before the valiant mien of the drug clerk. Sharp surprise and a palpable fear bourgeoned upon the Captain's face. And, verily, that face was one to rather call up such expressions upon the faces of others. The face of a libidinous heathen idol, small eyed, with carven folds in the heavy jowls, and a consuming, pagan license in its expression. In the gutter just beyond the store Tansey saw a closed carriage standing with its back toward him, and a motionless driver perched in his place.

"Why, it's Tansey!" exclaimed Captain Peek. "How are you, Tansey? H-have a cigar, Tansey?"

"Why, it's Peek!" cried Tansey, jubilant at his own temerity. "What deviltry are you up to now, Peek? Back streets and a closed carriage! Fie! Peek!"

"There's no one in the carriage," said the Captain, smoothly.

"Everybody out of it is in luck," continued Tansey, aggressively. "I'd love for you to know, Peek, that I'm not stuck on you. You're a bottle-nosed scoundrel."

"Why, the little rat's drunk!" cried the Captain, joyfully; "only drunk, and I thought he was on! Go home, Tansey, and quit bothering grown persons on the street."

But just then a white-clad figure sprang out of the carriage, and a shrill voice — Katie's voice — sliced the air: "Sam! Sam! — help me, Sam!"

Tansey sprang toward her, but Captain Peek interposed his bulky form. Wonder of wonders! the whilom spiritless youth struck out with his right, and the hulking Captain went over in a swearing heap. Tansey flew to Katie, and took her in his arms like a conquering knight. She raised her face, and he kissed her — violets! electricity! caramels! champagne! Here was the attainment of a dream that brought no disenchantment.

"Oh, Sam," cried Katie, when she could; "I knew you would rescue me. What do you suppose the mean things were going to do with me?"

"Have your picture taken," said Tansey, wondering at the foolishness of his remark.

"No, they were going to eat me. I heard them talking about it."

"Eat you!" said Tansey, after pondering a moment. "That can't be; there's no plates."

But a sudden noise warned him to turn. Down upon him were bearing the Captain and a monstrous long-bearded dwarf in a spangled cloak and red trunk hose. The dwarf leaped twenty feet and clutched him. The Captain seized Katie and hurled her, shrieking, back into the carriage, himself followed, and the vehicle dashed away. The dwarf lifted Tansey high above his head and ran with him into the store. Holding him with one hand, he raised the lid of an enormous chest half filled with cakes of ice, flung Tansey inside, and closed down the cover.

The force of the fall must have been great, for Tansey lost consciousness. When his faculties revived his first sensation was one of severe cold along his back and limbs. Opening his eyes, he found himself to be seated upon the limestone steps still facing the wall and convent of Santa Mercedes. His first thought was of the ecstatic kiss from Katie. The outrageous villainy of Captain Peek, the unnatural mystery of the situation, his preposterous conflict with the improbable dwarf — these things roused and angered him, but left no impression of the unreal.

"I'll go back there to-morrow," he grumbled aloud, "and knock the head off that comic opera squab. Running out and picking up perfect strangers, and shoving them into cold storage!"

But, the kiss remained uppermost in his mind. "I might have done that long ago," he mused. "She liked it, too. She called me 'Sam' four times. I'll not go up that street again. Too much scrapping. Guess I'll move down the other way. Wonder what she meant by saying they were going to eat her!"

Tansey began to feel sleepy, but after a while he decided to move along again. This time he ventured into the street to his left. It ran level for a distance, and then dipped gently downward, opening into a vast, dim, barren space — the old Military Plaza. To his left, some hundred yards distant he saw a cluster of flickering lights along the Plaza's border. He knew the locality at once.

Huddled within narrow confines were the remnants of the once famous purveyors of the celebrated Mexican national cookery. A few years before, their nightly encampments upon the historic Alamo Plaza, in the heart of the city, had been a carnival, a saturnalia that was renowned throughout the land. Then the caterers numbered hundreds; the patrons thousands. Drawn by the coquettish *senoritas,* the music of the weird Spanish minstrels, and the strange piquant Mexican dishes served at a hundred competing tables, crowds thronged the Alamo Plaza all night. Travelers, rancheros, family parties, gay gasconading rounders, sightseers and prowlers of polyglot, owlish San Antone mingled there at the center of the city's fun and frolic. The popping of corks, pistols and questions; the glitter of eyes, jewels and daggers; the ring of laughter and coin — these were the order of the night.

But now no longer. To some half dozen tents, fires and tables had dwindled the picturesque festival, and these had been relegated to an ancient disused plaza. Often had Tansey strolled down to these strands at night to partake of the delectable *chili-con-carne,* a dish evolved by the genius of Mexico, composed of delicate meats minced with aromatic herbs and the poignant *chili colorado* — a compound full of singular savor and a fiery zest delightful to the Southern's palate.

The titillating odor of this concoction came now, on the breeze, to the nostrils of Tansey, awakening in him hunger for it. As he turned in that direction he saw a carriage dash up to the Mexicans' tents out of the gloom of the Plaza. Some figures moved back and forward in the uncertain light of the lanterns, and then the carriage was driven swiftly away.

Tansey approached, and sat at one of the tables covered with gaudy oil cloth. Traffic was dull at the moment. A few half-grown boys noisily fared at another table; the Mexicans hung listless and phlegmatic about their wares. And it was still. The night hum of the city crowded to the wall of dark buildings surrounding the Plaza, and subsided to an indefinite buzz through which sharply perforated the crackle of the languid fires and the rattle of fork and spoon.

A sedative wind blew from the south-east. The starless firmament pressed down upon the earth like a leaden cover.

In all that quiet Tansey turned his head suddenly, and saw, without disquietude, a troop of spectral horsemen deploy into the Plaza and charge a luminous line of infantry that advanced to sustain the shock. He saw the fierce flame of cannon and small arms, but heard no sound. The careless victuallers lounged vacantly, not deigning to view the conflict. Tansey mildly wondered to what nations these mute combatants might belong; turned his back to them and ordered his chili and coffee from the Mexican woman who advanced to serve him. This woman was old and careworn; her face was lined like the rind of a cantaloupe. She fetched the viands from a vessel set by the smouldering fire, and then retired to a tent, dark within, that stood nearby.

Presently Tansey heard a turmoil in the tent; a wailing, broken-hearted pleading in the harmonious Spanish tongue, and then two figures stumbled out into the light of the lanterns. One was the old woman; the other was a man clothed with a sumptuous and flashing splendor. The woman seemed to clutch and beseech from him something against his will. The man broke from her, and struck her brutally back into the tent, where she lay, whimpering and invisible. Observing Tansey, he walked rapidly to the table where he sat. Tansey recognized him to be Ramon Torres, a Mexican, the proprietor of the stand he was patronizing.

Torres was a handsome, nearly full-blooded descendant of the Spanish, seemingly about thirty years of age, and of a haughty, but extremely courteous demeanor. To-night he was dressed with signal magnificence. His costume was that of a triumphant *matador,* made of purple velvet almost hidden by jeweled embroidery. Diamonds of enormous size flashed upon his garb and his hands. He reached for a chair, and, seating himself at the opposite side of the table, began to roll a finical cigarette.

"Ah, Meester Tansee," he said, with a sultry fire in his silky, black eyes, "I give myself pleasure to see you this evening. Meester Tansee, you have many times come to eat at my table. I theenk you a safe man — a verree good friend. How much would it please you to leeve forever?"

"Not come back any more?" inquired Tansey.

"No; not leave — *leeve;* the not-to-die."

"I would call that," said Tansey, "a snap."

Torres leaned his elbows upon the table, swallowed a mouthful of smoke, and spake — each word being projected in a little puff of gray:

"How old do you theenk I am, Meester Tansee?"

"Oh, twenty-eight or thirty."

"Thees day," said the Mexican, "ees my birthday. I am four hundred and three years of old to-day."

"Another proof," said Tansey, airily, "of the healthfulness of our climate."

"Eet is not the air. I am to relate to you a secret of verree fine value. Listen me, Meester Tansee. At the age of twenty-three I arrive in Mexico from Spain. When? In the year fifteen hundred nineteen, with the *soldados* of Hernando Cortez. I came to thees country seventeen fifteen. I saw your Alamo reduced. It was like yesterday to me. Three hundred ninety-six year ago I learn the secret always to leeve. Look at these clothes I wear — at these *diamantes!* Do you theenk I buy them with the money I make with selling the *chili-con-carne*, Meester Tansee?"

"I should think not," said Tansey, promptly. Torres laughed loudly.

"*Valgame Dios!* but I do. But it not the kind you eating now. I make a deeferent kind, the eating of which makes men to always leeve. What do you think! One thousand people I supply — *diez pesos* each one pays me the month. You see! ten thousand *pesos* everee month! *Que diable!* how not I wear the fine *rapa!* You see that old woman try to hold me back a little while ago? That ees my wife. When I marry her she is young — seventeen year — *bonita*. Like the rest she ees become old and — what you say! — tough? I am the same — young all the time. To-night I resolve to dress myself and find another wife befitting my age. This old woman try to scr-r-ratch my face. Ha! ha! Meester Tansee — same way they do *entre los Americanos.*"

"And this health food you spoke of?" said Tansey.

"Hear me," said Torres, leaning over the table until he lay flat upon it; "eet is the *chili-con-carne* made not from the beef or the chicken, but from the flesh of the *senorita* — young and tender. That ees the secret. Everee month you must eat of it, having care to do so before the moon is full, and you will not die any times. See how I trust you, friend Tansee! To-night I have bought one young ladee — verree pretty — so *fina, gorda, blandita!* To-morrow the *chili* will be ready. *Ahora se!* One thousand dollars I pay for thees young ladee. From an *Americano* I have bought — a verree tip-top man — *el Captain Peek — que es, Senor?*"

For Tansey had sprung to his feet, upsetting the chair. The words of Katie reverberated in his ears: "They're going to eat me, Sam." This, then, was the monstrous fate to which she had been delivered by her unnatural parent. The carriage he had seen drive up from the Plaza was Captain Peek's. Where was Katie? Perhaps already —

Before he could decide what to do a loud scream came from the tent. The old Mexican woman ran out, a flashing knife in her hand. "I have released her," she cried. "You shall kill no more. They will hang you — *ingrato!* — *encantador!*"

Torres, with a hissing exclamation, sprang at her.

"Ramoncito!" she shrieked; "once you loved me."

The Mexican's arm raised and descended. "You are old," he cried; and she fell and lay motionless.

Another scream; the flaps of the tent were flung aside, and there stood Katie, white with fear, her wrists still bound with a cruel cord.

"Sam!" she cried, "save me again."

Tansey rounded the table, and flung himself, with superb nerve, upon the Mexican. Just then a clangor began; the clocks of the city were tolling the midnight hour. Tansey clutched at Torres, and, for a moment, felt in his grasp the crunch of velvet and the cold facets of the glittering gems. The next instant, the bedecked caballero turned in his hands, to a shrunken, leather-visaged, white-bearded, old, old, screaming mummy, sandalled, ragged, and four hundred and three. The Mexican woman was crawling to her feet, and laughing. She shook her brown hand in the face of the whining *viego*.

"Go, now," she cried, "and seek your senorita. It was I, Ramoncito, who brought you to this. Within each moon you eat of the life-giving *chili*. It was I that kept the wrong time for you. You should have eaten *yesterday* instead of *to-morrow*. It is too late. Off with you, *hombre*, you are too old for me!"

"This," decided Tansey, releasing his hold of the graybeard, "is a private family matter concerning age, and no business of mine."

With one of the table knives he hastened to saw asunder the fetters of the fair captive; and then, for the second time that night he kissed Katie Peek — tasted again the sweetness, the wonder, the thrill of it, attained once more the maximum of his incessant dreams.

The next instant an icy blade was driven deep between his shoulders; he felt his blood slowly congeal; heard the senile cackle of the perennial Spaniard; saw the Plaza rise and reel till the zenith crashed into the horizon — and knew no more.

When Tansey opened his eyes again he was sitting upon those selfsame steps gazing upon the dark bulk of the sleeping convent. In the middle of his back was still the acute, chilling pain. How had he been conveyed back there again? He got stiffly to his feet and stretched his cramped limbs. Supporting himself against the stonework he revolved in his mind the extravagant adventures that had befallen him each time he had strayed from the steps that night. In reviewing them certain features strained his credulity. Had he really met Captain Peek or Katie or the unparalleled Mexican in his wanderings — had he really encountered them under commonplace conditions and his over-stimulated brain had supplied the incongruities? However that might be, a sudden, elating thought caused him an intense joy. Nearly all of us have at some point in our lives — either to excuse our own stupidity or placate our consciences — promulgated some theory of fatalism. We have set up an intelligent Fate that works by codes and signals. Tansey had done likewise; and now he read, through the night's incidents, the finger prints of destiny. Each excursion that he had made had led to the one paramount finale — to Katie and that kiss, which survived and grew strong and intoxicating in his memory. Clearly, Fate was holding up to him the mirror that night, calling him to observe what awaited him at the end of whichever road he might take. He immediately turned, and hurried homeward.

Clothed in an elaborate, pale blue wrapper, cut to fit, Miss Katie Peek reclined in an armchair before a waning fire, in her room. Her little, bare feet were thrust into house shoes rimmed with swan's down. By the light of a small lamp she was attacking the society news of the latest Sunday paper. Some happy substance, seemingly indestructible, was being rhythmically crushed between her small white teeth. Miss Katie read of functions and furbelows, but she kept a vigilant ear for outside sounds, and a frequent eye upon the clock over the mantel. At every footstep upon the asphalt sidewalk her smooth, round chin would cease for a moment its regular rise and fall, and a frown of listening would pucker her pretty brows.

At last she heard the latch of the iron gate click. She sprang up, tripped swiftly to the mirror, where she made a few of those feminine, flickering passes at her front hair and throat which are warranted to hypnotize the approaching guest.

The door bell rang, Miss Katie, in her haste, turned the blaze of the lamp lower instead of higher, and hastened noiselessly down stairs into the hall. She turned the key, the door opened, and Mr. Tansey side-stepped in.

"Why, the i-de-a!" exclaimed Miss Katie, "Is this you, Mr. Tansey? It's after midnight. Aren't you ashamed to wake me up at such an hour to let you in? You're just *awful!*"

"I was late," said Tansey, brilliantly.

"I should think you were! Ma was awfully worried about you. When you weren't in by ten, that hateful Tom McGill said you were out calling on another — said you were out calling on some young lady. I just despise Mr. McGill. Well, I'm not going to scold you any more, Mr. Tansey, if it is a little late — Oh! I turned it the wrong way!"

Miss Katie gave a little scream. Absent-mindedly she had turned the blaze of the lamp entirely out instead of higher. It was very dark.

Tansey heard a musical, soft giggle, and breathed an entrancing odor of heliotrope. A groping light hand touched his arm.

"How awkward I was! Can you find your way — Sam?"

"I — I think I have a match Miss K-Katie."

A scratching sound; a flame; a glow of light held at arm's length by the recreant follower of Destiny illuminating a tableau which shall end the ignominious chronicle — a maid with unkissed, curling, contemptuous lips slowly lifting the lamp chimney and allowing the wick to ignite; then waving a scornful and abjuring hand toward the staircase, the unhappy Tansey, erstwhile champion in the prophetic lists of fortune, ingloriously ascending to his just and certain doom, while (let us imagine) half within the wings stands the imminent figure of Fate jerking wildly at the wrong strings, and mixing things up in her usual able manner.

NOTES AND COMMENTS

This story is one of six Texas stories O. Henry wrote in Columbus, five of which he listed in his notebook. "The Enchanted Kiss" and "A Fog in Santone" have the entire action in San Antonio. Another of the stories written at Columbus, "Hygeia at the Solito," begins in San Antonio and continues on the ranch south of San Antonio in LaSalle County.

For a review of literary evaluation and additional notes and comments related to "The Enchanted Kiss," reference is made to Dr. Porter's essay, Part II, "The Imprisoned Splendor," *ante*, pp. 36–37.

Hygeia at the Solito

If you are knowing in the chronicles of the ring you will recall to mind an event in the early nineties when, for a minute and sundry odd seconds, a champion and a "would-be" faced each other on the alien side of an international river. So brief a conflict had rarely imposed upon the fair promise of true sport. The reporters made what they could of it, but, divested of padding, the action was sadly fugacious. The champion merely smote his victim, turned his back upon him, remarking, "I know what I done to dat stiff," and extended an arm like a ship's mast for his glove to be removed.

Which accounts for a train-load of extremely disgusted gentlemen in an uproar of fancy vests and neckwear being spilled from their Pullmans in San Antonio in the early morning following the fight. Which also partly accounts for the unhappy predicament in which "Cricket" McGuire found himself as he tumbled from his car and sat upon the depot platform, torn by a spasm of that hollow, racking cough so familiar to San Antonian ears. At that time, in the uncertain light of dawn, that way passed Curtis Raidler, the Nueces County cattleman — may his shadow never measure under six feet two.

First published in *Everybody's* magazine for February 1903, as by O. Henry.

Seventh of nineteen stories in *Heart of the West,* published by McClure Company, New York, in 1907.

The cattleman, out this early to catch the southbound for his ranch station, stopped at the side of the distressed patron of sport, and spoke in the kindly drawl of his ilk and region, "Got it pretty bad, bud?"

"Cricket" McGuire, ex-feather-weight prize-fighter, tout, jockey, follower of the "ponies," all-around sport, and manipulator of the gum balls and walnut shells, looked up pugnaciously at the imputation cast by "bud."

"G'wan," he rasped, "telegraph pole. I didn't ring for yer."

Another paroxysm wrung him, and he leaned limply against a convenient baggage truck. Raidler waited patiently, glancing around at the white hats, short overcoats, and big cigars thronging the platform. "You're from the no'th, ain't you, bud?" he asked when the other was partially recovered. "Come down to see the fight?"

"Fight!" snapped McGuire. "Puss-in-the-corner! 'Twas a hypodermic injection. Handed him just one like a squirt of dope, and he's asleep, and no tanbark needed in front of his residence. Fight!" He rattled a bit, coughed, and went on, hardly addressing the cattleman, but rather for the relief of voicing his troubles. "No more dead sure t'ings for me. But Rus Sage himself would have snatched at it. Five to one dat de boy from Cork wouldn't stay t'ree rounds is what I invested in. Put my last cent on, and could already smell the sawdust in dat all-night joint of Jimmy Delaney's on T'irty-seventh Street I was goin' to buy. And den — say, telegraph pole, what a gazaboo a guy is to put his whole roll on one turn of the gaboozlum!"

"You're plenty right," said the big cattleman; "more 'specially when you lose. Son, you get up and light out for a hotel. You got a mighty bad cough. Had it long?"

"Lungs," said McGuire comprehensively. "I got it. The croaker says I'll come to time for four months longer — maybe six if I hold my gait. I wanted to settle down and take care of myself. Dat's why I speculated on dat five to one perhaps. I had a t'ousand iron dollars saved up. If I winned I was goin' to buy Delaney's *café*. Who'd a t'ought dat stiff would take a nap in the foist round — say?"

"It's a hard deal," commented Raidler, looking down at the diminutive form of McGuire crumpled against the truck. "But you go to a hotel and rest. There's the Menger and the Maverick. and —"

"And the Fi'th Av'noo, and the Waldorf-Astoria," mimicked McGuire. "Told you I went broke. I'm on de bum, proper. I've got one dime left. Maybe a trip to Europe or a sail in me private yacht would fix me up — poi-per!"

He flung his dime at a newsboy, got his *Express,* propped his back against the truck, and was at once rapt in the account of his Waterloo as expanded by the ingenious press.

Curtis Raidler interrogated an enormous gold watch, and laid his hand on McGuire's shoulder.

"Come on, bud," he said. "We got three minutes to catch the train."

Sarcasm seemed to be McGuire's vein.

"You ain't seen me cash in any chips or call a turn since I told you I was broke, a minute ago, have you? Friend, chase yourself away."

"You're going down to my ranch," said the cattleman, "and stay till you get well. Six months'll fix you good as new." He lifted McGuire with one hand, and half-dragged him in the direction of the train.

"What about the money?" said McGuire, struggling weakly to escape.

"Money for what?" asked Raidler, puzzled. They eyed each other, not understanding, for they touched only as at the gear of bevelled cog-wheels-at right angles, and moving upon different axes.

Passengers on the south-bound saw them seated together, and wondered at the conflux of two such antipodes. McGuire was five feet one, with a countenance belonging to either Yokohama or Dublin. Bright-beady of eye, bony of cheek and jaw, scarred, toughened, broken and reknit, indestructible, grisly, gladiatorial as a hornet, he was a type neither new nor unfamiliar. Raidler was the product of a different soil. Six feet two in height, miles broad, and no deeper than a crystal brook, he represented the union of the West and South. Few accurate pictures of his kind have been made, for art galleries are so small, and the mutoscope as yet unknown in Texas. After all, the only possible medium of portrayal of Raidler's kind would be the fresco — something high and simple and cool and unframed.

They were rolling southward on the International. The timber was huddling into little dense, green motts at rare distances before the inundation of the downright, vert prairies. This was the land of the ranches; the domain of the kings of the kine.

McGuire sat, collapsed into his corner of the seat, receiving with acid suspicion the conversation of the cattleman. What was the "game" of this big "geezer" who was carrying him off? Altruism would have been McGuire's last guess. "He ain't no farmer," thought the captive, "and he ain't no con man, for sure. W'at's his lay? You trail in, Cricket, and see how many cards he draws. You're up against it, anyhow. You got a nickel and gallopin' consumption, and you better lay low. Lay low, and see w'at's his game."

At Rincon, a hundred miles from San Antonio, they left the train for a buckboard which was waiting there for Raidler. In this they travelled the thirty miles between the station and their destination. If anything could, this drive should have stirred the acrimonious McGuire to a sense of his ransom. They sped upon velvety wheels across an exhilarant savanna. The pair of Spanish ponies struck a nimble, tireless trot, which gait they occasionally relieved by a wild, untrammelled gallop. The air was wine and seltzer, perfumed, as they absorbed it, with the delicate redolence of prairie flowers. The road perished, and the buckboard swam the uncharted billows of the grass itself, steered by the practised hand of Raidler, to whom each tiny distant mott of trees was a signboard, each convolution of the low hills a voucher of course and distance. But McGuire reclined upon his spine, seeing nothing but a desert, and receiving the cattleman's advances with sullen mistrust. "W'at's he up to?" was the burden of his thoughts; "w'at kind of a gold brick has the big guy got to sell?" McGuire was only applying the measure of the streets he had walked to a range bounded by the horizon and the fourth dimension.

A week before, while riding the prairies, Raidler had come upon a sick and weakling calf deserted and bawling. Without dismounting he had reached and slung the distressed bossy across his saddle, and dropped it at the ranch for the boys to attend to. It was impossible for McGuire to know or comprehend that, in the eyes of the cattleman, his case and that of the calf were identical in interest and demand upon his assistance. A creature was ill and helpless; he had the power to render aid — these were the only postulates required for the cattleman to act. They formed his system of logic and the most of his creed. McGuire was the seventh invalid whom Raidler had picked up thus casually in San Antonio, where so many thousands go for the ozone that is said to linger about its contracted streets. Five of them had been guests of Solito Ranch until they had been able to leave, cured or better, and exhausting the vocabulary of tearful gratitude. One came too late, but rested very comfortably, at last, under a ratama tree in the garden.

So, then, it was no surprise to the ranch-hold when the buckboard spun to the door, and Raidler took up his debile *protégé* like a handful of rags and set him down upon the gallery.

McGuire looked upon things strange to him. The ranch-house was the best in the county. It was built of brick hauled one hundred miles by wagon, but it was of but one story, and its four rooms were completely encircled by a mud floor "gallery." The miscellaneous set-

ting of horses, dogs, saddles, wagons, guns, and cowpunchers' para-
phernalia oppressed the metropolitan eye of the wrecked sportsman.

"Well, here we are at home," said Raidler cheeringly.

"It's a h — l of a looking place," said McGuire promptly, as he
rolled upon the gallery floor in a fit of coughing.

"We'll try to make it comfortable for you, buddy," said the cattleman gently. "It ain't fine inside; but it's the out-doors, anyway,
that'll do you the most good. This'll be your room, in here. Anything
we got, you ask for it."

He led McGuire into the east room. The floor was bare and
clean. White curtains waved in the gulf breeze through the open
windows. A big willow rocker, two straight chairs, a long table covered with newspapers, pipes, tobacco, spurs, and cartridges stood in
the centre. Some well-mounted heads of deer and one of an enormous black javeli projected from the walls. A wide, cool cot-bed
stood in a corner. Nueces County people regarded this guest-cham-
ber as fit for a prince. McGuire showed his eye-teeth at it. He took
out his nickel and spun it up to the ceiling.

"T'ought I was lyin' about the money, did ye? Well, you can
frisk me if you wanter. Dat's the last simoleon in the treasury. Who's
goin' to pay?"

The cattleman's clear gray eyes looked steadily from under his
grizzly brows into the huckleberry optics of his guest. After a little he
said simply, and not ungraciously, "I'll be much obliged to you, son,
if you won't mention money any more,. Once was quite a plenty.
Folks I ask to my ranch don't have to pay anything, and they very
scarcely ever offers it. Supper'll be ready in half an hour. There's
water in the pitcher, and some, cooler, to drink, in that red jar hanging on the gallery."

"Where's the bell?" asked McGuire, looking about.

"Bell for what?"

"Bell to ring for things. I can't — see here," he exploded in a
sudden, weak fury, "I never asked you to bring me here. I never held
you up for a cent. I never give you a hard-luck story till you asked
me. Here I am, fifty miles from a bellboy or a cocktail. I'm sick. I
can't hustle. Gee! but I'm up against it!" McGuire fell upon the cot
and sobbed shiveringly.

Raidler went to the door and called. A slender, bright-complex-
ioned Mexican youth about twenty came quickly. Raidler spoke to
him in Spanish:

"Ylario, it is in my mind that I promised you the position of *vaquero* on the San Carlos range at the fall *rodea.*"

"*Si, señor,* such was your goodness."

"Listen. This *señorito* is my friend. He is very sick. Place yourself at his side. Attend to his wants at all times. Have much patience and care with him. And when he is well, or — and when he is well, instead of *vaquero* I will make you *mayordomo* of the Rancho de las Piedras. *Está Bueno?*"

"*Si, si* — *mil gracias, señor,*" Ylario tried to kneel upon the floor in his gratitude, but the cattleman kicked at him benevolently, growling, "None of your operyhouse antics, now."

Ten minutes later Ylario came from McGuire's room and stood before Raidler.

"The little *señor*," he announced, "presents his compliments" (Raidler credited Ylario with the preliminary) "and desires some pounded ice, one hot bath, one gin feez-z, that the windows be all closed, toast, one shave, one NewYorkheral', cigarettes, and to send one telegram."

Raidler took a quart bottle of whiskey from his medicine cabinet. "Here, take him this," he said.

Thus was instituted the reign of terror at the Solito Ranch. For a few weeks McGuire blustered and boasted and swaggered before the cow-punchers who rode in for miles around to see this latest importation of Raidler's. He was an absolutely new experience to them. He explained to them all the intricate points of sparring and the tricks of training and defence. He opened to their minds' view all the indecorous life of a tagger after professional sports. His jargon of slang was a continuous joy and surprise to them. His gestures, his strange poses, his frank ribaldry of tongue and principle fascinated them. He was like a being from a new world.

Strange to say, this new world he had entered did not exist to him. He was an utter egoist of bricks and mortar. He had dropped out, he felt, into open space for a time, and all it contained was an audience for his reminiscences. Neither the limitless freedom of the prairie days nor the grand hush of the close-drawn, spangled nights touched him. All the hues of Aurora could not win him from the pink pages of a sporting journal. "Get something for nothing," was his mission in life; "T'irty-seventh" Street was his goal.

Nearly two months after his arrival he began to complain that he felt worse. It was then that he became the ranch's incubus, its harpy, its Old Man of the Sea. He shut himself in his room like some venomous kobold or flibbertigibbet, whining, complaining, cursing, accusing. The keynote of his plaint was that he had been inveigled into a gehenna against his will; that he was dying of neglect and lack of comforts. With all his dire protestations of increasing illness, to the eye of others he remained unchanged. His currant-like eyes were as bright and diabolic as ever; his voice was as rasping; his callous face, with the skin drawn tense as a drumhead, had no flesh to lose. A flush on his prominent cheek bones each afternoon hinted that a clinical thermometer might have revealed a symptom, and percussion might have established the fact that McGuire was breathing with only one lung, but his appearance remained the same.

In constant attendance upon him was Ylario, whom the coming reward of the *mayordomo*ship must have greatly stimulated, for McGuire chained him to a bitter existence. The air — the man's only chance for life — he commanded to be kept out by closed windows and drawn curtains. The room was always blue and foul with cigarette smoke; whosoever entered it must sit, suffocating, and listen to the imp's interminable gasconade concerning his scandalous career.

The oddest thing of all was the relations existing between McGuire and his benefactor. The attitude of the invalid toward the cattleman was something like that of a peevish, perverse child toward an indulgent parent. When Raidler would leave the ranch, McGuire would fall into a fit of malevolent, silent sullenness. When he returned, he would be met by a string of violent and stinging reproaches. Raidler's attitude toward his charge was quite as inexplicable in its way. The cattleman seemed actually to assume and feel the character assigned him by McGuire's intemperate accusations — the character of tyrant and guilty oppressor. He seemed to have adopted the responsibility of the fellow's condition, and he always met his tirades with a pacific, patient, and even remorseful kindness that never altered.

One day Raidler said to him, "Try more air, son. You can have the buckboard and a driver every day if you'll go. Try a week or two in one of the cow camps. I'll fix you up plum comfortable. The ground, and the air next to it — them's the things to cure you. I knowed a man from Philadelphy, sicker than you are, got lost on the Guadalupe, and slept on the bare grass in sheep camps for two weeks. Well, sir, it started him getting well, which he done. Close to the ground — that's where the medicine in the air stays. Try a little hossback riding now. There's a gentle pony —"

"What've I done to yer?" screamed McGuire. "Did I ever double cross yer? Did I ask you to bring me here? Drive me out to yer camps if you wanter; or stick a knife in me and save trouble. Ride? I can't lift my feet. I couldn't side-step a jab from a five-year-old kid. That's what your d — d ranch has done for me. There's nothing to eat, nothing to see, and nobody to talk to but a lot of Reubens who don't know a punching-bag from a lobster salad."

"It's a lonesome place, for certain," apologized Raidler abashedly. "We got plenty, but it's rough enough. Anything you think of you want, the boys'll ride up and fetch it down for you."

It was Chad Murchison, a cow-puncher from the Circle Bar outfit, who first suggested that McGuire's illness was fraudulent. Chad had brought a basket of grapes for him thirty miles, and four out of his way, tied to his saddle-horn. After remaining in the smoke-tainted room for a while, he emerged and bluntly confided his suspicions to Raidler.

"His arm," said Chad, "is harder'n a diamond. He interduced me to what he called a shore-perplex-us punch, and 'twas like being kicked twice by a mustang. He's playin' it low down on you, Curt. He ain't no sicker'n I am. I hate to say it, but the runt's workin' you for range and shelter."

The cattleman's ingenuous mind refused to entertain Chad's view of the case, and when, later, he came to apply the test, doubt entered not into his motives.

One day, about noon, two men drove up to the ranch, alighted, hitched, and came in to dinner; standing and general invitations being the custom of the country. One of them was a great San Antonio doctor, whose costly services had been engaged by a wealthy cowman who had been laid low by an accidental bullet. He was now being driven to the station to take the train back to town. After dinner Raidler took him aside, pushed a twenty-dollar bill against his hand, and said:

"Doc, there's a young chap in that room I guess has got a bad case of consumption. I'd like for you to look him over and see just how bad he is, and if we can do anything for him."

"How much was that dinner I just ate, Mr. Raidler?" said the doctor bluffly, looking over his spectacles. Raidler returned the money to his pocket. The doctor immediately entered McGuire's room, and the cattleman seated himself upon a heap of saddles on the gallery, ready to reproach himself in the event the verdict should be unfavorable.

In ten minutes the doctor came briskly out. "Your man," he said promptly, "is as sound as a new dollar. His lungs are better than mine. Respiration, temperature, and pulse normal. Chest expansion five inches. Not a sign of weakness anywhere. Of course I didn't examine for the bacillus, but it isn't there. You can put my name on the diagnosis. Even cigarettes and a vilely close room haven't hurt him. Coughs, does he? Well, you tell him it isn't necessary. You asked if there is anything you could do for him. Well, I advise you to set him digging post-holes or breaking mustangs. There's our team ready. Good-day, sir." And like a puff of wholesome, blustery wind the doctor was off.

Raidler reached out and plucked a leaf from a mesquite bush by the railing, and began chewing it thoughtfully.

The branding season was at hand, and the next morning Ross Hargis, foreman of the outfit, was mustering his force of some twenty-five men at the ranch, ready to start for the San Carlos range, where the work was to begin. By six o'clock the horses were all saddled, the grub wagon ready, and the cow-punchers were swinging themselves upon their mounts, when Raidler bade them wait. A boy was bringing up an extra pony, bridled and saddled, to the gate. Raidler walked to McGuire's room and threw open the door. McGuire was lying on his cot, not yet dressed, smoking.

"Get up," said the cattleman, and his voice was clear and brassy, like a bugle.

"How's that?" asked McGuire, a little startled.

"Get up and dress. I can stand a rattlesnake, but I hate a liar. Do I have to tell you again?" He caught McGuire by the neck and stood him on the floor.

"Say, friend," cried McGuire wildly, "are you bughouse? I'm sick — see? I'll croak if I got to hustle. What've I done to yer?" — he began his chronic whine — "I never asked yer to —"

"Put on your clothes," called Raidler in a rising tone.

Swearing, stumbling, shivering, keeping his amazed, shiny eyes upon the now menacing form of the aroused cattleman, McGuire managed to tumble into his clothes. Then Raidler took him by the collar and shoved him out and across the yard to the extra pony hitched at the gate. The cow-punchers lolled in their saddles, open-mouthed.

"Take this man," said Raidler to Ross Hargis, "and put him to work. Make him work hard, sleep hard, and eat hard. You boys know I done what I could for him, and he was welcome. Yesterday the best doctor in San Antone examined him, and says he's got the lungs of a burro and the constitution of a steer. You know what to do with him Ross."

Ross Hargis only smiled grimly.

"Aw," said McGuire, looking intently at Raidler, with a peculiar expression upon his face, "The croaker said I was all right, did he? Said I was fakin', did he? You put him onto me. You t'ought I wasn't sick. You said I was a liar. Say, friend, I talked rough, I know, but I didn't mean most of it. If you felt like I did — aw! I forgot — I ain't sick, the croaker says. Well, friend, now I'll go work for yer. Here's where you play even."

He sprang into the saddle easily as a bird, got the quirt from the horn, and gave his pony a slash with it. "Cricket," who once brought in Good Boy by a neck at Hawthorne — and a 10 to 1 shot — had his foot in the stirrups again.

McGuire led the cavalcade as they dashed away for San Carlos, and the cow-punchers gave a yell of applause as they closed in behind his dust.

But in less than a mile he had lagged to the rear, and was last man when they struck the patch of high chaparral below the horse pens. Behind a clump of this he drew rein, and held a handkerchief to his mouth. He took it away drenched with bright, arterial blood, and threw it carefully into a clump of prickly pear. Then he slashed with his quirt again, gasped, "G'wan," to his astonished pony, and galloped after the gang.

That night Raidler received a message from his old home in Alabama. There had been a death in the family; an estate was to divide, and they called for him to come. Daylight found him in the buckboard, skimming the prairies for the station. It was two months before he returned. When he arrived at the ranch house, he found it well-nigh deserted save for Ylario, who acted as a kind of steward during his absence. Little by little the youth made him acquainted with the work done while he was away. The branding camp, he was informed, was still doing business. On account of many severe storms the cattle had been badly scattered, and the branding had been accomplished but slowly. The camp was now in the valley of the Guadalupe, twenty miles away.

"By the way," said Raidler, suddenly remembering, "that fellow I sent along with them — McGuire — is he working yet?"

"I not know," said Ylario. "Mans from the camp come verree few times to the ranch. So plentee work with the leetle calves. They no say. Oh, I think that fellow McGuire he dead much time ago."

"Dead!" said Raidler. "What you talking about?"

"Verree sick fellow, McGuire," replied Ylario, with a shrug of his shoulder. "I theenk he no live one, two month when he go away."

"Shucks!" said Raidler. "He humbugged you, too, did he? The doctor examined him and said he was sound as a mesquite knot."

"That doctor," said Ylario, smiling, "he tell you so? That doctor no see McGuire."

"Talk up," ordered Raidler. "What the devil do you mean?"

"McGuire," continued the boy tranquilly, "he getting drink water outside when that doctor come in room. That doctor take me and pound me all over here with his fingers" — putting his hand to his chest — "I not know for what. He put his ear here and here and here, and listen — I not know for what. He put little glass stick in my mouth. He feel my arm here. He make me count like whisper — so — twenty, *treinta, cuarenta* times. Who knows," concluded Ylario, with a deprecating spread of his hands, "for what that doctor do those ver-ree droll and suchlike things?"

"What horses are up?" asked Raidler shortly.

"Paisano is grazing but behind the little corral, *señor.*"

"Ensillamele, prontito."

Within a very few minutes the cattleman was mounted and away. Paisano, well named after that ungainly but swift-running bird, struck into his long lope that ate up the road like a strip of mac-aroni. In two hours and a quarter Raidler, from a gentle swell, saw the branding camp by a water hole in the Guadalupe. Sick with ex-pectancy of the news he feared, he rode up, dismounted, and dropped Paisano's reins. So gentle was his heart that at that moment he would have pleaded guilty to the murder of McGuire.

The only being in the camp was the cook, who was just arrang-ing the hunks of barbecued beef, and distributing the tin coffee cups for supper. Raidler evaded a direct question concerning the one sub-ject in his mind.

"Everything all right in camp, Pete?" he managed to inquire.

"So, so," said Pete conservatively. "Grub give out twice. Wind scattered the cattle, and we've had to rake the brush for forty mile. I need a new coffee-pot. And the mosquitos is some more hellish than common."

"The boys — all well?"

Pete was no optimist. Besides, inquiries concerning the health of cow-punchers were not only superfluous, but bordered on flaccid-ity. It was not like the boss to make them.

"What's left of 'em don't miss no calls to grub." the cook con-ceded.

"What's left of 'em?" repeated Raidler in a husky voice. Me-chanically he began to look around for McGuire's grave. He had in his mind a white slab such as he had seen in the Alabama church-yard. But immediately he knew that was foolish. Of course they would cover his grave with pear to keep the coyotes from it.

"Sure," said Pete; "what's left. Cow camps change in two months. Some's gone."

Raidler nerved himself.

"That — chap — I sent along — McGuire — did — he —"

"Say," interrupted Pete, rising with a chunk of corn bread in each hand, "that was a dirty shame, sending that poor, sick kid to a cow camp. A doctor that couldn't tell he was graveyard meat ought to be skinned with a cinch buckle. Game as he was, too — it's a scandal among snakes. Lemme tell you what he done. First night in camp the boys started to initiate him in the leather breeches degree. Ross Hargis busted him one swipe with his chaparreras, and what do you reckon the poor child did? Got up, the little skeeter, and licked Ross. Licked Ross Hargis. Licked him good. Hit him plenty and everywhere and hard. Ross'd just get up and pick out a fresh place to lay down on agin.

"Then that McGuire goes off there and lays down with his head in the grass and bleeds. A hem-ridge they calls it. He lays there eighteen hours by the watch, and they can't budge him. The grass is red all round him. Then Ross Hargis, who loves any man who can lick him, goes to work and damns the doctors from Greenland to Poland Chiny; and him and Green Branch Jonson they gets McGuire in a tent, and spells each other feedin' him chopped raw meat and whiskey.

"But it looks like the kid ain't got no appetite to git well, for they misses him from the tent in the night and finds him rootin' in the grass, and likewise a drizzle fallin'. 'G'wan,' he says, 'lemme go and die like I wanter. He said I was a liar and a fake' — McGuire says — 'and I was playin' sick. Lemme alone.'

"Two weeks," went on the cook, "he laid around, not noticin' nobody, and then — "

A sudden thunder filled the air, and a score of galloping centaurs crashed through the brush into camp.

"Illustrious rattlesnakes!" exclaimed Pete, springing all ways at once; "here the boys come, and I'm an assassinated man if supper ain't ready in three minutes."

But Raidler saw only one thing. A little, brownfaced, grinning chap, springing from his saddle in the full light of the fire. McGuire was not like that, and yet —

In another instant the cattleman was holding him by the hand and shoulder.

"Son, son, how goes it?" was all he found to say.

"Close to the ground, says you," shouted McGuire, crunching Raidler's fingers in a grip of steel; "and dat's where I found it — healt' and strengt', and tumbled to what a cheap skate I been actin'. T'anks fer kickin' me out, old man. And — say! the joke's on dat croaker, ain't it? I looked t'rough the window and see him playin' tag on dat Dago kid's solar plexus."

"You son of a tinker," growled the cattleman, "why'n't you talk up and say the doctor never examined you?"

"Aw — g'wan!" said McGuire, with a flash of his old asperity, "nobody can't bluff me. You never ast me. You made your spiel, and you t'rowed me out, and I let it go at dat. And, say, friend, dis chasin' cows is outer sight. Dis is de whitest bunch of sports I ever travelled with. You'll let me stay, won't yer, old man?"

Raidler looked wonderingly toward Ross Hargis.

"That cussed little runt," remarked Ross tenderly, "is the Jo-dartin'est hustler — and the hardest hitter in anybody's cow camp."

NOTES AND COMMENTS

This story opens in San Antonio early one February morning in 1896 with a Southern Pacific passenger train disgorging its load of unhappy sportsmen arriving from Langtry, Texas, some 250 miles west of San Antonio. The day before, the sporting crowd had waded the Rio Grande into Mexico to witness a prize fight between Bob Fitzsimmons and Peter Maher, in which Fitzsimmons flattened the hapless Maher in ninety-five seconds of the first round. The Texas Legislature a short time before had outlawed prize fights in Texas, and Texas Rangers were on hand to see that the law was enforced in Texas.

The title of this story was well chosen by O. Henry. "Cricket" McGuire, as one of the unhappy sportsmen, was suffering from tuberculosis, and in time, with guidance from Curtis Raidler, McGuire recovered his health. Hygeia in Greek mythology was the goddess of health. At the Solito ranch, where Raidler took McGuire, the only customary cure for tuberculosis in those days was "close to the ground. . . where the medicine in the air stays." Solito in music means "in the usual customary manner," a meaning known to O. Henry, an accomplished musician. Thus O. Henry gives McGuire restored health in the usual and customary manner.

For a review of literary evaluation and additional notes and comments related to "Hygeia at the Solito," reference is made to Dr. Porter's essay, part II, "The Imprisoned Splendor," *ante*, pp. 38–39.

Rouge et Noir

I. DICKY'S DIGRESSION.

Nobody knew exactly where Dicky Maloney hailed from or how he reached Puerto Rey. He appeared there one day, and that was all. He afterward said that he came on the fruit steamer *Thor*, but, an inspection of the *Thor's* passenger list of that date would have found it to be Maloneyless. Curiosity, however, soon perished, and Dicky took his place among the heterogeneous litter of the coast — the stranded adventurers, refugees and odd fish from other countries that line the shore of the Caribbean.

He was an active, devil-may-care, rollicking fellow with an engaging gray eye, the most irresistible grin, a rather dark, or much sun-burned complexion, and a head of the fieriest red hair ever seen in that country. Speaking the Spanish language as well as he spoke English, and seeming always to have plenty of silver in his pockets, it was not long before he was a welcome companion both with the natives and the resident foreigners. He developed an extreme fond-

---

First published in *Ainslee's* magazine for December 1901, as by Olivier Henry. This was the first of ten stories originally published under the pen name "Olivier Henry."

This short story was never published in book form but supplied Chapter XV and Chapter XVI of *Cabbages and Kings,* the first book and the only novel by O. Henry, published by McClure, Phillips & Co., New York, in November 1904.

ness for *vino blancho;* could drink more of it than any three men in the
port, and to meet Dicky Maloney's brilliant head and smile coming
down the street meant, to any of his acquaintances, the consumption
of from one to three bottles of strong, white wine. Everybody called
him Dicky; everybody cheered up at sight of him — especially the
natives to whom his marvelous ruddy hair and his free and easy style
were a constant delight and envy. Anywhere about the port you
would soon see Dicky and hear his genial laugh, and find around
him a group of admirers, who appreciated both him and the *vino
blancho* he was so ready to buy.

A considerable amount of speculation still existed concerning
the object of his stay in Puerto Rey, but one day he silenced this by
opening a small shop for the sale of cigars, *dulces* and the handiwork
of the interior Indians — fiber and silk woven goods, deerskin *zapatos,* and basketwork of *tule* reeds. Even then he did not change his
habits, for he was drinking and playing cards half the day and night
with the comandante, the collector of the port, the Jefe Politico, and
other gay dogs among the native officials. The care of the shop he
left entirely to Pasa. And now it is both desirable and fitting to make
Pasa's acquaintance, for she was Dicky's Digression.

La Madama Timotea Buencaminos y Salazar de las Yglesias
kept a rum shop in Calle numero ocho. No disgrace, mind you, for
rum-making is a government monopoly, and to keep a government
dispensary assures respectability if not supereminence. Moreover,
the saddest of precisians could find no fault with the conduct of the
shop. Customers drank there in the lowest of spirits and fearsomely,
as in the shadow of the dead, for la madama's ancient but vaunted
lineage counteracted even the rum's behest to be joyful. For, was she
not of the Yglesias who landed with Pizarro? And had her deceased
husband not been Comisionado de Caminos y Puentes for the district?

In the next room, seated in the cane rocking-chair, dreamily
strumming a guitar, could generally be found her daughter Pasa —
"La Santita Navanjada" the young men had named her. *Navanjada* is
the Spanish word for a certain shade of color that you must go to
more trouble to describe in English. By saying: "The little saint,
tinted the most beautiful-delicate-slightly-orange-golden" you will
approximate the description of Doña Pasa Buencaminos y Salazar
de las Yglesias.

Every evening a row of visiting young caballeros would occupy
the prim line of chairs set against the wall of this room. They were
there to besiege the heart of "La Santita." Their method (which is
not proof against intelligent competition) consisted of expanding the

chest, looking valorous, and silently consuming a gross or two of cigarettes. Even saints, delicately oranged, prefer to be wooed differ-
ently. Doña Pasa was accustomed to tide over the vast chasms of ni-
cotinized silence with her guitar, and wondered if the romances she
had read about gallant and more — more — contiguous cavaliers
were all lies. At somewhat regular intervals la madama would glide
in from the dispensary with a sort of draught-suggesting look in her
eye, and there would follow a great rustling of stiff white duck trousers as one of the caballeros would suggest a visit to the bar.

That Dicky Maloney would, sooner or later, explore this field
was a thing to be foreseen. There were few doors in Puerto Rey his
red head had not been poked into.

He saw Pasa one afternoon sitting by the door with an unusually saintly look upon her face. Dicky rushed off to find one of the
white duck wall-flowers to present him. In an incredibly short time
he was seated close beside the cane rocking-chair. There were no
back-against-the-wall poses with Dicky. At close range, was his theory of subjection. To carry the fortress with one concentrated, ar-
dent, eloquent, irresistible *escalade* — that was Dicky's way.

Pasa was descended from the proudest Spanish families in the
country. Moreover, she had had unusual advantages. Two years in
a New Orleans school had elevated her ambitions and fitted her for
a fate above the ordinary maidens of her native land. And yet here
she succumbed to the first red-haired scamp with a glib tongue and
a charming smile that came along and courted her properly. For,
very soon Dicky took her quietly to the little church next to the Tea-
tro Nacional and then to his little shop in the grass-grown street
where customers seldom troubled him. And it was her fate to sit,
with her patient, saintly eyes and figure like a bisque Psyche, behind
its sequestered counter, while Dicky drank and philandered with his
frivolous acquaintances.

The women, with their naturally fine instinct, saw a chance for
vivisection, and delicately taunted her with his habits. She turned
upon them in a beautiful, steady blaze of sorrowful contempt.

"You meat-cows," she said, in her level, crystal-clear tones;
"you know nothing of a man. Your men are *maromeros*. They are fit
only to roll cigarettes in the shade until the sun strikes and shrivels
them up. They drone in your hammocks and you comb their hair
and feed them with fresh fruit. My man is of no such blood. Let him
drink of the wine. When he has taken sufficient of it to drown one of
your *flaccitos* he will come home to me *mas hombre* than one thousand
of your *pobrecitos*. My hair he smoothes and braids; he sings to me; he
himself removes my *zapatos*, and there, there, upon each instep

leaves a kiss. He holds — Oh, you will never understand! Blind ones who have never known a *man.*"

Sometimes mysterious things happened at night about Dicky's shop. While the front of it was dark, in the little room back of it Dicky and a few of his friends would sit about a table carrying on some kind of very quiet *negocios* until quite late. Finally he would let them out the front door very carefully, and go upstairs to his little saint. These visitors were generally conspirator-like men with dark clothes and hats. Of course, these dark doings were noticed after a while, and talked about. At the Hotel Internacional, where the English-speaking colony mostly congregated, it was openly stated that this fellow Maloney was a card sharp that made his money by skinning the native talent. This charge, however, was considered quite a tepid one, coming from this source, for most of the foreign population of Puerto Rey were fugitives from some sort of justice — uneasy exiles who watched every incoming steamer with poorly-concealed anxiety.

Quite a number of letters arrived, addressed to "Mr. Dicky Maloney," or "Señor Dickee Maloney," to the considerable pride of Pasa. That so many people should desire to write to him only confirmed her own suspicion that the light from his red head shone around the world. As to their contents she never felt curiosity. There was a wife for you!

The one mistake Dicky made in Puerto Rey was to run out of money at the wrong time. Where his money came from was a puzzle, for the sales of his shop were next to nothing, but that source failed, and at a peculiarly unfortunate time. It was when the comandante, Don Señor el Coronel Encarnacion Casablanca looked upon the little saint seated in the shop and felt his heart go pitapat.

The comandante, who was versed in all the intricate arts of gallantry, first delicately hinted at his sentiments by donning his dress uniform and strutting up and down fiercely before her window. Pasa, glancing demurely with her saintly eyes, instantly perceived his resemblance to her parrot, Chichi, and was diverted to the extent of a smile. The comandante saw the smile, which was not intended for him. Convinced of an impression made, he entered the shop, confidently, and advanced to open compliment. Pasa froze; he pranced; she flamed royally; he was charmed to injudicious persistence; she commanded him to leave the shop; he tried to capture her hand, and Dicky entered, broadly smiling, full of white wine and the devil.

Five minutes later he pitched the comandante out the door upon the stones of the street, senseless. That five minutes Dicky had spent in punishing him scientifically and carefully, so that the pain might be prolonged as far as possible.

A barefooted policeman who had been watching the affair from across the street, now blew a whistle and a squad of eight soldiers came running from the *cuartel* just around the corner. When they saw that Dicky was the offender they stopped and blew more whistles, which brought out re-enforcements of twelve.

Dicky, being thoroughly imbued with the martial spirit, stooped and drew the comandante's sword which was girded about him, and charged his foe. He chased the standing army four squares, playfully prodding its squealing rear, and hacking its bare, ginger-colored heels. He was not so successful with the civic authorities. Eight muscular, nimble policemen overpowered him, and conveyed him, triumphantly but warily to jail. *"El Diablo Colorado,"* they dubbed him, and derided the military for its defeat.

Dicky, with the rest of the prisoners, could look out the barred door at the grass of a little plaza, a row of orange trees, and the red tile roofs and 'dobe walls of a line of insignificant *tiendas*. At sunset, along a path across this plaza, came a melancholy procession of sad-faced women bearing plantains, bread, *casaba* and fruit — each coming with food to some wretch behind those bars to whom she still clung. Thrice a day, morning, noon and sunset, they were permitted to come. Water was furnished her guests by the republic, but no food.

Dicky's name was called by the sentry, and he stepped before the door. There stood his little saint, a black mantilla draped about her head and shoulders, her face like glorified melancholy, her clear eyes gazing longingly at him as if they might draw him between the bars to her. She brought a chicken, some oranges, *dulces,* and a loaf of white bread. A soldier inspected the food, and passed it in to Dicky. Pasa spoke calmly, as she always did, and briefly, in her thrilling, flute-like tones. "Angel of my life," she said, "let it not be long that thou art away from me. Thou knowest that life is not a thing to be endured with thou not at my side. Tell me if I can do aught in this matter. If not, I will wait — a little while. I come again in the morning."

Dicky, with his shoes removed so as not to disturb his fellow prisoners, tramped the floor of the jail half the night condemning his lack of money and the cause of it — whatever that might have been. He knew very well that money would have bought his release at once.

For two days succeeding Pasa came at each appointed time and brought him food. He eagerly inquired each time if a letter or package had come for him, and she mournfully shook her head.

On the morning of the third day she brought only a small loaf of bread. There were dark circles under her eyes. She seemed as calm as ever.

"By jingo," said Dicky, who seemed to speak in English or Spanish as the whim seized him, "this is dry provender, *muchachita.* Is this the best you can dig up for a fellow?"

Pasa looked at him as a mother looks at a beloved but capricious babe.

"Think better of it," she said, in a low voice; "since for the next meal there will be nothing. The last *centavo* is spent." She pressed closer against the grating.

"Sell the goods in the shop — take anything for them."

"Have I not tried? Did I not offer them for one-tenth their cost? Not even one *peso* would any one give. There is not one *real* in this town to assist Dickee Malonee."

Dick clenched his teeth grimly. "That's the comandante," he growled. "He's responsible for that sentiment. Wait, oh, wait till the cards are all out."

Pasa lowered her voice to almost a whisper. "And, listen, heart of my heart," she said, "I have endeavored to be brave, but I cannot live without thee. Three days now —"

Dicky caught a faint gleam of steel from the folds of her mantilla. For once she looked in his face and saw it without a smile, stern, menacing and purposeful. Then he suddenly raised his hand and his smile came back like a gleam of sunshine. The hoarse signal of an incoming steamer's siren sounded in the harbor. Dicky called to the sentry who was pacing before the door:

"What steamer comes?"

"The *Catarina.*"

"Of the Vesuvius line?"

"Without doubt, of that line."

"Go you, *picarilla,*" said Dicky, joyously to Pasa, "to the American consul. Tell him I wish to speak with him. See that he comes at once. And you, let me see a different look in those eyes, for I promise your head shall rest upon this arm tonight."

It was an hour before the consul came. He was a spectacled young man, a greedy botanist who was utilizing his office to study the tropic flora. He held a green umbrella under his arm, and mopped his forehead impatiently.

"Now, see here, Maloney," he began, captiously, "you fellows seem to think you can cut up any kind of row, and expect me to pull you out of it. I'm neither the War Department nor a gold mine. This country has its laws, you know, and there's one against pounding the senses out of the regular army. You Irish are forever getting into trouble. I don't see what I can do. Anything like tobacco, now, to make you comfortable — or newspapers —"

"Son of Eli," interrupted Dicky, gravely, "you haven't changed an iota. That is almost a duplicate of the speech you made when old Koen's donkeys and geese got into the chapel loft, and the culprits wanted to hide in your room."

"Oh, heavens!" exclaimed the consul, hurriedly adjusting his spectacles. "Are you a Yale man, too? Were you in that crowd? I don't seem to remember any one with red — any one named Maloney. Such a lot of college men seem to have misused their advantages. One of the best mathematicians of the class of '91 is selling lottery tickets in Belize. A Cornell man dropped off here last month. He was second steward on a guano boat. I'll write to the Department if you like, Maloney. Or if there's any tobacco, or newspa —"

"There's nothing," interrupted Dicky, shortly, "but this. You go tell the captain of the *Catarina* that Dicky Maloney wants to see him as soon as he can conveniently come. Tell him where I am. Hurry. That's all."

The consul, glad to be let off so easily, hurried away. The captain of the *Catarina,* a stout man, Sicilian born, soon appeared, shoving, with little ceremony, through the guards to the jail door. The Vesuvius Fruit Company had a habit of doing things that way in Puerto Rey.

"I am exceeding sorry — exceeding sorry," said the captain, "to see this occur. I place myself at your service, Mr. Maloney. Whatever you need shall be furnished. Whatever you say shall be done."

Dicky looked at him unsmilingly. His red hair could not detract from his attitude of severe dignity as he stood, tall and calm, with his now grim mouth forming a horizontal line.

"Captain De Lucco, I believe I still have funds in the hands of your company — ample and personal funds. I ordered a remittance last week. The money has not arrived. You know what is needed in this game. Money and money and more money. Why has it not been sent?"

"By the *Cristobal,*" replied De Lucco, gesticulating, "it was dispatched. Where is the *Cristobal?* Off Cape Antonio I spoke her with a broken shaft. A tramp coaster was towing her back to New Orleans. I brought money ashore thinking your need for it might not withstand delay. In this envelope is one thousand dollars. There is more if you need it, Mr. Maloney."

"For the present it will suffice," said Dicky, softening as he crinkled the envelope and looked down at the half inch thickness of smooth, dingy bills.

"The long green!" he said, gently, with a new reverence in his gaze. "Is there anything it will not buy, captain?"

"I had three friends," replied De Lucco, who was a bit of a philosopher. "who had money. One of them speculated in stocks and made ten million; another is in heaven, and the third married a poor girl whom he loved."

"The answer, then," said Dicky, "is held by the Almighty, Wall Street and Cupid. So, the question remains."

"This," queried the captain, including Dicky's surroundings in a significant gesture of his hand; "is it — it is not — it is not connected with the business of your little shop? There is no failure in your plans?"

"No, no," said Dicky. "This is merely the result of a little private affair of mine, a digression from the regular line of business. They say for a complete life a man must know poverty, love and war. But they don't go well together, *capitan mio*. No; there is no failure in my business. The little shop is doing very well."

When the captain had departed Dicky called the sergeant of the jail squad and asked:

"Am I *preso* by the military or by the civil authority?"

"Surely there is no martial law in effect now, señor."

"*Bueno*. Now go or send to the alcalde, the Juez de la Paz and the Jefe de los Policios. Tell them I am prepared at once to satisfy the demands of justice." A folded bill of the "long green" slid into the sergeant's hand.

Then Dicky's smile came back again, for he knew that the hours of his captivity were numbered, and he hummed, in time with the sentry's tread:

> "They're hanging men and women now
> For lacking of the green."

So, that night Dicky sat by the window of the room over his shop and his little saint sat close by, working at something silken and dainty. Dicky was thoughtful and grave. His red hair was in an unusual state of disorder. Pasa's fingers often ached to smooth and arrange it, but Dicky would never allow it. He was poring, to-night, over a great litter of maps and books and papers on his table until that perpendicular line came between his brows that always dis-

tressed Pasa. Presently she went and brought his hat, and stood with
it until he looked up, inquiringly.

"It is sad for you here," she explained. "Go out and drink *vino
blanco*. Come back when you get that smile you used to wear. That is
what I wish to see."

Dicky laughed and threw down his papers. "The *vino blanco*
stage is past. It has served its turn. Perhaps, after all, there was less
entered my mouth and more my ears than people thought. But,
there will be no more maps or frowns to-night. I promise you that.
Come."

They sat upon a reed *silleta* at the window and watched the quivering gleams from the lights of the *Catarina* reflected in the harbor.

Presently Pasa rippled out one of her infrequent chirrups of audible laughter.

"I was thinking," she began, anticipating Dicky's question, "of
the foolish things girls have in their minds. Because I went to school
in the states I used to have ambitions. Nothing less than to be the
President's wife would satisfy me. And, look thou, red picaroon, to
what obscure fate hast thou stolen me!"

"Don't give up hope," said Dicky, smiling. "There was a dictator of Chili named O'Higgins. Why not a President Maloney of
this country? Say the word, and I'll make the race. We'll capture the
Irish vote, easy running, by a head."

"No,no,no,no, *cabeza colorada!*" cooed Pasa, pointing the allusion with the tip of her finger against Dicky's brilliant locks, "I am
content" — she laid her head against his arm — "here."

II.   THE VESUVIUS PLAYS.

The banana republic of Costaragua has, practically, two capi-
tals. The one officially recognized is San Mateo, seventy miles in the
interior. But, during the hot season, from May to October, the entire
administration removes to Puerto Rey, where the sea breeze renders
the pursuit of business and pleasure possible. Custom had so established this annual hegira of the executive that a commodious government building had been erected on the beach at Puerto Rey for the
use of the President and his official family during their sojourn.
Thus Puerto Rey claimed, with reason, equal honor with San Mateo
as capital of the republic.

It is during this season that Puerto Rey may actually be said to
live. The pleasure-loving people make it one long holiday of amusement and rejoicing. *Fiestas, bailes,* games, sea bathing, processions,
and small theatres contribute to their enjoyment.

The famous Swiss band of forty pieces plays in the little Plaza Nacional every night, while the fourteen carriages in Puerto Rey circle in funereal but complacent procession. Los Indios, looking like prehistoric stone idols, come down from the mountains to peddle their handiwork in the streets. The people throng the sidewalks, a chattering, careless, happy stream of buoyant humanity. Preposterous children, with the shortest of ballet skirts, gilt wings and grimy, bare legs, howl underfoot among the effervescent crowds. Especially is the arrival of the presidential party, on the fifteenth day of May, attended with pomp, show and public demonstrations of enthusiasm and delight.

But now, this year, though the middle of May was almost come, the heart of the people was not stirred to the customary joyous preparation. Throughout the entire republic there seemed to be a spirit of silent, sullen discontent. The administration of President Zarilla had made him far from a popular idol. Fresh taxes, fresh import duties, and, more than all, his tolerance of the outrageous oppression of the citizens by the military had rendered him the most obnoxious President since the despised Alforan. The majority of his own cabinet were out of sympathy with him. The army, which he courted by giving it license to tyrannize, had been his main, and, thus far, adequate bulwark.

But the most impolitic of the administration's moves had been when it antagonized the Vesuvius Fruit Company of New Orleans, an organization plying twelve steamships, and with a cash capital something larger than Costaragua's surplus and debt combined. Naturally, an established concern like the Vesuvius would become irritated at having a small, retail republic with no rating at all attempt to squeeze it. So, when the government proxies applied for subsidy they encountered a polite refusal. The President retaliated by clapping an export duty of one *real* per bunch on bananas — a thing unprecedented in fruit growing countries. But the Vesuvius Company had built costly iron piers and wharves at three points along the Costaraguan coast. The company's agents had erected fine homes in the towns where they had their headquarters, and the company had invested large sums in banana plantations and timber lands of the republic. It would cost an immense sum if it should be compelled to move out. The selling price of bananas from Vera Cruz to Trinidad was three *reals* per bunch. This duty of one *real* would have fallen as a loss upon the growers, but the Vesuvius seemed to prefer Costaraguan fruit, and they continued to buy it, paying four *reals* without a murmur.

This apparent victory deceived His Excellency, and he hungered for its fruits. An emissary requested an interview with a representative of the company. The Vesuvius sent Mr. Franzoni, a little, stout, cheerful man always whistling Verdi. Señor Ortiz, secretary to the Minister of Finance, attempted the sandbagging in behalf of Costaragua.

Señor Ortiz opened negotiations by the announcement that the government contemplated the building of a railroad to skirt the alluvial coast lands. After touching upon the benefits such an improvement would confer upon the interests of the Vesuvius, he reached the definite suggestion that a contribution to the road's expense of one hundred thousand *pesos* would not be more than an equivalent to benefits received.

Mr. Franzoni denied any benefits from the contemplation of a road. He was authorized, however, to offer a contribution of five hundred to the contemplators.

Did Señor Ortiz understand Mr. Franzoni to mean five hundred *thousand?*

By no means. Five hundred *pesos*. And in silver; not gold.

"Your offer insults my government," said Señor Ortiz, rising indignantly.

"Then," cried Mr. Franzoni, in a warning voice, "we will change it!"

The offer was never changed. Mr. Franzoni must have meant something else.

So, when the fifteenth day of May arrived the signs were that the presidential advent would not be celebrated by unlimited rejoicing.

Although the rainy season was long over, the day seemed to hark back to reeking February. A fine drizzle of rain fell all during the forenoon. A narrow gauge railroad runs from Puerto Rey to within ten miles of San Mateo. The train conveying the executive party rolled into the summer capital at a speed of fifteen miles an hour at four in the afternoon. Colonel Rocas, with a regiment of the regular army, and Captain Cruz, with his famous troop of one hundred light horse "El Ciento Huilando," the President's personal escort, had marched down by easy stages from San Mateo, arriving the previous afternoon.

President Zarilla was a little, elderly man, grizzly bearded, with a considerable ratio of Indian blood revealed in his cinnamon complexion. As he was assisted into his carriage, his sharp, beady eyes glanced around for the expected demonstration of welcome, but he faced a stolid, unenthused array of curious citizens. Sightseers the Costaraguans are by birth and habit, and they turned out to the last able-bodied unit to witness the scene, but they maintained an accusive silence. They crowded the streets to the very wheel ruts, they covered the red tile roofs to the eaves, but there was never a "Viva!" among them. No wreaths of palm and lemon branches or gorgeous strings of paper roses hung from the windows and balconies as was the custom. There was an apathy, a dull, dissenting, disapprobation that was the more ominous because it puzzled. No one feared an outburst, a revolt of the discontents, for they had no leader. The President and those loyal to him had never even heard whispered a name among them capable of crystallizing the dissatisfaction into opposition. No, there could be no danger. The people always procured a new idol before they destroyed an old one.

At length, after a prodigious galloping and curvetting of red-sashed majors, goldlaced colonels and epauletted generals, the procession formed for its annual formal progress down the principal street — the Camino Real — to the government building at its end.

The Swiss band led the line of march. After it pranced the local comandante, mounted, and a detachment of his troops. Next came a carriage with four members of the cabinet, conspicuous among them the Minister of War, old General Pilar, with his white mustache and his soldierly bearing. Then the President's vehicle, containing also the alcalde and the Ministers of Finance and State; and surrounded by Captain Cruz's light horse formed in a close double file of fours. Following them the rest of the officials of state, and judges and distinguished military and social ornaments of public and private life.

As the band struck up, and the movement began, like a bird of ill omen the *S. J. Pizzoni, Jr.*, the swiftest steamship of the Vesuvius line, glided into the harbor in plain view of the President and his train. Of course, there was nothing menacing about its arrival — a business firm does not go to war with a nation — but it reminded Señor Ortiz and others in those carriages that the Vesuvius Fruit Company was undoubtedly carrying something up its sleeve for them.

By the time the van of the procession had reached the government building, Captain Cronin, of the *S. J. Pizzoni, Jr.*, and Mr Vincenti, member of the Vesuvius Company, had landed and were pushing their way, bluff, hearty and nonchalant, through the crowd on the narrow sidewalk. Clad in white linen, big, debonair, with an air of good-humored authority, they made conspicuous figures among the dark mass of unimposing Costaraguans. They penetrated to within a few yards of the steps of the brown stone building Casa Moreno, the brown White House of Costaragua. Looking easily above the heads of the crowd, they perceived another that towered above the undersized natives. It was the fiery poll of Dicky Maloney against the wall close by the lower step, and his broad, seductive grin showed that he recognized their presence.

Dicky had attired himself becomingly for the festive occasion in a well-fitting black suit. Pasa was close by his side, her head covered with the ubiquitous black mantilla.

Mr. Vincenti looked at her attentively.

"Botticelli's Madonna," he remarked, gravely. "I wonder when she got into the game. I don't like his getting tangled with the woman. I hoped he would keep away from them."

Captain Cronin's laugh almost drew attention from the parade.

"With that head of hair! Keep away from the women! And a Maloney! Hasn't he got a license? But, nonsense aside, what do you think of the prospects? It's a species of filibustering out of my line."

Vincenti glanced again at Dicky's head and smiled.

"Rouge et noir," he said. "There you have it. Make your play, gentlemen. Our money is on the red."

"The lad's game," said Cronin, with a commending look at the tall, easy figure by the steps. "But 'tis all like fly-by-night theatricals to me. The talk's bigger than the stage; there's a smell of gasoline in the air, and they're their own audience and scene-shifters."

They ceased talking, for General Pilar had descended from the first carriage and had taken his stand upon the top step of Casa Morena. As the oldest member of the cabinet, custom had decreed that he should make the address of welcome, presenting the keys of the official residence to the President at its close.

General Pilar was the most distinguished citizen of the republic. Hero of three wars and innumerable revolutions, he was an honored guest at European courts and camps. An eloquent speaker and a friend to the people, he represented the highest type of the Costaraguans.

Holding in his hand the gilt keys of Casa Morena, he began his address in a historical form, touching upon each administration and the advance of civilization and prosperity from the first dim striving after liberty down to present times. Arriving at the régime of President Zarilla, at which point, according to precedent, he should have delivered a eulogy upon its wise conduct and the happiness of the people, General Pilar paused. Then he silently held up the bunch of keys high above his head, with his eyes closely regarding it. The ribbon with which they were bound fluttered in the breeze.

"It still blows," cried the speaker, exultantly. "Citizens of Costaragua, give thanks to the saints this night that our air is still free."

Thus disposing of Zarilla's administration, he abruptly reverted to that of Olivarra, Costaragua's most popular ruler. Olivarra had been assassinated nine years before while in the prime of life and usefulness. A faction of the Liberal party led by Zarilla himself had been accused of the deed. Whether guilty or not, it was eight years before the ambitious and scheming Zarilla had gained his goal.

Upon this theme General Pilar's eloquence was loosed. He drew the picture of the beneficent Olivarra with a loving hand. He reminded the people of the peace, the security and the happiness they had enjoyed during that period. He recalled in vivid detail and with significant contrast the last summer sojourn of President Olivarra in Puerto Rey, when his appearance at their *fiestas* was the signal for thundering *vivas* of love and approbation.

The first public expression of sentiment from the people that day followed. A low, sustained murmur went among them like the surf rolling along the shore.

"Ten dollars to a dinner at the Saint Charles." remarked Mr. Vincenti, "that *rouge* wins."

"I never bet against my own interests," said Captain Cronin, lighting a cigar. "Long-winded old boy, for his age. What's he talking about?"

"My Spanish," replied Vincenti, "runs about ten words to the minute; his is something around two hundred. Whatever he's saying, he's getting them warmed up."

"Friends and brothers," General Pilar was saying, "could I reach out my hand this day across the lamentable silence of the grave to Olivarra 'the Good,' to the ruler who was one of you, whose tears fell when you sorrowed, and whose smile followed your joy — I would bring him back to you, but — Olivarra is dead — dead at the hands of a craven assassin!"

The speaker turned and gazed boldly into the carriage of the President. His arm remained extended aloft as if to sustain his peroration. The President was listening, aghast, at this remarkable address of welcome. He was sunk back upon his seat, trembling with rage and dumb surprise, his dark hands tightly gripping the carriage cushions.

"Who says that Olivarra is dead?" suddenly cried the speaker, his voice, old as he was, sounding like a battle trumpet. "His body lies in the grave, but, to the people he loved he has bequeathed his spirit — yes, more — his learning, his courage, his kindness — yes, more — his youth, his image — people of Costaragua, have you forgotten the son of Olivarra?"

Cronin and Vincenti, watching closely, saw Dicky Maloney suddenly raise his hat, tear off his shock of red hair, leap up the steps and stand at the side of General Pilar. The Minister of War laid his arm across the young man's shoulders. All who had known President Olivarra saw again his same lion-like pose, the same frank, undaunted expression, the same high forehead with the peculiar line of the clustering, crisp black hair.

General Pilar was an experienced orator. He seized the moment of breathless silence that preceded the storm.

"Citizens of Costaragua," he trumpeted, holding aloft the keys to Casa Morena, "I am here to deliver these keys — the keys to your homes and liberty — to your chosen President. Shall I deliver them to Enrico Olivarra's assassin, or to his son?"

"Olivarra! Olivarra!" the crowd shrieked and howled. All vociferated the magic name — men, women, children and the parrots.

And the enthusiasm was not confined to the blood of the plebs. Colonel Rocas ascended the steps and laid his sword theatrically at young Ramon Olivarra's feet. Four members of the cabinet embraced him. Captain Cruz gave a command and twenty of El Ciento Huilando dismounted and arranged themselves in a cordon about the steps of Casa Morena.

But Ramon Olivarra seized that moment to prove himself a born genius and politician. He waved those soldiers aside, and descended the steps to the street. There, without losing his dignity or the distinguished elegance that the loss of his red hair brought him, he took the proletariat to his bosom — the barefooted, the dirty, Indians, Caribs, babies, beggars, old, young, saints, soldiers and sinners — he missed none of them.

While this act of the drama was being produced the scene-shifters had been busy at the duties assigned them. Two of Cruz's dragoons had seized the bridle reins of President Zarilla's horses, others formed a close guard, and they galloped off with the tyrant and his two malodorous ministers. No doubt a place had been prepared for them. There are quite a number of well-barred stone apartments in Puerto Rey.

"*Rouge* wins," said Mr. Vincenti, calmly lighting another cigar.

Captain Cronin had been intently watching the vicinity of the steps for some time.

"Good boy!" he exclaimed, suddenly, as if relieved. "I was wondering if he was going to forget his Kathleen Mavourneen."

Young Olivarra had reascended the steps and spoken a few words to General Pilar. That distinguished veteran descended to the walk and approached Pasa, who still stood, calm and wonder-eyed, where Dicky had left her. With his hat in his hand, and his medals and decorations shining on his breast, the general gave her his arm, and they went up the steps together. And then Ramon Olivarra stepped forward and took both her hands before all the people.

And while the cheering was breaking out afresh everywhere Captain Cronin and Mr. Vincenti turned and walked back toward the landing where the ship's gig was waiting for them.

"There'll be another *Presidente proclamada* in the morning," said Vincenti, musingly. "As a rule, they are not as reliable as the elected ones. But this youngster seems to have good stuff in him. He planned and maneuvered the whole campaign. Olivarra's widow, you know, was wealthy. She gave the boy eight years of the best education in the States. The company hunted him up and backed him in the little game."

"It's a glorious thing," said Cronin, half jestingly, "to be able to discharge a government and insert one of your own choosing, these days."

"It's business," stated Vincenti, stopping to offer his cigar to a monkey swinging from a lime tree; "and that is what moves the world of to-day. That extra *real* on the price of bananas had to go. We took the quickest way of removing it."

NOTES AND COMMENTS

For a review of literary evaluation and notes and comments related to "Rouge et Noir," reference is made to Dr. Porter's essay, Part II, "The Imprisoned Splendor," *ante,* pp. 29–32.

The Duplicity
of Hargraves

When Major Pendleton Talbot, of Mobile, sir, and his daughter, Miss Lydia Talbot, came to Washington to reside, they selected, for a boarding place, a house that stood fifty yards back from one of the quietest avenues. It was an old fashioned brick building, with a portico upheld by tall white pillars. The yard was shaded by stately locusts and elms, and a catalpa tree, in season, rained its pink and white blossoms upon the grass. Rows of high box bushes lined the fence and walks. It was the Southern style and aspect of the place that pleased the eyes of the Talbots.

In this pleasant private boarding house they engaged rooms, including a study for Major Talbot, who was adding the finishing chapters to his book, "Anecdotes and Reminiscences of the Alabama Army, Bench, and Bar."

Major Talbot was of the old, old South. The present day had little interest or excellence in his eyes. His mind lived in that period before the Civil War, when the Talbots owned thousands of acres of

First published in *Junior Munsey* for February 1902, as by O. Henry.

Thirteenth of twenty-five stories in *Sixes and Sevens*, published by Doubleday, Page & Company, Garden City, New York, in 1911.

fine cotton land and the slaves to till them; when the family mansion
was the scene of princely hospitality, and drew its guests from the aristocracy of the South. Out of that period he had brought all its old
pride and scruples of honor, an antiquated and punctilious polite-
ness, and (you would think) its wardrobe.

Such clothes were surely never made within fifty years. The
major was tall, but whenever he made that wonderful, archaic gen-
uflexion he called a bow, the corners of his frock coat swept the
floor. That garment was a surprise even to Washington, which has
long ago ceased to shy at the frocks and broad brimmed hats of
Southern Congressmen. One of the boarders christened it a "Father
Hubbard," and it certainly *was* high in the waist and full in the skirt.

But the major, with all his queer clothes, his immense area of
pleated, raveling shirt bosom, and the little black string tie with the
bow always slipping on one side, was both smiled at and liked in
Mrs. Vardeman's select boarding house. Some of the young department clerks would often "string him," as they called it, getting him
started upon the subject dearest to him — the traditions and history
of his beloved Southland. During his talks he would quote freely
from the "Anecdotes and Reminiscences." But they were very careful not to let him see their designs, for, in spite of his sixty-eight
years, he could make the boldest of them uncomfortable under the
steady regard of his piercing gray eyes.

Miss Lydia was a plump little old maid of thirty five, with
smoothly drawn, tightly twisted hair that made her look still older.
Old fashioned, too, she was; but ante bellum glory did not radiate
from her as it did from the major. She possessed a thrifty common
sense; and it was she who handled the finances of the family, and
met all comers when there were bills to pay. The major regarded
board bills and wash bills as contemptible nuisances. They kept
coming in so persistently and so often. Why, the major wanted to
know, could they not be filed and paid in a lump sum at some convenient period — say when the "Anecdotes and Reminiscences" had
been published and paid for? Miss Lydia would calmly go on with
her sewing and say, "We'll pay as we go as long as the money lasts,
and then perhaps they'll have to lump it."

Most of Mrs. Vardeman's boarders were away during the day,
being nearly all department clerks and business men; but there was one
of them who was about the house a great deal from morning to night.
This was a young man named Henry Hopkins Hargraves — every one
in the house addressed him by his full name — who was engaged at one
of the popular vaudeville theaters. Vaudeville has risen to such a respectable plane in the last few years, and Mr. Hargraves was such a

modest and well mannered person, that Mrs. Vardeman could find no objection to enrolling him upon her list of boarders.

At the theater Hargraves was known as an all round dialect comedian, having a large repertoire of German, Irish, Swede, and black face specialties. But Mr. Hargraves was ambitious, and often spoke of his great desire to succeed in legitimate comedy.

This young man appeared to conceive a strong fancy for Major Talbot. Whenever that gentleman would begin his Southern reminiscences, or repeat some of the liveliest of the anecdotes, Hargraves could always be found, the most attentive among his listeners.

For a time the major showed an inclination to discourage the advances of the "play actor," as he privately termed him; but soon the young man's agreeable manner and indubitable appreciation of the old gentleman's stories completely won him over.

It was not long before the two were like old chums. The major set apart each afternoon to read to him the manuscript of his book. During the anecdotes Hargraves never failed to laugh at exactly the right point. The major was moved to declare to Miss Lydia one day that young Hargraves possessed remarkable perception and a gratifying respect for the old régime. And when it came to talking of those old days — if Major Talbot liked to talk, Mr. Hargraves was entranced to listen.

Like almost all old people who talk of the past, the major loved to linger over details. In describing the splendid, almost royal, days of the old planters, he would hesitate until he had recalled the name of the negro who held his horse, or the exact date of certain minor happenings, or the number of bales of cotton raised in such a year; but Hargraves never grew impatient or lost interest. On the contrary, he would advance questions on a variety of subjects connected with the life of that time, and he never failed to extract ready replies.

The fox hunts, the 'possum suppers, the hoe downs and jubilees in the negro quarters, the banquets in the plantation house hall, when invitations went for fifty miles around; the occasional feuds with the neighboring gentry, the major's duel with Rathbone Culbertson about Kitty Chalmers, who afterwards married a Thwaite of South Carolina; the private yacht races for fabulous sums on Mobile Bay; the quaint beliefs, improvident habits, and loyal virtues of the old slaves — all these were subjects that held both the major and Hargraves absorbed for hours at a time.

Sometimes, at night, when the young man would be coming up stairs to his room after his turn at the theater was over, the major would appear at the door of his study and beckon archly to him.

Going in, Hargraves would find a little table set with a decanter, sugar bowl, fruit, and a big bunch of fresh green mint.

"It occurred to me," the major would begin — he was always ceremonious — "That perhaps you might have found your duties at the — at your place of occupation sufficiently arduous to enable you, Mr. Hargraves, to appreciate what the poet might well have had in his mind when he wrote, 'tired Nature's sweet restorer' — one of our Southern juleps."

It was a fascination to Hargraves to watch him make it. He took rank among artists when he began, and he never varied the process. With what delicacy he bruised the mint; with what exquisite nicety he estimated the ingredients; with what solicitous care he capped the compound with the scarlet fruit glowing against the dark green fringe! And then the hospitality and grace with which he offered it, after the selected oat straws had been plunged into its tinkling depths!

After about four months in Washington, Miss Lydia discovered, one morning, that they were almost without money. The "Anecdotes and Reminiscences" was completed, but publishers had not jumped at the collected gems of Alabama sense and wit. The rental of a small house which they still owned in Mobile was two months in arrears. Their board money for the month would be due in three days. Miss Lydia called her father to a consultation.

"No money?" said he with a surprised look. "It is quite annoying to be called on so frequently for these petty sums. Really, I —"

The major searched his pockets. He found only a two dollar bill, which he returned to his vest pocket.

"I must attend to this at once, Lydia," he said. "Kindly get me my umbrella, and I will go down town immediately. The Congressman from our district, General Fulghum, assured me some days ago that he would use his influence to get my book published at an early date. I will go to his hotel at once and see what arrangement has been made."

With a sad smile, Miss Lydia watched him button the "Father Hubbard," and depart, pausing at the door, as he always did, to bow profoundly.

That evening, at dark, he returned. It seemed that Congressman Fulghum had seen the publisher who had the major's manuscript for reading. That person had said that if the Anecdotes, etc., were carefully pruned down about one half, in order to eliminate the sectional and class prejudice with which the book was dyed from end to end, he might consider its publication.

The major was in a white heat of anger, but regained his equanimity, according to his code of manners, as soon as he was in Miss Lydia's presence.

"We must have money," said Miss Lydia, with a little wrinkle above her nose. "Give me the two dollars, and I will telegraph to Uncle Ralph for some tonight."

The major drew a small envelope from his upper vest pocket and tossed it on the table.

"Perhaps it was injudicious," he said mildly, "but the sum was so merely nominal that I bought tickets to the theater tonight. It's a new war drama, Lydia. I thought you would be pleased to witness its first production in Washington. I am told that the South has very fair treatment in the play. I confess I should like to see the performance myself."

Miss Lydia threw up her hands in silent despair.

Still, as the tickets were bought, they might as well be used. So that evening, as they sat in the theater listening to the lively overture, even Miss Lydia was minded to relegate their troubles, for the hour, to second place. The major in spotless linen, with his extraordinary coat showing only where it was closely buttoned, and his white hair smoothly roached, looked really fine and distinguished. The curtain went up on the first act of "A Magnolia Flower," revealing a typical Southern plantation scene, Major Talbot betrayed some interest.

"Oh, see!" exclaimed Miss Lydia, nudging his arm, and pointing to her program.

The major put on his glasses and read the line in the cast of characters that her finger indicated.

Colonel Webster Calhoun. . . H. Hopkins Hargraves.

"It's our Mr. Hargraves," said Miss Lydia. "It must be his first appearance in what he calls 'the legitimate.' I'm so glad for him."

Not until the second act did *Colonel Webster Calhoun* appear upon the stage. When he made his entry Major Talbot gave an audible sniff, glared at him, and seemed to freeze solid. Miss Lydia uttered a little, ambiguous squeak and crumpled her program in her hand. For *Colonel Calhoun* was made up as nearly resembling Major Talbot as one pea does another. The long, thin, white hair, curly at the ends, and the aristocratic beak of a nose, the crumpled, wide raveling shirt front, the string tie with the bow nearly under one ear, were almost exactly duplicated. And then, to clinch the imitation, he wore the twin to the major's supposed to be unparalleled coat. High collared, baggy, empire waisted, ample skirted, hanging a foot lower in front than behind, the garment could have been designed from no other pattern. From then on, the major and Miss Lydia sat bewitched, and saw the counterfeit presentment of a haughty Talbot "dragged," as the major afterwards expressed it, "through the slanderous mire of a corrupt stage."

Mr. Hargraves had used his opportunities well. He had caught the major's little idiosyncrasies of speech, accent, and intonation, and his pompous courtliness, to perfection — exaggerating all to the purposes of the stage. When he performed that marvelous bow that the major fondly imagined to be the pink of all salutations, the audience sent forth a sudden round of hearty applause.

Miss Lydia sat immovable, not daring to glance towards her father. Sometimes her hand next to him would be laid against her cheek, as if to conceal the smile which, in spite of her disapproval, she could not entirely suppress.

The culmination of Hargraves' audacious imitation took place in the third act. The scene is where *Colonel Calhoun* entertains a few of the neighboring planters in his "den."

Standing at a table in the center of the stage, with his friends grouped about him, he delivers that inimitable, rambling, character monologue so famous in "A Magnolia Flower," at the same time that he deftly makes juleps for the party.

Major Talbot, sitting quietly, but white with indignation, heard his best stories retold, his pet theories and hobbies advanced and expanded, and the cream of the "Anecdotes and Reminiscences" served, exaggerated and garbled. His favorite narrative — that of his duel with Rathbone Culbertson — was not omitted, and it was delivered with more fire, egotism, and gusto than the major himself put into it.

The monologue concluded with a quaint, delicious, witty little lecture on the art of concocting a julep, illustrated by the act. Here Major Talbot's delicate but showy science was reproduced to a hair's breadth — from his dainty handling of the fragrant weed — "the one thousandth part of a grain too much pressure, gentlemen, and you extract the bitterness, instead of the aroma, of this heaven bestowed plant" — to his solicitous selection of the oaten straws.

At the close of the scene the audience raised a tumultuous roar of appreciation. The portrayal of the type was so exact, so sure and thorough, that the leading characters in the play were forgotten. After repeated calls, Hargraves came before the curtain and bowed, his rather boyish face bright and flushed with the knowledge of success.

At last Miss Lydia turned and looked at the major. His thin

nostrils were working like the gills of a fish. He laid both shaking hands upon the arms of his chair to rise.

"We will go, Lydia," he said chokingly. "This is an abominable — desecration."

Before he could rise, she pulled him back into his seat.

"We will stay it out," she declared. "Do you want to advertise the copy by exhibiting the original coat?" So they remained to the end.

Hargraves' success must have kept him up late that night, for neither at the breakfast nor at the dinner table did he appear.

About three in the afternoon he tapped at the door of Major Talbot's study. The major opened it, and Hargraves walked in with his hands full of the morning papers — too full of his triumph to notice anything unusual in the major's demeanor.

"I put it all over 'em last night, major," he began exultantly. "I had my inning, and I think I scored. Here's what the *Post* says:

> His conception and portrayal of the old time Southern colo-
> nel, with his absurd grandiloquence, his eccentric garb, his quaint
> idioms and phrases, his moth eaten pride of family, and his really
> kind heart, fastidious sense of honor, and lovable simplicity, is the
> best delineation of a character rôle on the boards today. The coat
> worn by *Colonel Calhoun* is itself nothing less than an evolution of
> genius. Mr. Hargraves has captured his public.

How does that sound, major, for a first nighter?"

"I had the *honor*"— the major's voice sounded ominously frigid — "of witnessing your very remarkable performance, sir, last night."

Hargraves looked disconcerted.

"You were there? I didn't know you ever — I didn't know you cared for the theater. Oh, I say, Major Talbot," he exclaimed frankly, "don't you be offended. I admit I did get a lot of pointers from you that helped me out wonderfully in the part. But it's a type, you know — not individual. The way the audience caught on shows that. Half the patrons of that theater are Southerners. They recognized it."

"Mr. Hargraves," said the major, who had remained standing, "you have put upon me an unpardonable insult. You have burlesqued my person, grossly betrayed my confidence, and misused my hospitality. If I thought you possessed the faintest conception of what is the sign manual of a gentleman, or what is due one, I would call you out, sir, old as I am. I will ask you to leave the room, sir."

The actor appeared to be slightly bewildered, and seemed hardly to take in the full meaning of the old gentleman's words.

"I am truly sorry you took offense," he said regretfully. "Up here we don't look at things just as you people do. I know men who would buy out half the house to have their personality put on the stage so the public would recognize it."

"They are not from Alabama, sir," said the major haughtily.

"Perhaps not. I have a pretty good memory, major; let me quote a few lines from your book. In response to a toast at a banquet given in — Milledgeville, I believe — you uttered, and intend to have printed, these words:

> The Northern man is utterly without sentiment or warmth except in so far as the feelings may be turned to his own commercial profit. He will suffer without resentment any imputation cast upon the honor of himself or his loved ones that does not bear with it the consequence of pecuniary loss. In his charity, he gives with a liberal hand; but it must be heralded with the trumpet and chronicled in brass.

Do you think that picture is *fairer* than the one you saw of *Colonel Calhoun* last night?"

"The description," said the major, frowning, "is — not without grounds. Some exag — latitude must be allowed in public speaking."

"And in public acting," replied Hargraves.

"That is not the point," persisted the major, unrelenting. "It was a personal caricature. I positively decline to overlook it, sir."

"Major Talbot," said Hargraves, with a winning smile, "I wish you would understand me. I want you to know that I never dreamed of insulting you. In my profession, all life belongs to me. I take what I want, and what I can, and return it over the footlights. Now, if you will, let's let it go at that. I came in to see you about something else. We've been pretty good friends for some months, and I'm going to take the risk of offending you again. I know you are hard up for money — never mind how I found out; a boarding house is no place to keep such matters secret — and I want you to let me help you out of the pinch. I've been there often enough myself. I've been getting a fair salary all the season, and I've saved some money. You're welcome to a couple of hundred — or even more — until you get — "

"Stop!" commanded the major, with his arm outstretched. "It seems that my book didn't lie, after all. You think your money salve will heal all the hurts of honor. Under no circumstances would I accept a loan from a casual acquaintance; and as to you, sir, I would starve before I would consider your insulting offer of a financial adjustment of the circumstances we have discussed. I beg to repeat my request relative to your quitting the apartment."

Hargraves took his departure without another word. He also

left the house the same day, moving, as Mrs. Vardeman explained at the supper table, nearer the vicinity of the down town theater, where "A Magnolia Flower" was booked for a week's run.

Critical was the situation with Major Talbot and Miss Lydia. There was no one in Washington to whom the major's scruples allowed him to apply for a loan. Miss Lydia wrote a letter to Uncle Ralph, but it was doubtful whether that relative's constricted affairs would permit him to furnish help. The major was forced to make an apologetic address to Mrs. Vardeman regarding the delayed payment for board, referring to "delinquent rentals" and "delayed remittances" in a rather confused strain.

Deliverance came from an entirely unexpected source.

Late one afternoon the door maid came up and announced an old colored man who wanted to see Major Talbot. The major asked that he be sent up to his study. Soon an old darky appeared in the doorway, with his hat in hand, bowing, and scraping with one clumsy foot. He was quite decently dressed in a baggy suit of black. His big, coarse shoes shone with a metallic luster suggestive of stove polish. His bushy wool was gray — almost white. After middle life, it is difficult to estimate the age of a negro. This one might have seen as many years as had Major Talbot.

"I be bound you don't know me, Mars' Pendleton," were his first words.

The major rose and came forward at the old, familiar style of address. It was one of the old plantation darkies without a doubt; but they had been widely scattered, and he could not recall the voice or face.

"I don't believe I do," he said kindly — "unless you will assist my memory."

"Don't you 'member Cindy's Mose, Mars' Pendleton, what 'migrated 'mediately after de war?"

"Wait a moment," said the major, rubbing his forehead with the tips of his fingers. He loved to recall everything connected with those beloved days. "Cindy's Mose," he reflected. "You worked among the horses — breaking the colts. Yes, I remember now. After the surrender, you took the name of — don't prompt me — Mitchell, and went to the West — to Nebraska."

"Yassir, yassir," — the old man's face stretched with a delighted grin — "dat's him, dat's it. Newbraska. Dat's me — Mose Mitchell. Old Uncle Mose Mitchell, dey calls me now. Old mars', your pa, gimme a pah of dem mule colts when I lef', fur to staht me goin' with. You 'member dem colts, Mars' Pendleton?"

"I don't seem to recall the colts," said the major. "You know, I was married the first year of the war, and living at the old Follinsbee place. But sit down, sit down, Uncle Mose. I'm glad to see you. I hope you have prospered."

Uncle Mose took a chair and laid his hat carefully on the floor beside it.

"Yassir; of late I done mouty famous. When I first got to Newbraska, dey folks come all roun' me to see dem mule colts. Dey ain't see no mules like dem in Newbraska. I sold dem mules for three hunderd dollars. Yassir — three hunderd.

"Den I open a blacksmith shop, suh, and made some money, and bought some lan'. Me and my old 'oman done raised up seb'm chillun, and all doin' well 'cept two of 'em what died. Fo' year ago a railroad come along and staht a town slam ag'inst my lan', and, sur, Mars' Pendleton, Uncle Mose am worth leb'm thousand dollars in money, property, and lan'."

"I'm glad to hear it," said the major heartily. "Glad to hear it."

"And dat little baby of yo'n, Mars Pendleton — one what you name Miss Lyddy — I be bound dat little tad done grown up tell nobody wouldn't know her."

The major stepped to the door and called: "Lydia dear, will you come?"

Miss Lydia, looking quite grown up, and a little worried, came in from her room.

"Dar, now! What'd I tell you? I knowed dat baby done be plum growed up. You don't 'member Uncle Mose, child?"

"This is Aunt Cindy's Mose, Lydia," explained the major. "He left Sunnymead for the West when you were two years old."

"Well," said Miss Lydia, "I can hardly be expected to remember you, Uncle Mose, at that age. And, as you say, I'm 'plum growed up,' and was a blessed long time ago. But I'm glad to see you, even if I can't remember you."

And she was. And so was the major. Something alive and tangible had come to link them with the happy past. The three sat and talked over the olden times, the major and Uncle Mose correcting or prompting each other as they reviewed the plantation scenes and days.

The major inquired what the old man was doing so far from his home."

"Uncle Mose am a delicate," he explained, "to de grand Baptis' convention in dis city. I never preached none, but, bein' a 'residin' elder in de church, and able fur to pay my own expenses, dey sent me along."

"And how did you know we were in Washington?" inquired Miss Lydia.

"Dey's a cullud man works in de hotel whar I stops, what comes f'om Mobile. He told me he seen Mars' Pendleton comin' outen dish here house one mawnin'.

"What I come fur," continued Uncle Mose, reaching into his pocket — "besides de sight of home folks — was to pay Mars' Pendleton what I owes him."

"Owe me?" said the major, in surprise.

"Yassir — three hunderd dollars." He handed the major a roll of bills. "When I lef' old mars' says: 'Take dem mule colts, Mose, and, if it be so you gits able, pay fur 'em.' Yassir — dem was his words. De war had done lef' old mars' po' hisself. Old mars' bein' 'long ago dead, de debt descends to Mars' Pendleton. Three hunderd dollars. Uncle Mose is plenty able to pay now. When dat railroad buy my lan' I laid off to pay fur dem mules. Count de money, Mars Pendleton. Dat's what I sold dem mules fur. Yassir."

Tears were in Major Talbot's eyes. He took Uncle Mose's hand and laid his other upon his shoulder.

"Dear, faithful old servitor," he said in an unsteady voice, "I don't mind saying to you that 'Mars'' Pendleton spent his last dollar in the world a week ago. We will accept this money, Uncle Mose, since, in a way, it is a sort of payment, as well as a token of the loyalty and devotion of the old régime. Lydia, my dear, take the money. You are better fitted than I to manage its expenditure."

"Take it, honey," said Uncle Mose. "Hit belongs to you. Hit's Talbot money."

After Uncle Mose had gone, Miss Lydia had a good cry — for joy; and the major turned his face to a corner, and smoked his clay pipe volcanically.

The succeeding days saw the Talbots restored to peace and ease. Miss Lydia's face lost its worried look. The major appeared in a new frock coat, in which he looked like a wax figure personifying the memory of his golden age. Another publisher who read the manuscript of the "Anecdotes and Reminiscences" thought that, with a little retouching and toning down of the highlights, he could make a really bright and salable volume of it. Altogether, the situation was comfortable, and not without the touch of hope that is often sweeter than arrived blessings.

One day, about a week after their piece of good luck, a maid brought a letter for Miss Lydia to her room. The postmark showed that it was from New York. Not knowing any one there, Miss Lydia, in a mild flutter of wonder, sat down by her table and opened the letter with her scissors. This was what she read:

DEAR MISS TALBOT:

I thought you might be glad to learn of my good fortune. I have received and accepted an offer of two hundred dollars per week by a New York stock company to play *Colonel Calhoun* in "A Magnolia Flower."

There is something else I wanted you to know. I guess you'd better not tell Major Talbot. I was anxious to make him some amends for the great help he was to me in studying the part, and for the bad humor he was in about it. He refused to let me, so I did it anyhow. I could easily spare the three hundred.

Sincerely yours,

H. HOPKINS HARGRAVES.

P.S. How did I play *Uncle Mose?*

Major Talbot, passing through the hall, saw Miss Lydia's door open, and stopped.

"Any mail for us this morning, Lydia dear?" he asked.

Miss Lydia slid the letter beneath a fold of her dress.

"The Mobile *Chronicle* came," she said promptly. "It's on the table in your study."

NOTES AND COMMENTS

For a review of literary evaluation and notes and comments related to "The Duplicity of Hargraves," reference is made to Dr. Porter's essay, Part II, "The Imprisoned Splendor," *ante.* pp. 39.

The Marionettes

The policeman was standing at the corner of Twenty-fourth
Street and a prodigiously dark alley near where the elevated
railroad crosses the street. The time was two o'clock in the
morning; the outlook a stretch of cold, drizzling, unsociable black-
ness until the dawn.

A man, wearing a long overcoat, with his hat tilted down in
front, and carrying something in one hand, walked softly but rapidly
out of the black alley. The policeman accosted him civilly, but with
the assured air that is linked with conscious authority. The hour, the
alley's musty reputation, the pedestrian's haste, the burden he carried — these easily combined into the "suspicious circumstances"
that required illumination at the officer's hands.

The "suspect" halted readily and tilted back his hat, exposing,
in the flicker of the electric lights, an emotionless smooth countenance with a rather long nose and steady dark eyes. Thrusting his
gloved hand into a side pocket of his overcoat, he drew out a card
and handed it to the policeman. Holding it to catch the uncertain

First published in *Black Cat* magazine for April 1902, as by O. Henry.

Fifth of stories and sketches in *Rolling Stones,* published by Doubleday, Page &
Company, Garden City, New York, in 1912.

light, the officer read the name "Charles Spencer James, M.D." The
street and number of the address were of a neighborhood so solid
and respectable as to subdue even curiosity. The policeman's downward glance at the article carried in the doctor's hand — a handsome medicine case of black leather, with small silver mountings —
further endorsed the guarantee of the card.

"All right, Doctor," said the officer, stepping aside, with an air
of bulky affability. "Orders are to be extra careful. Good many bur-
glaries and hold-ups lately. Bad night to be out. Not so cold, but —
clammy."

With a formal inclination of his head, and a word or two corro-
borative of the officer's estimate of the weather, Dr. James continued his somewhat rapid progress. Three times that night had a pa-
trolman accepted his professional card and the sight of his paragon
of a medicine case as vouchers for his honesty of person and purpose.
Had any one of those officers seen fit, on the morrow, to test the evidence of that card he would have found it borne out by the doctor's
name on a handsome door-plate, his presence, calm and well
dressed, in his well-equipped office — provided it were not too early,
Dr. James being a late riser — and the testimony of the neighborhood to his good citizenship, his devotion to his family, and his success as a practitioner the two years he had lived among them.

Therefore, it would have much surprised any one of those zeal-
ous guardians of the peace could they have taken a peep into that
immaculate medicine case. Upon opening it, the first articles to be
seen would have been an elegant set of the latest conceived tools
used by the "box man," as the ingenious safe burglar now denomi-
nates himself. Specially designed and constructed were the imple-
ments — the short but powerful "jimmy," the collection of curiously
fashioned keys, the blued drills and punches of the finest temper —
capable of eating their way into chilled steel as a mouse eats into a
cheese, and the clamps that fasten like a leech to the polished door of
a safe and pull out the combination knob as a dentist extracts a
tooth. In a little pouch in the inner side of the "medicine" case was
a four-ounce vial of nitroglycerine, now half empty. Underneath the
tools was a mass of crumpled bank-notes and a few handfuls of gold
coin, the money, altogether, amounting to eight hundred and thirty
dollars.

To a very limited circle of friends, Dr. James was known as
"The Swell 'Greek.'" Half of the mysterious term was a tribute to
his cool and gentlemanlike manners; the other half denoted, in the
argot of the brotherhood, the leader, the planner, the one who, by
the power and prestige of his address and position, secured the infor-

mation upon which they based their plans and desperate enterprises.

Of this selected circle the other members were Skitsie Morgan and Gum Decke., expert "box men," and Leopold Pretzfelder, a jeweller down town, who manipulated the "sparklers" and other ornaments collected by the working trio. All good and loyal men, as loose-tongued as Memnon and as fickle as the North Star.

That night's work had not been considered by the firm to have yielded more than a moderate repayal for their pains. An old-style two-story side-bolt safe in the dingy office of a very wealthy old-style dry-goods firm on a Saturday night should have excreted more than twenty-five hundred dollars. But that was all they found, and they had divided it, the three of them, into equal shares upon the spot, as was their custom. Ten or twelve thousand was what they expected. But one of the proprietors had proved to be just a trifle too old-style. Just after dark he had carried home in a shirt box most of the funds on hand.

Dr. James proceeded up Twenty-fourth Street, which was, to all appearance, depopulated. Even the theatrical folk, who affect this district as a place of residence, were long since abed. The drizzle had accumulated upon the street; puddles of it among the stones received the fire of the arc lights, and returned it, shattered into a myriad liquid spangles. A captious wind, shower-soaked and chilling, coughed from the laryngeal flues between the houses.

As the practitioner's foot struck even with the corner of a tall brick residence of more pretension than its fellows, the front door popped open, and a bawling negress clattered down the steps to the pavement. Some medley of words came from her mouth, addressed, like as not, to herself — the recourse of her race when alone and beset by evil. She looked to be one of that old vassal class of the South — voluble, familiar, loyal, irrepressible; her person pictured it — fat, neat, aproned, kerchiefed.

This sudden apparition, spewed from the silent house, reached the bottom of the steps as Dr. James came opposite. Her brain transferring its energies from sound to sight, she ceased her clamor and fixed her pop-eyes upon the case the doctor carried.

"Bress de Lawd!" was the benison the sight drew from her. "Is you a doctor, suh?"

"Yes, I am a physician," said Dr. James, pausing.

"Den fo' God's sake come and see Mister Chandler, suh. He done had a fit or sump'n. He layin' jist like he wuz dead. Miss Amy sont me to get a doctor. Lawd know whar old Cindy'd a skeared one up from, if you, suh, hadn't come along. Ef old Mars' knowed one

ten-hunderdth part of dese doins dey'd be shootin' gwine on, suh —
pistol shootin' — leb'm feet marked off on de ground, and ev'ybody
a-duelin'. And dat po' lamb, Miss Amy —"

"Lead the way," said Dr. James, setting his foot upon the step,
"if you want me as a doctor. As an auditor I'm not open to engage-
ments."

The negress preceded him into the house and up a flight of
thickly carpeted stairs. Twice they came to dimly lighted branching
hallways. At the second one the now panting conductress turned
down a hall, stopping at a door and opening it.

"I done brought de doctor, Miss Amy."

Dr. James entered the room, and bowed slightly to a young lady
standing by the side of a bed. He set his medicine case upon a chair,
removed his overcoat, throwing it over the case and the back of the
chair, and advanced with quiet self-possession to the bedside.

There lay a man, sprawling as he had fallen — a man dressed
richly in the prevailing mode, with only his shoes removed; lying relaxed, and as still as the dead.

There emanated from Dr. James an aura of calm force and reserve strength that was as manna in the desert to the weak and desolate among his patrons. Always had women, especially, been attracted by something in his sick-room manner. It was not the
indulgent suavity of the fashionable healer, but a manner of poise, of
sureness, of ability to overcome fate, of deference and protection and
devotion. There was an exploring magnetism in his steadfast, luminous brown eyes; a latent authority in the impassive, even priestly,
tranquillity of his smooth countenance that outwardly fitted him for
the part of confidant and consoler. Sometimes, at his first professional visit, women would tell him where they hid their diamonds at
night from the burglars.

With the ease of much practice, Dr. James's unroving eyes estimated the order and quality of the room's furnishings. The ap-
pointments were rich and costly. The same glance had secured cognizance of the lady's appearance. She was small and scarcely past
twenty. Her face possessed the title to a winsome prettiness, now ob-
scured by (you would say) rather a fixed melancholy than the more
violent imprint of a sudden sorrow. Upon her forehead, above one
eyebrow, was a livid bruise, suffered, the physician's eye told him,
within the past six hours.

Dr. James's fingers went to the man's wrist. His almost vocal
eyes questioned the lady.

"I am Mrs. Chandler," she responded, speaking with the plaintive Southern slur and intonation. "My husband was taken sud-

denly ill about ten minutes before you came. He has had attacks of heart trouble before — some of them were very bad." His clothed state and the late hour seemed to prompt her to further explanation. "He had been out late; to — a supper, I believe."

Dr. James now turned his attention to his patient. In whichever of his "professions" he happened to be engaged he was wont to honor the "case" or the "job" with his whole interest.

The sick man appeared to be about thirty. His countenance bore a look of boldness and dissipation, but was not without a symmetry of feature and the fine lines drawn by a taste and indulgence in humor that gave the redeeming touch. There was an odor of spilled wine about his clothes.

The physician laid back his outer garments, and then, with a penknife, slit the shirt-front from collar to waist. The obstacles cleared, he laid his ear to the heart and listened intently.

"Mitral regurgitation?" he said, softly, when he rose. The words ended with the rising inflection of uncertainty. Again he listened long; and this time he said, "Mitral insufficiency," with the accent of an assured diagnosis.

"Madam," he began, in the reassuring tones that had so often allayed anxiety, "there is a probability — " As he slowly turned his head to face the lady, he saw her fall, white and swooning, into the arms of the old negress.

"Po' lamb! po' lamb! Has dey done killed Aunt Cindy's own blessed child? May de Lawd 'stroy wid his wrath dem what stole her away; what break dat angel heart; what left —"

"Lift her feet," said Dr. James, assisting to support the drooping form. "Where is her room? She must be put to bed."

"In here, suh." The woman nodded her kerchiefed head toward a door. "Dat's Miss Amy's room."

They carried her in there, and laid her on the bed. Her pulse was faint, but regular. She passed from the swoon, without recovering consciousness, into a profound slumber.

"She is quite exhausted," said the physician. "Sleep is a good remedy. When she wakes, give her a toddy — with an egg in it, if she can take it. How did she get that bruise upon her forehead?"

"She done got a lick there, suh. De po' lamb fell — No, suh" — the old woman's racial mutability swept her into a sudden flare of indignation — "old Cindy aint gwineter lie for dat debble. He done it, suh. May de Lawd wither de hand what — dar now! Cindy promise her sweet lamb she aint gwine tell. Miss Amy got hurt, suh, on de head."

Dr. James stepped to a stand where a handsome lamp burned, and turned the flame low.

"Stay here with your mistress," he ordered, "and keep quiet so she will sleep. If she wakes, give her the toddy. If she grows any weaker, let me know. There is something strange about it."

"Dar's mo' strange t'ings dan dat 'round here," began the negress, but the physician hushed her in a seldom-employed peremptory, concentrated voice with which he had often allayed hysteria itself. He returned to the other room, closing the door softly behind him. The man on the bed had not moved, but his eyes were open. His lips seemed to form words. Dr. James bent his head to listen. "The money! the money!" was what they were whispering.

"Can you understand what I say?" asked the doctor, speaking low, but distinctly.

The head nodded slightly.

"I am a physician, sent for by your wife. You are Mr. Chandler, I am told. You are quite ill. You must not excite or distress yourself at all."

The patient's eyes seemed to beckon to him. The doctor stooped to catch the same faint words.

"The money — the twenty thousand dollars."

"Where is this money? — in the bank?"

The eyes expressed a negative. "Tell her" — the whisper was growing fainter — "the twenty-thousand dollars — her money" — his eyes wandered about the room.

"You have placed this money somewhere?" — Dr. James's voice was toiling like a siren's to conjure the secret from the man's failing intelligence — "Is it in this room?"

He thought he saw a fluttering assent in the dimming eyes. The pulse under his fingers was as fine and small as a silk thread.

There arose in Dr. James's brain and heart the instincts of his other profession. Promptly, as he acted in everything, he decided to learn the whereabouts of this money, and at the calculated and certain cost of a human life.

Drawing from his pocket a little pad of prescription blanks, he scribbled upon one of them a formula suited, according to the best practice, to the needs of the sufferer. Going to the door of the inner room, he softly called the old woman, gave her the prescription, and bade her take it to some drug store and fetch the medicine.

When she had gone, muttering to herself, the doctor stepped to the bedside of the lady. She still slept soundly; her pulse was a little stronger; her forehead was cool, save where the inflammation of the bruise extended, and a slight moisture covered it. Unless disturbed, she would yet sleep for hours. He found the key in the door, and locked it after him when he returned.

Dr. James looked at his watch. He could call half an hour his own, since before that time the old woman could scarcely return from her mission. Then he sought and found water in a pitcher and a glass tumbler. Opening his medicine case he took out the vial containing the nitroglycerine — "the oil," as his brethren of the brace-and-bit term it.

One drop of the faint yellow, thickish liquid he let fall in the tumbler. He took out his silver hypodermic syringe case, and screwed the needle into its place. Carefully measuring each modicum of water in the graduated glass barrel of the syringe, he diluted the one drop with nearly half a tumbler of water.

Two hours earlier that night, Dr. James had, with that syringe, injected the undiluted liquid into a hole drilled in the lock of a safe, and had destroyed, with one dull explosion, the machinery that controlled the movement of the bolts. He now purposed, with the same means, to shiver the prime machinery of a human being — to rend its heart — and each shock was for the sake of the money to follow.

The same means, but in a different guise. Whereas that was the giant in its rude, primary dynamic strength, this was the courtier, whose no less deadly arms were concealed by velvet and lace. For the liquid in the tumbler and in the syringe that the physician carefully filled was now a solution of glonoin, the most powerful heart stimulant known to medical science. Two ounces had riven the solid door of an iron safe; with one-fiftieth part of a minim he was now about to still forever the intricate mechanism of a human life.

But not immediately. It was not so intended. First there would be a quick increase of vitality; a powerful impetus given to every organ and faculty. The heart would respond bravely to the fatal spur; the blood in the veins return more rapidly to its source.

But, as Dr. James well knew, over-stimulation in this form of heart disease means death, as sure as by a rifle shot. When the clogged arteries should suffer congestion from the increased flow of blood pumped into them by the power of the burglar's "oil," they would rapidly become "no thoroughfare," and the fountain of life would cease to flow.

The physician bared the chest of the unconscious Chandler. Easily and skillfully he injected, subcutaneously, the contents of the syringe into the muscles of the region over the heart. True to his neat habits in both professions, he next carefully dried his needle and re-inserted the fine wire that threaded it when not in use.

In three minutes Chandler opened his eyes, and spoke, in a

voice faint but audible, inquiring who attended upon him. Dr. James again explained his presence there.

"Where is my wife?" asked the patient.

"She is asleep — from exhaustion and worry," said the doctor. "I would not awaken her, unless —"

"It isn't — necessary." Chandler spoke with spaces between his words caused by his short breath that some demon was driving too fast. "She wouldn't — thank you — to disturb her — on my — account."

Dr. James drew a chair to the bedside. Conversation must not be squandered.

"A few minutes ago," he began, in the grave, candid tones of his other profession, "you were trying to tell me something regarding some money. I do not seek your confidence, but it is my duty to advise you that anxiety and worry will work against your recovery. If you have any communication to make about this — to relieve your mind about this — twenty thousand dollars, I think, was the amount you mentioned — you would better do so."

Chandler could not turn his head, but he rolled his eyes in the direction of the speaker.

"Did I — say where this — money is?"

"No," answered the physician. "I only inferred, from your scarcely intelligible words, that you felt a solicitude concerning its safety. If it is in this room —"

Dr. James paused. Did he only seem to perceive a flicker of understanding, a gleam of suspicion upon the ironical features of his patient? Had he seemed too eager? Had he said too much? Chandler's next words restored his confidence.

"Where — should it be," he gasped, "but in — the safe — there?"

With his eyes he indicated a corner of the room, where now, for the first time, the doctor perceived a small iron safe, half-concealed by the trailing end of a window curtain.

Rising, he took the sick man's wrist. His pulse was beating in great throbs, with ominous intervals between.

"Lift your arm," said Dr. James.

"You know — I can't move, Doctor."

The physician stepped swiftly to the hall door, opened it, and listened. All was still. Without further circumvention he went to the safe, and examined it. Of a primitive make and simple design, it afforded little more security than protection against light fingered servants. To his skill it was a mere toy, a thing of straw and pasteboard. The money was as good as in his hands. With his clamps he could draw the knob, punch the tumblers and open the door in two minutes. Perhaps, in another way, he might open it in one.

Kneeling upon the floor, he laid his ear to the combination plate, and slowly turned the knob. As he had surmised, it was locked at only a "day com." — upon one number. His keen ear caught the faint warning click as the tumbler was disturbed; he used the clue — the handle turned. He swung the door wide open. The interior of the safe was bare — not even a scrap of paper rested within the hollow iron cube.

Dr. James rose to his feet and walked back to the bed.

A thick dew had formed upon the dying man's brow, but there was a mocking, grim smile on his lips and in his eyes.

"I never — saw it before," he said, painfully, "medicine and — burglary wedded? Do you — make the — combination pay — dear Doctor?"

Than that situation afforded, there was never a more rigorous test of Dr. James's greatness. Trapped by the diabolic humor of his victim into a position both ridiculous and unsafe, he maintained his dignity as well as his presence of mind. Taking out his watch, he waited for the man to die.

"You were — just a shade — too — anxious — about that money. But it never was — in any danger — from you, dear Doctor. It's safe. Perfectly safe. It's all — in the hands — of the bookmakers. Twenty — thousand — Amy's money. I played it at the races — lost every — cent of it. I've been a pretty bad boy, Burglar — excuse me — Doctor, but I've been a square sport. I don't think — I ever met — such an — eighteen-carat rascal as you are, Doctor — excuse me — Burglar, in all my rounds. Is it contrary — to the ethics — of your — gang, Burglar, to give a victim — excuse me — patient, a drink of water?"

Dr. James brought him a drink. He could scarcely swallow it. The reaction from the powerful drug was coming in regular, intensifying waves. But his moribund fancy must have one more grating fling.

"Gambler — drunkard — spendthrift — I've been those, but — a doctor-burglar!"

The physician indulged himself to but one reply to the other's caustic taunts. Bending low to catch Chandler's fast crystallizing gaze, he pointed to the sleeping lady's door with a gesture so stern and significant that the prostrate man half-lifted his head, with his remaining strength, to see. He saw nothing; but he caught the cold words of the doctor — the last sounds he was to hear:

"I never yet — struck a woman."

It were vain to attempt to con such men. There is no curriculum that can reckon with them in its ken. They are offshoots from the types whereof men say, "He will do this," or "He will do that." We only know that they exist; and that we can observe them, and tell one another of their bare performances, as children watch and speak of the marionettes.

Yet it were a droll study in egoism to consider these two — one an assassin and a robber, standing above his victim; the other baser in his offenses, if a lesser lawbreaker, lying, abhorred, in the house of the wife he had persecuted, spoiled and smitten, one a tiger, the other a dog-wolf — to consider each of them sickening at the foulness of the other; and each flourishing out of the mire of his manifest guilt his own immaculate standard — of conduct, if not of honor.

The one retort of Dr. James must have struck home to the other's remaining shreds of shame and manhood, for it proved the *coup de grâce*. A deep blush suffused his face — an ignominious *rosa mortis;* the respiration ceased, and, with scarcely a tremor, Chandler expired.

Close following upon his last breath came the negress, bringing the medicine. With a hand gently pressing upon the closed eyelids, Dr. James told her of the end. Not grief, but a hereditary *rapprochement* with death in the abstract, moved her to a dismal, watery snuffling, accompanied by her usual jeremiad.

"Dar now! It's in de Lawd's hands. He am de jedge ob de transgressor, and de suppo't of dem in distress. He gwine hab suppo't us now. Cindy done paid out de last quarter fer dis bottle of physic, and it nebber come to no use."

"Do I understand," asked Dr. James, "that Mrs. Chandler has no money?"

"Money, suh? You know what make Miss Amy fall down, and so weak? Stahvation, suh. Nothin' to eat in dis house but some crumbly crackers in three days. Dat Angel sell her finger rings and watch mont's ago. Dis fine house, suh, wid de red cyarpets and shiny bureaus, it's all hired; and de man talkin' scan'lous about de rent. Dat debble — 'scuse me, Lawd — he done in yo' hands fer jedgment, now — he made way wid everything."

The physician's silence encouraged her to continue. The history that he gleaned from Cindy's disordered monologue was an old one, of illusion, wilfulness, disaster, cruelty and pride. Standing out from the blurred panorama of her gabble were little clear pictures — an ideal home in the far South; a quickly repented marriage; an unhappy season, full of wrongs and abuse, and, of late, an inheritance of money that promised deliverance; its seizure and waste by the dog-wolf during a two months' absence, and his return in the midst of a scandalous carouse. Unobtruded, but visible between every line, ran a pure white thread through the smudged warp of the story — the simple, all-enduring, sublime love of the old negress, following her mistress unswervingly through everything to the end.

When at last she paused, the physician spoke, asking if the house contained whiskey or liquor of any sort. There was, the old woman informed him, half a bottle of brandy left in the sideboard by the dog-wolf.

"Prepare a toddy as I told you," said Dr. James. "Wake your mistress; have her drink it, and tell her what has happened."

Some ten minutes afterward, Mrs. Chandler entered, supported by old Cindy's arm. She appeared to be a little stronger since her sleep and the stimulant she had taken. Dr. James had covered with a sheet, the form upon the bed.

The lady turned her mournful eyes once, with a half-frightened look, toward it, and pressed closer to her loyal protector. Her eyes were dry and bright. Sorrow seemed to have done its utmost with her. The fount of tears was dried; feeling itself paralyzed.

Dr. James was standing near the table, his overcoat donned, his hat and medicine case in his hand. His face was calm and impassive — practice had inured him to the sight of human suffering. His lambent brown eyes alone expressed a discreet professional sympathy.

He spoke kindly and briefly, stating that, as the hour was late, and assistance, no doubt, difficult to procure, he would himself send the proper persons to attend to the necessary finalities.

"One matter, in conclusion," said the doctor, pointing to the safe with its still wide open door; "Your husband, Mrs. Chandler, toward the end, felt that he could not live; and directed me to open the safe, giving me the number upon which the combination is set. In case you may need to use it, you will remember that the number is forty-one. Turn several times to the right; then to the left once; stop at forty-one. He would not permit me to waken you, though he knew the end was near.

"In that safe he said he had placed a sum of money — not large — but enough to enable you to carry out his last request. That was that you should return to your old home, and, in after days, when time shall have made it easier, forgive his many sins against you."

He pointed to the table, where lay an orderly pile of banknotes, surmounted by two stacks of gold coins.

"The money is there — as he described it — eight hundred and thirty dollars. I beg to leave my card with you, in case I can be of any service later on."

So, he had thought of her — and kindly — at the last! So late! And yet the lie fanned into life one last spark of tenderness where she had thought all was turned to ashes and dust. She cried aloud "Rob! Rob!" She turned, and, upon the ready bosom of her true servitor, diluted her grief in relieving tears. It is well to think, also, that in the years to follow the murderer's falsehood shone like a little star above the grave of love, comforting her, and gaining the forgiveness that is good in itself, whether asked for or no.

Hushed and soothed upon the dark bosom, like a child, by a crooning, babbling sympathy, at last she raised her head — but the doctor was gone.

NOTES AND COMMENTS

It is noted that O. Henry wrote at least three stories in which an intentional murder was committed. The man killed in each story was the husband of the woman in the story and had physically mistreated her in addition to other mistreatment. The two other stories were "A Municipal Report," a Tennessee story, and "A Departmental Case," a Texas story.

For a review of literary evaluation and additional notes and comments related to "The Marionettes," reference is made to Dr. Porter's essay, Part II, "The Imprisoned Splendor," *ante*, p.40.

Detail of O. Henry map (1888) showing the Goddess of Liberty atop the Texas State Capitol Dome. The statue was removed for repairs in 1985.

Old General Land Office designed by C. C. Stremme, German architect, showing the west entrance used in Will Porter's time. This is the setting of "Georgia's Ruling" and "Bexar Scrip No. 2692." "In the old General Land Office Will Porter learned Texas history from primary sources in an archive without parallel." (Texas State Library Archives)

Will Porter in the teller's cage with Bob Brackenridge behind counter to right. "I am absolutely innocent of wrongdoing in that bank matter." Austin History Center, Austin (Texas) Public Library.

The Federal Courthouse in downtown Austin, now O. Henry Hall and part of The University of Texas administrative system. Will Porter was tried on the second floor. "It was in Austin that Will Porter ran the gamut of emotional experience from joy and love to sorrow and humiliation." (Austin History Center)

On the left, the jail where O. Henry was held after his trial, before being taken to Columbus. It was located on 11th Street, across the street from the old Land Office. Austin History Center, Austin (Texas) Public Library.

The old First National Bank of Austin, designed by Abner Cook, located on the northwest corner of Sixth and Congress where One American Center now stands.

The quaint Old Bakery building, an Austin landmark and the setting for "Witches' Loaves," in which Will Porter is doubtless the young man smoking a pipe. It was but a short walk from the Land Office to the Old Bakery on Congress Avenue, and it was very close also to Porter's home, the "Honeymoon Cottage" on 11th Street which Judge O'Quinn sought to preserve. Austin History Center, Austin (Texas) Public Library.

O. Henry in the Land Office, second from left in the back row, in vest with no visible tie. "Whenever you visit Austin you should by all means go to see the General Land Office." It is easy to imagine the model for the bearded Blumberger of "Witches' Loaves" was among this group. Austin History Center, Austin (Texas) Public Library.

The desk O. Henry used in 1885 when he was a bookkeeper for Maddox Brothers and Anderson. (In the Judge's Collection, Austin History Center) All photographs of O. Henry furniture by Jim Flinn, Seattle, Washington.

down the past and make something of myself yet if I can seize a chance.

If you can & will send me the $75.00, as soon as you get this, I will repay it out of the McClure check which, as you see by his letter, will be in not later than April.

I am very anxious to go to N.Y. at the earliest possible date, as "Ainslee's" are expecting me, and I have an idea they will make me a solid & permanent offer, as they have hinted at several times

Please answer at once, returning the letters, and helping me if you can. I will return the money promptly out of the first check I get.

Yours very truly
W. S. Porter
119 Fourth Ave.

An O. Henry letter, written in Pittsburgh to Frank Maddox of Austin, asking for a loan of $75 so that he can go to New York and pursue his writing. (The Judge's Collection, Austin History Center)

Pages from the original manuscript of O. Henry's "A Fog in Santone," first given by its author to Witter Bynner and recently acquired by Judge Trueman E. O'Quinn and now in his private collection. This somber story, set in San Antonio, reveals O. Henry's contemplation of suicide.

A Fog in Santone

A Meteorological Sketch

The drug clerk looks sharply at the white face half concealed by the high turned overcoat collar.

"I would rather not supply you," he says, doubtfully. "I sold you a dozen morphia tablets less than an hour ago."

The customer smiles wanly. "The fault is in your crooked streets. I didn't intend to call upon you twice, but I guess I got tangled up. Excuse me."

He draws his collar higher, and moves out, slowly.

the big man drops the curtains
and passes on.

The orchestra ceases
playing suddenly, and an important voice can be heard
loudly talking in one of the
boxes farther down the aisle. No
doubt some citizen entertains there
some visitor to the town, and
Miss Rosa leans back in her chair
and smiles at some of the words
she catches:

"Surest Atmosphere . . . .
in the world . . . . Litmus paper
all along . . . . nothing hurtful
. . . . our city . . . . nothing but
pure ozone."

The waiter returns for
the tray and glasses. As he enters,
the girl crushes a little empty pasteboard box in her hand, and throws
it in a corner. She is stirring something in her glass with her hat pin.

"Why, Miss Rosa," says the
waiter, with the civil familiarity he uses,
— "Putting salt in your beer this early
in the night!"

"Not on your Uncle Mark Hanna," responds Toledo, "will we get drunk. We've . . . been vaccinated with whiskey and . . . cod liver oil. What would send you to the police station . . . only gives us a thirst. S–s set out another bottle."

It is slow work trying to meet death by that route. Some quicker way must be found. They leave the saloon, and plunge again into the mist. The sidewalks are mere flanges at the base of the houses; the street a cold ravine, the fog filling it like a freshet. Not far away is the Mexican quarter. Conducted as if by wires along the heavy air comes a guitar's tinkle, and the demoralizing voice of some Señorita singing:

"En las tardes sombrillos del invierno
En el prado á llorar me reclino,
Y maldigo mi fausto destino —
Una vida la mas infeliz."

Page of "A Fog in Santone" MS in O. Henry's unmistakable handwriting, showing the Spanish quatrain which sets the tone of the story. O. Henry's Spanish has been incorrectly printed in standard editions of his works, thereby destroying a poignant key element of this work. (Reproduced by permission of Trueman E. O'Quinn)

Round walnut table where one could place a sandwich and a drink while he dealt the cards or played dominoes. Will Porter and his Land Office friend, Charles ("Count") Scrivener played cards at this table. (In the Judge's Collection)

The walnut chair and table Will Porter used at Zerchausky's Saloon on Congress Avenue. Will playfully carved a notch in the table to show that it was his favorite place to sit. (The Judge's Collection, Austin History Center)

*The Larkin desk where William Sidney Porter wrote "The Miracle of Lava Canyon,"
in Austin (1897). (The Judge's Collection, Austin History Center)*

Beautiful old curly pine mantel with beveled mirrors saved by Judge Trueman O'Quinn from the Joe Harrell home at 1008 Lavaca Street. Will used to sit before this fireplace to read and write. (The Judge's Collection, Austin History Center)

INDEX

SC

Henry, O
AUTHOR

Time to write
TITLE

DATE DUE	BORROWER'S NAME
SEP 2 1 1994	885

SC

HARDEMAN COUNTY PUBLIC LIBRARY
TUESDAY, WEDNESDAY 9:30 TO 5:30
THURSDAY, FRIDAY 12:30 TO 5:30
SATURDAY 9:30 TO 3:30
PHONE: 663 - 8149